THE
PRESERVATIONIST'S
PROGRESS

Also by Hugh Howard

How Old Is This House?
Baseball by the Rules (co-author)
I'm Not Doing It Myself
The Home Inspection Handbook

THE
PRESERVATIONIST'S
PROGRESS

Architectural Adventures in
Conserving Yesterday's Houses

HUGH HOWARD

Farrar, Straus and Giroux
New York

Published simultaneously in Canada by HarperCollins*CanadaLtd.*
Printed in the United States of America
Designed by Marjorie Anderson
First edition, 1991
Library of Congress Cataloging-in-Publication Data

Howard, Hugh.
The preservationist's progress : architectural adventures in
conserving yesterday's houses / Hugh Howard. — 1st ed.
p.   cm.
Includes index.
1. Architecture, Domestic—United States—Conservation and
restoration.   I. Title.
NA7205.H735   1991
728′.028′8—dc20   90-24138

Photographs, except those credited to other sources, were taken
by the author.

The photograph of the sprung-roof porch on the title page was taken at
Robert Herron's home in Austerlitz, New York. The elliptical blind
pictured on page one is located in the gable of a house on Main Street in
Essex, New York. The salvaged columns at the end of Chapter 12 were
photographed at Eastfield Village. The photograph accompanying the
Notes on Sources at the close of this book is of the abandoned terrace of
the New York Cancer Hospital.

The endpapers are a wallpaper pattern attributed to Moses Grant of
Boston. Believed to have been made originally between 1810 and 1817,
the wallpaper was reproduced by Brunschwig and Fils, Inc. from samples
found on the walls of the Emerson Bixby house at Old Sturbridge Village
(see Chapter 4).

For my father,
J. Philip Howard,
from whom I learned
to look to history

ACKNOWLEDGMENTS

This book could not have been written without the help of the preservationists. First and foremost, then, I must thank Robert Adam, Donald Carpentier, John Curtis, Christopher Gray, Robert Herron, Clem Labine, Chester Liebs, Charles Lyle, William McMillen, John Mesick, Thomas Monaghan, and Andrea di Pietro.

Many other people have given me their time, too, including Denise Carpentier, Bruno Freschi, Robert Hammerslag, James Murray Howard, Philip C. Marshall, Lauren Murphy, John O'Hern, Norman Young, and others I have no doubt forgotten to mention. My appreciation, too, to Thurston and Antonia Clarke, who acquainted us with Essex. Many thanks to each of you.

I am indebted to my publisher, Roger W. Straus III, and my editor, Elisabeth Dyssegaard, of Farrar, Straus & Giroux, Inc. They are patient people who made their way through this book in its several earlier incarnations. They made me think and taught me things along the way. My thanks, too, to Ida Veltri, Bridget Marmion and Judy Klein, and the others at Farrar, Straus who have helped me find the audience that cares about these houses, as well as to Seán O'Loinsaigh, who detected more than a few literary lapses in the manuscript.

My appreciation to Stephen Drucker at *The New York Times*'s Home section, who commissioned several pieces that were the germ of several chapters in this book, and to Mervyn Kaufman of *House Beautiful.*

To Marjorie Anderson, I extend my affection and thanks for her design and guidance; to Jean Atcheson and Judy Grant, my appreciation for catching what everyone else missed.

A final word to acknowledgment must go to John Bunyan. The title of this book is, obviously, intended to echo that of his classic, *The Pilgrim's Progress.*

The Preservationist's Progress is not an allegory, nor is its subject religious faith, yet I believe there is a certain thematic affinity between Bunyan's work and this one. To borrow the words of Roger Sharrock (author of the standard Bunyan biography and editor of his *Works*), Bunyan attempted in his writing "an examination of his past experience and a translation of it into a form which would provide a recognizable pattern of hope."

I believe that description applies, too, to the preservationists I have met. It is my hope that their faith and confidence in the worth of the past is to be heard in these pages.

CONTENTS

Our eyes, even if we know clearly what serious architecture is, have to search for it questioningly in a welter of commercial and municipal monstrosities. It is as though one had to tune a violin in the midst of a railway accident.

—Geoffrey Scott
The Architecture of Humanism (1914)

THE PRESERVATIONIST'S PROGRESS

1
Cultural
Conservatism

———

Old truths, old laws, old boots, old books, and old friends are the best.

—Polish proverb

One day when I was about nine, my mother volunteered me to help her move some old junk around the cellar. One of the musty objects was an antique footlocker. Forgetting my plight momentarily, I was compelled by curiosity to open the chest.

Inside was a pair of leather boots that had belonged to an ancestor. Perhaps it was the spirit of the fellow who had worn them, or it might have been the innate playfulness of a lad of nine, but something about those boots made me want to wear them.

They appeared to be of military issue, but playing army had never had much appeal to me. It was more a matter of where those boots had been. I discovered then what fantasies can fill a boy's head when marching about in a pair of boots with such a storied past.

I learned from my mother that they had been the property of a man named Wheeler, a surname last found in my family tree three generations back on my mother's side. Three generations earlier still, this particular Wheeler had held the rank

3

of captain in Washington's army, which entitled him to the boots. He survived the war and returned to his family in central Massachusetts. Captain Wheeler once again became Freeman Wheeler, and resumed farming the stony New England soil.

Three years later, he found himself involved in another armed conflict. Like many farmers in more recent years, Adam Wheeler and his neighbors faced foreclosure and the loss of their farms. He was not about to accept the loss of his land passively, so he joined the ranks of other insurrectionists under the leadership of Daniel Shays. They put up what our culture has come to call the good fight.

No doubt there are many stories to be learned about Captain Wheeler's exploits. I know I imagined some. But the one that has come down by word of mouth through the generations of my family concerns his arrest in 1787, during Shays's Rebellion.

Wheeler was captured and imprisoned after he and his men had laid siege to the federal armory at Springfield, Massachusetts. He was promptly sentenced to death. When I first heard the story, the details were too few for my eager and impressionable ears, but the bottom line was that he managed to escape. Not only that, but he survived to father the son who, in turn, fathered other sons and daughters, leading eventually to my birth. That's a nuance I came to appreciate as an adult.

As a child, I was more intrigued by the clever way in which he outwitted his pursuers. He got himself delivered over the Canadian border in a box. It was a coffin, to be exact, and in my mind he has always emerged from his premature burial box wearing his boots.

Though I coveted them, I never got to wear the boots out to play. My mother forbade me to wear them at all. She told me something like "They don't fit, so they're bad for your feet." Even more vaguely, I remember my father's explanation: "Those are not toys, son. They're a part of history."

The world is full of easy distinctions. For the purposes of this book, a convenient one is between the savers and the throwers.

If this were a lifestyle magazine, you would now be invited to embark on a round of twenty questions. You might be asked whether you still have your notebooks from college and if your closets and drawers contain more than a few clothes you haven't worn (or been able to wear) in years. One of these theoretical questions might even venture into the field of genetics: How about your parents? Do they have boxes of musty old photos or other memorabilia in the attic?

You probably know without totaling your yeas and nays whether you are a saver or a thrower. You may have guessed that, by virtue of both nature and nurture, I am a saver. You will encounter a number of savers in the pages that follow.

Yet categories like savers and throwers are too simple. There is another word that offers more of the subtle nuances and echoes needed. A second childhood anecdote suggests something of the complexity and flexibility required here.

One day in fifth grade our teacher was giving us a vocabulary lesson. She asked the twenty-five-odd children present if we knew what the word "cute" meant.

One of my classmates suggested that to be cute was to be bowlegged. We all laughed. But Mrs. Hemmi made it clear to us that while not precisely synonymous, there certainly could be instances in which someone "bowlegged" might indeed be "cute."

At the time, I thought she was protecting the sensitive child who had offered the definition. In recent years, though, I've thought often how apt that usage is when applied to a toddler walking. The plump feet, the chubby legs, the awkward stance— my classmate was right, it is the bowlegged gait that makes the new walker's attempts at upright locomotion humorous, charming, and, well, cute.

The meanings of words are forever changing. Sometimes, as in the very narrow context of my fifth-grade class, a word takes on a whole new range of meaning quite apart from its original definition. I don't think it has even been used interchangeably with "bowlegged," but "conservatism" is a word that has had more than its share of shadings and even transformations.

By instinct, I resist labels. I don't have problems with facts. As a writer, I find qualifiers that are clearly defined very useful. When it comes to adjectives like "grayish," "interesting," and "cool," I grow a little uneasy. But upon meeting up with ideological labels like "liberal" or "Republican," the sensation is almost physical. They're like a wool sweater on bare skin. They itch and irritate and usually I find myself throwing them off.

"Conservatism" is a word with which I've had such experiences. To Chaucer and other medieval and Renaissance writers, it was essentially synonymous with "preservative," identifying a tendency to keep intact or unchanged. Today, mention of the word tolls a veritable chorus of political bells, yet it wasn't until 1830 that it assumed any political connotation at all. The usage I have in mind lies somewhere in the vast range between Chaucer and Ronald Reagan.

This book isn't about politics. Conservative electoral politics as currently practiced in America involves a range of assumptions far different from those with which conservatism's early theorists were concerned. The world's balance of economic and military power today is of such a vastly different order that what we know as political conservatism would be almost unrecognizable to the early conservative thinkers of the late eighteenth and early nineteenth centuries.

Yet the subject of this book is the instinct that the word "conservative" originally signified. There has been in the last decade an undeniable shift in this country to understand, cherish, and *conserve* artifacts and aspects of America's past, and even to integrate them into the present. In part to avoid unwanted political connotations, I have taken to calling the breed of savers, or preservationists, with which this book is concerned, "cultural conservators."

A clear definition is in order, but on the way there let us recall Captain Wheeler's boots for a moment.

"They're a part of history," I was told. The message was that there was something intangible about them that made them too precious for mere child's play. They could never have any utility, nor were they likely to provide anyone with any aesthetic satisfaction. They weren't beautiful or comfortable. They were stiff and musty leather boots from an old trunk in a damp cellar.

Yet some objects are endowed with an essential "historicalness." I suspect I sensed that for the first time when I discovered the boots. The ability to recognize and appreciate the presence of that historicalness in an object is one of the qualifications of a cultural conservator.

To amplify: Cultural conservators are people who value their place in the continuum of time. History is more than a subject taught in school; it's an influence throughout life. To a cultural conservator, that influence may be felt as often as a familiar object sparks a synapse to connect it to a remembered moment, or as rarely as the antiquated construction "fourscore and seven" recalls the image of Honest Abe.

Cultural conservators act as custodians, preserving objects for posterity. Yet they are concerned not only with artifacts but with the intellectual qualities and even the moral lessons of the past. Fundamental is the notion of the conservative philosopher George Santayana: "Those who cannot remember the past are condemned to repeat it."

Most simply put, then, a cultural conservator recognizes the moral, intellectual, and even physical importance of the past. He works in some fashion to preserve those vestiges. Finally, he engages that appreciation of the past in living his (or her) daily life.

I believe the work of the cultural conservator is best understood as a physical act, and in this book I will use architecture to try to understand the urge to conserve and to employ that intangible historicalness. Perhaps another of the arts might have served as well, but buildings, specifically houses, offer a unique combination of objects and of lives lived. Houses are more than artifacts, as they are also vessels in which the voyage of life is continually undertaken. As the needs of residents or users change; as technology advances; as economic, demographic, and other shifts occur, buildings forever evolve.

Buildings are among the most valuable records of a culture. If the play of history is to be seen as continual change, then individual buildings provide physical records—or at least significant clues—that can help us understand something of those who came before us. In turn, what we do to a building will help those who come after to understand us.

As an adult, I have found that I have a certain affinity for houses, one that began with working on them but which has often led me to write about them. Those writings—a trio of books and many articles—led to the writing of this book. The people I've come to know in learning about houses inspired me as well.

Colloquially, these people are most often called preservationists. To borrow Henry James's words, they have "a lurking esteem for things that show the marks of having lasted." The decision to try to understand old buildings—and it is understanding that these men are after, not merely paychecks—isn't a career choice. It's akin to discovering you have a religious vocation.

These people are believers. Their confidence isn't so much in progress as it is in the essential worth of the buildings our ancestors constructed on this continent. They share some instinctual, largely unspoken connection to older houses.

A variety of professions are represented in these pages. Individual chapters concern an architect, a professor, a museum curator, a historian, a craftsman, a publisher, a collector of architectural artifacts, and others involved with old buildings. I've traveled thousands of miles over a period of several years in order to talk to them, learning as much as possible about them, the houses on which they lavish their care, and American houses in general.

Although this book purports to be about old buildings, the changes made in them over time, and the men involved with them today, there is a dimly murmuring undercurrent. Like an underground stream on a hillside that springs to the surface only to disappear again into another crevice, an urge to conserve appears here, as it does in the everyday life of the "savers," to return to that simplistic but identifiable characterization.

At first, the hillside seems constant, as do the men and the buildings in these pages. But beneath the vegetation, water is forever in motion, nourishing and sustaining life. In the same way, we all are subject to the informing, energizing, and stabilizing influences of the past.

All of us, to a greater or lesser degree, share a native will to conserve, savers and throwers alike. By examining one area of human activity, namely the preservation of old houses, I will attempt to suggest how these cultural conservators, these preservationists, became sensitized to the historicalness of things and how their inclination to conserve has enriched their lives. I believe we can learn from them.

2
An Architectural Assay

The longer they have lasted . . . the more we cherish them.
—Edmund Burke, Reflections on the
Revolution in France *(1790)*

There are countless different ways to discover new things. Magazines, books, radio, and TV bring many new places, people, objects, and ideas to the attention of millions of us every day. So do coincidence, nosy neighbors, serendipity, and, I've learned, unexpected illnesses.

One weekend back in 1987, my wife and I were visiting friends in upstate New York, less than an hour from the Canadian border. Our hostess woke up Sunday morning feeling ill. Instead of relaxing with our hosts and their babies for the day, our best course seemed to be an early departure. Assured there was nothing we could do to help, off we went.

In a matter of minutes, we found ourselves in the town of Essex, New York. Our hosts had told us there were some impressive old houses there and indeed the town was a gem, with a dozen or more Great Houses in a picturesque setting on the shore of Lake Champlain. The downtown area has been on the National Register of Historic Places since 1975.

"Great House," by the way, is almost a term of art. Architects, preservationists, architectural historians, and other professional house fanciers use it the way sportswriters say "All-Star." The term often refers to size, though not always. It can be used to describe both broken-down wrecks and meticulously restored structures. But Great House always implies a house of a certain age and of evident architectural quality.

Few communities can claim two or three Great Houses, so Essex's collection was a wonderful surprise to us on that drizzly September Sunday. A drive through the little hamlet is rather like a real-life browse through an architectural field guide. There are Federal houses, an Italianate or two, Greek Revivals, and a Second Empire. Some are Great Houses, fancy and formal; others are plain and simple. Next to none have been mistreated so badly they look like something else.

I wished immediately that I lived there.

Essex is also distinguished by the fact that it stopped growing around 1860. The railroads had arrived in the area in 1849, and over the next decade replaced the water-bound lake trade. Essex's principal industries, shipping and shipbuilding, went out of business.

The period of financial hardship that followed must have been particularly galling to the nineteenth-century mind with its confidence in progress and its belief that technological advances would lead inevitably to growth, development, and universal improvement.

Essex's change in fortune ran counter to the expectations of the era. During the 1850s, Essex lost a third of its population. Over the next century, it lost another third, leaving it with its present population of about nine hundred citizens.

The failure of economic growth also meant there wasn't a great deal of money to spend on lifting the face of the town or its individual dwellings. The shrinking population made new housing unnecessary. For the architectural historian of our time, this produced a long-term benefit, the unspoiled visage the town offers to visitors today. As Essex's prospects faded, an accidental blending of geographic, economic, and other factors created a rare medium for preservation. Like the bonsai dwarfed and shaped by the gardener, Essex became an architectural and demographic miniature.

On the day we first visited, one house didn't quite fit the picture-book look. With a major renovation underway, the house was obscured by a fence, scaffolding, and mounds of both demolition debris and new building materials. We later learned it was known as the Ralph Hascall house.

Subsequently we also discovered that, quite unlike the average house restoration, the Hascall house was the subject of a public preservation debate. Whether to save it was not at issue; the community's desire to preserve was a given in Essex. Rather, it was a more philosophical discussion touching upon some of the essential conflicts of preservation.

The restoration and the accompanying public deliberations provide a convenient case study. One dilemma concerned the selection of the moment in the life of the building to which it was to be restored. To some, its original appearance was sacred. Others thought that its present appearance should be conserved. Upon close investigation, still other options from intervening years were identified.

The process itself is illuminating. Preserving the Hascall house required an in-depth study of the building, both as an architectural artifact and as evidence of changes in the life of its inhabitants and even that of the town and region around it. At public hearings, the villagers were briefed on the findings of the investigators. The wishes of the community were identified, then the fragile structure was preserved along those lines.

The Hascall house debate and restoration provide an opportunity to look at architectural preservation as it is practiced today.

Michelangelo described the process of sculpture as "liberating the figure from the marble that imprisons it." The restoration task at the Hascall house required a similar process of revelation. The building isn't made of marble, of course, but until recently the original house was virtually obscured by later architectural accretions.

In December 1985, the house was purchased by the Essex Community Heritage Organization (ECHO), a nonprofit membership organization concerned with local preservation, housing, and ecological issues. ECHO, which was founded in 1969, planned to convert the one-family house into two apartments for moderate-income rentals. The organization had applied for and received a $35,000 grant for the conversion from the New York State Rural Area Revitalization Program.

At that time, the house was known in the community as the Ed Sherman house, after the man who had owned it since 1946. The Sherman connection went back at least another decade. Prior to purchasing the house, the Sherman family had lived in it as a rental. During the Shermans' half century of residence, a large barn on the property had been removed and an ell off

In its as-found condition in 1985, the Ralph Hascall house in Essex, New York. *ECHO*

the back demolished and replaced by a porch. Numerous other changes were made inside.

According to an ECHO report: "As the [Sherman] family drifted away to other pursuits, the maintenance of the house became more and more of a burden." In translation: the house ECHO bought was a mess.

The building's wooden frame was severely decayed. The porches also bore the signs of a losing battle with the rigorous northern climate, as portions were rotted. The working systems were outmoded and, to put it generously, the interior finish was hardly of the kind or condition to appeal to prospective tenants.

Everyone agreed that a wholesale renovation was required. What wasn't so clear was how to proceed, so the decision was postponed. An exhaustive study of the house was commissioned to identify what was beneath the superficial changes that so obviously postdated the original construction of the house. The study was conducted by an architect, a free-lance writer, and a preservation contractor, all of whom were residents of the town.

The proverbial peeling of the onion then commenced, a process of removing layers to see what lay beneath. The house as it appeared in 1985 was an eclectic display of various architectural styles and forms. Starting with the porches, the most obvious aspect of the building's façade, the investigators were able to identify distinct stages in the life of the house.

They determined that the enclosed porch on the second story was the last major structural change. A so-called Saranac Lake "cure porch," it had been added around 1910, one of thousands constructed according to the theories of Dr. E. L. Trudeau. Trudeau's base of operations was Saranac Lake, amid the nearby Adirondack Mountains. He believed that total rest and the outdoor air of such open, unheated sleeping porches were useful in treating tuberculosis. The owner of the house at the time, Dr. Frank E. Sweatt, was divorced, and local lore has it that he built the cure porch for an ailing lady friend.

The researchers also uncovered a circa 1902 photograph of the house. It revealed that the first-floor porch alone had then dominated the front elevation, giving the house a distinctly Victorian air with its gingerbread decoration. Other evidence of the Victorian era includes the round-headed window centered over the front door and the rest of the window sash which had two panes of glass each (making them two-over-two windows, in the parlance of the architectural historian).

While the house as pictured in 1902 seems very much of a piece, this is an illusion. Porches weren't to be found only on Victorian houses, since innumerable dwellings predating the nineteenth-century vogue for such open outdoor spaces have had porches grafted onto them.

The first-story porch had actually been added, either by Dr. Sweatt or by the previous owner, around 1900. The two-over-two windows were also a later improvement; the original twelve-over-twelves had been removed, probably after the Civil War.

This photograph is thought to have been taken in 1902. The porch was new, as was the horseless carriage out front, one of the first cars in the area. *Robert F. Sweatt/ECHO*

Only one original twelve-over-twelve remained. Located on an end wall, it later proved to be a convenient and valuable clue.

The biggest surprise was the attic. The inspection of the house had involved an all-fours tour of the attic space. There the rafters supporting the roof pitched low overhead, reaching a height of less than three feet at its highest point. Unlike the attic within, however, the roof without was steep and tall.

One of the investigators realized that the observations didn't compute. Further study revealed that the roofline had been changed. A steep gable roof had been constructed atop the older one, leaving most of the original hip roof intact in the attic, complete with its covering of wood shingles.

Examination of the original roof structure revealed a hand-hewn timber frame and suggested a date prior to 1850 for the construction of the house. The round-headed window was not exactly what it appeared to be upon first glance. It was actually a Palladian window, a configuration of three attached windows, featuring a central arched opening flanked by a pair of shorter, square-headed windows. Numerous decorative details in the interior, including an elegant cornice in the parlor, the baluster on the stairs, the doors, and various pieces of hardware (hinges and latches, for example), and other evidence confirmed an earlier-than-Victorian date.

The researchers concluded that the house had been built about 1810 for a state legislator and district attorney named Ralph Hascall. It was identified as having been constructed in the Georgian style, a classically inspired mode widely used during the rules of the Georges, the Hanoverian English kings. The doorway, obscured somewhat by the porches, most clearly identified the house as Georgian, with its arched fan sash, pilasters (flattened half columns), and other classical decorations. An analysis of nails and other evidence revealed that the house was not constructed prior to 1800, and wills and deeds and other documents pointed to a date of around 1810.

Though out of fashion by the time of construction, the use of the Georgian style in the Hascall house has been explained by the hypothesis that Ralph Hascall chose the style out of fond

Inside the attic (above), the rough-hewn frame of the roof looms low. Further study (and demolition) revealed that the roof without concealed an entirely independent roof. The later, taller roof has been removed in this photo (below). *ECHO*

recollection of another house or perhaps because its traditional grandeur was consistent with his prominent place in the community.

So the Hascall house wasn't simply a tumbledown twentieth-century house of no particular quality. The dwelling ECHO bought wasn't solely a Victorian house of evident character. And it was more than a rare house of Georgian inspiration and one of the earliest buildings in town.

Actually, the house was all of these.

Different communities address their concerns in different ways. They may vote out the incumbent mayor or vote in a big bond issue. There's never universal agreement about anything; that just isn't human nature. But a collective groping for consensus is essential to our sense of community, not to mention democracy. It is ECHO's ability to take the pulse of an entire town that earned it my nominating vote to the preservationists' pantheon.

Robert Hammerslag lives in an old house, a spacious 1824 Federal on the outskirts of Essex. And he is professionally concerned with other houses in his community. He managed the Hascall house project as ECHO's executive director, along with ECHO's community preservation specialist, Lauren Murphy. She also owns an early house, an 1842 Greek Revival mill-worker's dwelling one town south of Essex.

Once the study of the Hascall house was completed, the next step was to decide what to do with the house. Rather than making an arbitrary decision to preserve the house as it was or to restore it to some semblance of one of its former appearances, Hammerslag, Murphy, and ECHO took the discussion public. Residents of the town and a broader community of professional preservationists were invited to express their views and help determine the future appearance of the building. With the results of the study in hand, the lines of the debate had already been drawn, and the Ralph Hascall house became a

The interior of the Hascall house offered its share of surprises,
including the ghost of a dentil molding beneath the intricate cornice.
It appeared upon the removal of later wall surfaces. *ECHO*

textbook case of the difficulties posed by a much remodeled
early house.

The debate can be characterized as a choice: Should ECHO
opt for *preservation, restoration,* or *rehabilitation?* A definition of these terms is in order.

According to the Standards of the Secretary of the Interior
(under whose jurisdiction are the Historic American Buildings
Survey, the National Park Service, and the Preservation Assistance Division), *preservation* is "the act or process of applying
measures to sustain the existing form, integrity, and material
of a building or structure, and the existing form and vegetative
cover of a site. It may include stabilization work, where necessary, as well as ongoing maintenance of the historic building
materials."

Restoration is different. According to the Department of the
Interior, it is "the act or process of accurately recovering the
form and details of a property and its setting as it appeared at

a particular period of time by means of the removal of later work or by the replacement of missing earlier work."

Finally, *rehabilitation* is defined as "the act or process of returning a property to a state of utility through repair or alteration which makes possible an efficient contemporary use while preserving those portions or features of the property which are significant to its historical, architectural, and cultural values."

So which was it to be? "There was a state-of-the-art debate in this community about preservation versus restoration," Bob Hammerslag told me on one of my trips to Essex. "Everybody in town had opinions about what, even in the field, are relatively esoteric matters."

ECHO sponsored a series of public meetings during 1986 at which architectural professionals offered their views. Among them were Professor Chester H. Liebs, director of the University of Vermont Historic Preservation Graduate Program; architect John Mesick, of the Albany, New York, firm of Mesick, Cohen & Waite; and Bates Lowry, director of the National Building Museum in Washington, D.C. Articles describing the house, its history, and the ongoing discussions appeared in local papers and such national publications as the National Building Museum's membership newsletter, *Blueprints*.

Some experts endorsed restoration. John Mesick said, "Underneath was the early-nineteenth-century house. It was simply a matter of subtraction. . . . Not a lot of guesswork was involved, so a restoration could be done without conjecture. There were sufficient pieces so that the whole artifact could be restored."

Certain structural findings also supported restoration. The presence of the porches had led to considerable decay in the main structure. Close analysis of the building suggested that, if left uncorrected, some of the changes would continue to damage it. A poured-concrete floor on the first-floor porch in particular posed a threat to the structure's timber frame, as it caused rainwater to flow directly into the building's outer wall.

Another consideration that argued for restoration was that the Hascall house was the only Georgian-style house in town.

Essex is a community attuned to architectural issues, with its fine array of carefully preserved structures. But the British army had swept through the town during the Revolution, leaving no building in Essex intact. Since the vogue for Georgian buildings had passed by the war's end, the Hascall house was a unique, if anachronistic, specimen.

In January 1986, after further public testimony and discussion, ECHO's board voted unanimously to restore the house to its original, circa 1810 appearance. While everyone recognized that the building needed to be stabilized, not everyone agreed with the final decision. One outspoken opponent of the restoration—before, during, and after—was Professor Chester Liebs.

"I think something very valuable was lost," Liebs told me later. "There was a powerful layering of time, and now what we have is a version of just one period of time. I think that there's a constant urge to make the old new . . . and restoration is often the easiest route. It's sort of like surgery: it's easy to go in and cut. . . . Everyone likes to see, rather than imagine."

Liebs went on to express his admiration for ECHO's use of the building and the way the general public was involved in the decision-making process. But for him, that wasn't enough. "Really a restoration might be very appropriate for a museum or an exhibit building . . . but here we have a very special town and to early-it-up is to end up with a community that was neither then nor now. And to erase some very interesting history in the process."

The restoration was completed in 1988 and the house is now inhabited. One of the oldest houses in town has been stabilized. In the process, several local workers, under the auspices of a grant from the New York State Council on the Arts, were given employment and training in restoration woodworking and plastering techniques. (ECHO sold the house in 1989 for $128,000. The purchase agreement came complete with an architectural easement prohibiting changes to the exterior and to the restored parts of the interior, as well as the requirement that both apartments be rented to low- or moderate-income tenants for a period

The end result, the hip-roofed, porchless Hascall house, in 1988, much as it had originally appeared circa 1810.

of fifteen years. In return, the purchaser received ten years of low-income-housing tax credits.)

The Hascall house was a paradigm of clashing architectural styles: The Georgian met the Victorian, only to be transformed again, a generation or two later, into Adirondack vernacular. And now it's back to the Georgian.

Did they do the right thing?

Philip C. Marshall led the investigation team that found the old roof in the attic. Marshall, now director of the Architectural Artisanry Program at Southeastern Massachusetts University, remembered that at first "I took the side that, in theory, I wanted to keep all those additions on. But ECHO engaged the community in a very participatory sense . . . it seemed to be two groups with two different opinions on whether to preserve the house as it existed with all its later additions or to preserve it to a target date of its original construction. In retrospect, I've changed my mind. Today it's a real good example of a partnership of community and restoration."

Upon visiting the restored house for the first time, I found myself admiring the finished architectural product. Yet afterward I couldn't help but consider how fond I personally am of reading my newspaper on the porch of a summer evening—and you can't do that any longer at the white house on Main Street, Essex, New York.

That opposition is too easy, of course. But after giving it a great deal of thought, I've come to believe that such conflicts don't lend themselves to simple right and wrong answers.

Yet I do believe they can serve to deepen our understanding of the urge to conserve.

I am fascinated that Essex and ECHO opted to take what I would describe as the conservative path. At this juncture, it's important to explore further the nature of that word "conservative."

It takes a certain kind of person to care about conserving an old house. Lately we've been seeing more and more of that sort of person exercising his or her instincts. A Sunday drive through almost any century-old community in this country will produce evidence of the trend. But a whole community that appears to be concerned? Maybe it's something in the water.

ECHO has done more than save the Hascall house. Under Hammerslag's leadership, it has also initiated litigation to prevent further development in their village. There was a prolonged fight about a proposed marina expansion that would add more slips and would carve a parking lot out of the rear yards of some of the houses on Main Street. It would have brought dollars into the community, but it would have brought outsiders in, too, and offered the townspeople few or no advantages. ECHO eventually negotiated a settlement with the sponsors that reduced the development.

There is another, continuing debate over the possible reopening of quarries within the town limits. Once an important local industry, the quarries fell into disuse decades ago. Mining anew would produce jobs. But at what cost? ask its critics. The fragile infrastructure of the town might be strained by the enormous trucks that would, dozens of times a day, pound its streets. Then there's noise, dust, and the physical dangers inherent in such an operation.

ECHO's record in opposing such proposals is impressive. Things don't just happen in Essex. Thanks to Hammerslag and the rest of those involved with ECHO and, I suspect, an inbred Yankee suspicion of change, much discussion precedes decisions regarding significant changes in the community. ECHO has demonstrated an ability to gather the information necessary to consider such proposals; then it gets together some intelligent people to support or fight them. Everyone on its board and the bulk of its membership live in Essex, and ECHO clearly tries to act in the interests of most of the townspeople. There is a continuing tension in the town between conserving its essential qualities and dealing with the demands of the present.

In Essex and elsewhere, preservationists are concerned with continuity. When the political movement we know as conservatism was born in England at the turn of the nineteenth century and in America shortly thereafter, it was a reaction to both the French and the industrial revolutions. The anarchy in France in 1789 was abhorrent to the conservatives, while the changes that industrialism wrought on the fabric of society were enormous.

Almost overnight, an agricultural world was giving way to an industrial explosion. Its impact on human life was great— it produced the urban nightmare that provided the setting for several of Charles Dickens's best-known novels. Its other effects were equally significant, reaching into our own time, as the closing decades of this century have been given over to one round after another of the continuing fight to stem environmental destruction consequent to industrialism.

There's no point in debating the desirability of industrialism; it is an unstoppable juggernaut, and one long necessary to our economic system and to allowing us to live in the manner to which we have become accustomed. But the changes it produced in the nineteenth century were largely despised by the conservatives. It is in that tradition that the conservers in Essex are working to preserve a pristine little village. And today is a time when, thanks to developing technologies and an increased understanding of our world, the path of the juggernaut may at least be altered.

In the nineteenth century, the townspeople of Essex learned that progress comes with no guarantees. We're learning that same lesson as we are forced to acknowledge that there are limits to growth, to energy consumption, and to the amounts of garbage which we can safely dispose of.

I'm not suggesting that the Essex economic model—a boom, a bust, and a prolonged period of contraction—is one that any community should seek to emulate. On the other hand, Essex today is again a growing community, a lakeside resort increasingly attractive to summer and weekend residents. And the goal of progress, denied Essex in the 1850s, has been replaced by a quest for continuity.

Change and even growth may be inevitable, but they are means, not ends. What is desirable is to retain the character, the stability, and the integrity of the town. By accident then and by intention now, Essex has avoided becoming drunk with possibility. Instead, its sobriety has both rendered this little community worth preserving and provided it with the will to do so.

In the chapters that follow, we will meet a number of architectural wayfarers and some of the houses with which they are involved. All of these people are professionals in the field of architectural restoration and preservation. Frequently they disagree, like the two you've already heard from, John Mesick and Chester Liebs, who quite by accident found themselves cast as antagonists in the Hascall house discussion. Yet there is one underlying assumption that all these cultural conservators share: Preserving the old is a greater good. The issue isn't to save or not to save; the operative assumption throughout this volume is that buildings of a certain age and quality are, in principle, worth saving.

In truth, none of us is able to focus on the present without at least fleeting reference to the past or the future. We're anxious about or we eagerly anticipate the events of tomorrow or next week or next year. We regret missed opportunities or we fondly recall occurrences of yesterday. The concept of "now" and the fleeting sequence of moments we call "the present" aren't completely separable from earlier or later times.

Yet Americans have always been future-focused. Our short history doesn't reach back to antiquity as do European and Asian cultures. As a young country, the United States has traditionally been more concerned with the business at hand.

Now, in a world filled with countries only a few decades old, it grows more difficult to identify the United States as young. Perhaps as its middle age approaches, it is appropriate to come gradually to appreciate the past, to acknowledge that tomorrow isn't by definition better than today and that the passage of time is not synonymous with progress. On the contrary, perhaps we need routinely to consider how historic buildings can inform us as we think about our houses and our world, now and in the future.

3
The Admirable Craftsman

History with its flickering lamp stumbles along the trail of the past, trying to reconstruct its scenes, to review its echoes, and kindle with pale gleams the passion of former days.
—Winston Churchill, House of Commons tribute to Neville Chamberlain (1940)

Several years ago, I enrolled in a carpentry restoration workshop at a rather unorthodox academy called Eastfield Village. One summer morning the class went on a field trip to examine the streetscape of a nearby upstate New York town.

Among the houses we looked at was a sadly ill-used farmhouse. It probably hadn't been painted in more than twenty years, as the clapboards were past the peeling stage. No paint remained and the wood shone gray in the sunlight. Innocently, I made a remark along the lines of "My, now isn't *that* place ripe for restoration."

I was speaking to the instructor, Donald Carpentier. Approaching his fortieth birthday, Carpentier is trim and muscular. His attire is a contemporary blend of comfortable and practical, and on that summer day he wore a T-shirt, long trousers, and work boots. (In colder temperatures, it's a flannel shirt, long trousers, and work boots, and a neatly trimmed beard that comes and goes with the seasons.)

Carpentier looked at me, his eyes slightly narrowed. It's a look I've come to recognize as his impatient "Is this guy a jerk

Eastfield Village is located about twenty miles southeast of Albany, New York, in the town of East Nassau. Even in midwinter, seen across a barren field, this one-man collection of architectural artifacts is impressive.

or what?'' look. He paused before responding.

Oddly, I can remember his words precisely. He said, "That's because no yo-yo has destroyed it yet."

Looking at a house with him, whatever its condition, is to see it in a wholly new light.

The highway was built in the 1960s with funds from the 1956 Federal Highway Act. It is wide and straight, the builders having cut a deep and regular swath across the rolling countryside. After the highway comes a parkway. Its construction was begun in the 1930s, and its roadbed curves and bounds its way northward. It has no breakdown lane, and trees and branches

encroach on every turn. The parkway's concrete surface seems applied to the landscape rather than sculptured into it as the superhighway's had been.

On the 150-mile trip north from New York City to Eastfield Village, a series of winding, two-way secondary roads are next. Each is lined with an alternating pattern of pastures and commercial buildings and houses. Some of the buildings are so close to the road that it is immediately obvious that they predate the automobile. When the byway had been a narrow cart path, it hadn't encroached upon the frontage of those structures.

Then there are dirt roads, the last of them called Mud Pond Road. I remember wondering the first time I traveled its length if perhaps the muddy quality of the roadway itself had inspired the name. The last instruction directs you into a dirt driveway, and a "parking lot," a rather grandiose term when applied to a grassy bank adjacent to a small pond. You continue on foot, past a stone wall, and along a rutted road on which only a horse pulling a carriage would feel at home.

In retrospect, it seems only appropriate that the roads themselves represent a sort of time travel, culminating in a perfect meadow and a view of a village amid the tree line at the far edge. Donald Carpentier lives in this collection of buildings, which is less than a village but more than a museum.

You won't find Eastfield Village in your Rand McNally Road Atlas. It is a village in name only, though it has a church, two taverns, a doctor's office, a blacksmith shop, a carpentry shop, and several dwelling houses, a total of more than twenty buildings, all of which date from between 1787 and 1840. Carpentier, his wife, Denise, and their toddler daughter, Hannah, are the lone permanent residents.

Carpentier has earned a national reputation among preservationists for the workshops he has given there each summer since 1976. Morgan Phillips of the Society for the Preservation of New England Antiquities told *The New York Times* a decade ago, "Don is an undiscovered treasure. [He's] a real resource, someone who can teach a lot of us a lot of things."

Carpentier's reputation has grown despite the fact that none of his buildings has been restored to a state of Instamatic perfection. Rip Van Winkle, had he awakened a century or so later, would have felt quite at home here. The weathered clapboards, the absence of power lines, and the outhouses are straight out of Washington Irving's era. If a polished patina is essential to your appreciation of a restoration, then Eastfield probably isn't for you. Carpentier himself says, "I don't want it to look all neat and polished like a museum. The buildings will always be a little run-down, just for the fun of it and to make the place seem real."

Eastfield is not a "visitor's village" like Colonial Williamsburg or Old Sturbridge Village. Though the founders of Sturbridge (which is the subject, in part, of the next chapter) and Eastfield shared a concern for preserving the past, their approaches had little in common beyond that initial motivation. Sturbridge Village was the conspicuous project of a wealthy family named Wells. They bought acreage on the open market, hired noted architects, and invested considerable funds in buying and restoring buildings. They hired attorneys to draft nonprofit corporation papers and, in general, went about establishing their village in the manner of people of means, even to the point of composing detailed articles of organization.

Donald Carpentier has never applied for nonprofit status or financial grants. He composed no written statement of intent. He started later (he wasn't even born until 1951). When he reconstructed his first building at Eastfield in 1971, Old Sturbridge Village was thirty-five years old. Carpentier began with resources that consisted of little more than a pickup truck and his father's reluctant permission to construct a building on an eight-acre woodlot adjacent to the "east field" of the family's dairy farm.

No ticket offices or souvenir shops are to be found at Eastfield. No one is dressed in period costume. Even if he wanted to run the place as a tourist stop—which he most emphatically does not—Carpentier would probably balk at the cost of the insurance required and that would be that.

Carpentier hates insurance bills almost as much as he hates circular-saw marks. Not that he has anything against Skil saws. It's just that a saw with a circular blade was rarely used in domestic construction until about 1820. So he gets angry when he sees a well-funded restoration village displaying careless reproductions. He has been known to react to the presence of circular-saw marks on an allegedly eighteenth-century door-jamb the way most people respond to a skunk in their path. He goes in the other direction as quickly as possible, personally offended by the whole matter.

Eastfield Village is an act of Don Carpentier's imagination; he is its creator and director. Pursuing his unusual life's work has meant that Carpentier has had to endure a certain amount of derision from friends, neighbors, and family. Years ago, some

One of the village streets at Eastfield. In the foreground is a Greek Revival doctor's office that, when restored, will serve as the Village library. Next are a gambrel-roofed tavern (center) and the blacksmith shop. *Eastfield Village*

locals took to calling him "the Squire of Eastfield," an appel-
lation that, upon occasion, was accompanied by a condescend-
ing chuckle or harrumph. They may have thought it folly then,
but today the Squire does have his very own village.

Don Carpentier is a bit like the softhearted animal lover who
nurses wounded birds back to health. But in his case it's old
buildings rather than wild animals, and his ministrations tend
to the disciplines of restoration and preservation.

He's saved buildings from a range of fates. His blacksmith
shop had become a pigpen, the weaver's house was scheduled
to be used for firefighting practice, his tin shop was about to
be smashed asunder by the blade of a 'dozer.

Eastfield Village is intended for the workers of the antiques
and restoration worlds, not the dealers or the drones. Carpentier
is a gifted craftsman, one who has mastered an astonishing
variety of old-time trades. He's a carpenter and a joiner and a
cabinetmaker. His self-taught skills also include tinsmithing and
blacksmithing, grain painting, shoemaking, printing, plastering,
bricklaying, stonecutting, and pottery. All of these trades fuel
his dual passions, doing things right and doing them the way
they used to be done.

Carpentier has been a consultant to other restorations such
as Hancock Shaker Village and Old Sturbridge Village. He's
worked on several movies as a consultant on period sets, props,
and furnishings (notably *The Bostonians*, *The Europeans*, and
Ironweed). Municipalities (including New York's state capital,
Albany), individuals, and even real estate developers have hired
him to help restore specific structures. But his greatest influence
is probably not what he himself does but what his acolytes have
done.

At Eastfield, Carpentier has created a unique educational
institution. Each summer, Eastfield Village offers a dozen or
so workshops in historic preservation and in trades Carpentier
himself has mastered, like housewrighting, joinery, tinsmithing,
restoration carpentry, grain painting, wood carving, and

coopering. He teaches some himself and hires experts in the field to teach others. "I was tired of stuffy organizations that required master's degrees of their students," Carpentier once told me. "And I thought it would be fun to have a school that taught the kinds of things I wanted to learn."

Some of the courses are taught nowhere else. Carpentier has spent his life readying himself to teach "Dismantling Historic Structures." All the buildings at the Village were photographed and diagrammed, then disassembled and loaded piece by piece into Carpentier's pickup, and brought to Eastfield for reassembly. He started moving buildings as a teenager and has been at it ever since.

Teaching at Eastfield isn't formal schooling. There's always a certain amount of storytelling. Some courses include a slide show, and shop talk and problem solving are usually to be heard. That's inevitable when you get the sort of students Eastfield draws. They range from housewives who want to fix up their old houses to full-time craftsmen. In my many visits over the past several years, I've met architects and contractors; restoration professionals from Canada, Winterthur, several universities, and New York City's Landmarks Preservation Commission; and teachers and policemen and antiques dealers and, mostly, homeowners.

Carpentier and the other instructors are hands-on craftsmen who know their materials as few instructors do. So they talk rather than lecture. Invariably, *everyone*, teacher and student alike, takes tool in hand and does a bit of work. According to Carpentier: "You can read books and articles, and look at things in museums. And you may think that you understand what life and work was like back then, but only after you try to do something yourself do you realize how many questions you still need to ask."

Given Carpentier's education, none of this is surprising. While pursuing a degree in historic preservation and architecture, he discovered that neither his lecturers nor the books in the library could answer his questions. He had to go about discovering the explanations for himself. He earned a degree

In the dismantling
process every part must
be labeled and keyed to
detailed drawings.
Pictured is the joint
between a rafter, post,
and beam of a timber-
frame structure, a small
shed ready for dismantling.

from Empire State College in Saratoga Springs, New York, but
it was the result of a string of independent studies.

The degree wasn't the point anyway. For Don Carpentier,
more than two decades of the most intimate architectural recon-
structive surgery imaginable have given him an understanding
of old buildings shared by very few people. When he looks at
a building, he doesn't see surfaces; he sees structures within.
To him, plaster cracks aren't worrisome, they're keyholes
through which to peek. Textures can be read for the information
they offer about changes made over time.

One day I rode along to watch him inspect a house in Rens-
selaer, New York, just outside of Albany. The house looked as
though a battalion of angry escaped convicts had camped there
for several days. Most of the windows were broken, and the
interior was full of trash and smelled dank and moldy. The

mess hardly mattered, as a bulldozer was scheduled to arrive in a few days to crush the structure into its own foundation in order to make room for an enormous housing development.

When we arrived at the house, Carpentier told me it had been built in the Dutch style at the turn of the nineteenth century. He had been to the spot once before and had concluded on the basis of that short visit that it was just another old building rehabbed beyond recognition.

The windows had been replaced. "See the Victorian two-over-twos?" he asked. "They were once twelve-over-twelves." The floor plan had been changed radically and he pointed out that a pair of late-nineteenth-century ells had been added (their age was evident to him from the clapboards and windows). Most of the original architectural details seemed to be gone.

He was there to study and learn from the house; I was doing research for an article about him. What I found myself involved in was what I have come to recognize as the process of "reading a house."

You start with the skin, Carpentier instructed, working from the outside in. You look at materials and how they are used. You identify the kinds of fasteners (nails and screws) and look for layers of paint and anything that tells you something about the house. You break through the skin where it is not original and pick up evidence as you go. A story develops.

Don Carpentier reads clues and reaches conclusions faster than Jessica Fletcher ever could. We knocked a hole in the plaster ceiling of the first floor, and smooth hand-hewn and hand-planed beams emerged, reinforcing Carpentier's conclusion that the house was Dutch. What made the discovery remarkable was that the paint appeared to be the original coat of Prussian blue.

A key word in Carpentier's lexicon is "original." He used it often as the Dutch house was revealed. Original means unchanged, not rehabilitated, not distorted beyond recognition. He inspected the chimney foundation of the Dutch house, standing in several inches of mud, surrounded by spiderwebs and a ceiling so low that every beam threatened like the boom of a sailboat. But when he found that the original eight-foot-square "crib" foundation of stone and mortar was intact, he practically jumped for joy. The stones told him where the hearths had been, and despite the dirt and dark, he exclaimed, "It's beautiful, isn't it? Just look at that!" To Carpentier, finding the original is like catching the big fish or cooking the perfect soufflé.

Like "original," the words "early" and "late" are endowed with special meanings for old-building fanciers. Depending upon context, they can be used to refer to a time in a given period (early Victorian is pre-Civil War, late is more like 1890). Or if the period is unspecified, a more general reference is intended, usually to the era before or after machine-made goods came into widespread use. Circa 1830 is generally accepted as the dividing line. Thus, a 1790 house is termed "early," while an 1850 one is "late."

"Period" also has a special meaning in restoration jargon. It implies that an object was made in a specified era rather than being a later copy. An 1810 Federal mantel is "period," but a copy made a hundred years later during the Colonial Revival is termed "Federal-style."

As we completed our inspection, a clear profile of the old house emerged. The abandoned, tumbledown building was a good deal more than simply a vague remnant of what it once had been. The house remained, in fact, a fine example of an early American Dutch house. Today, of course, it is long gone.

The loss—in this case, the demolition—of such houses is one reason why Carpentier does what he does. He has an enduring fascination with old things and old ways, one that he remembers first recognizing early in his adolescence when he found some old bottles on the family property, bottles unlike those he encountered in his middle-class home in 1960s America.

Often he found them secreted in the niches on the fieldstone walls. "The bottoms had dates like 1882 stamped on them. I just couldn't believe they could be lying around outside and not be in a museum somewhere," Carpentier remembers.

He discovered handmade bottles, too. The imperfections were so numerous that no two had exactly the same shape. The colors varied in shade and intensity.

The bottles may have helped focus Carpentier's thinking, but buildings are what have always absorbed his imagination. There the character of the handmade is even more evident. Every square inch of the skeleton of a pre-machine-age building bears the marks of human muscle power, since every beam had to be shaped by hand using a broadax. Only after the middle of the nineteenth century were saws in general use that were capable of cutting a long, large-dimension beam. In an early house, each piece—every one of thousands—had to be made or shaped by hand. Carpentier remembers experimenting with old timber-framed buildings as early as age nine or ten.

Recently I asked Carpentier about the appeal of old things. What made him devote his life to them? We were having a leisurely after-dinner conversation, one that ranged from his new pottery experiments to a little schoolhouse he had just purchased for the Village.

He answered immediately, without so much as a philosophical "Well . . ."

"There was never any question. It wasn't like I sat down and made a decision. It just happened. I remember thinking after college that, someday, you're going to have to get a real job like real people, but it never happened." That was it. He's very matter-of-fact, at times clear and direct almost to the point of abruptness.

I decided to take it a step further, and asked what the common denominator was. Was it things *old*?

"I don't think it was just that things were old, it was the style somehow." There he paused. Later, I played back the tape of the conversation and realized he hadn't been satisfied with his choice of words. "Style" didn't quite do it.

"I think it was that here was something *handmade*," he continued. "Growing up when we did, there wasn't much handmade. People looked down on it. Only later with the hippies and the Bicentennial did people begin to like the handmade again."

There was another factor, too. "I've always wanted to know how things worked and how they were made."

So the proverbial die was cast? Understanding how these old, handmade things were made did it for you?

"The old didn't matter as much as the quality of the crafts-manship."

It was only fitting, actually, that our exchange ended with craftsmanship, for more than any of the other things he is— teacher, consultant, antiques dealer, and so on—Carpentier is a craftsman. He can make or restore objects made of wood, tin, brass, or pottery. The finished products, whether they are Palladian windows for his tavern or creamware mocha bowls, are always of the highest quality.

With that standard in mind, let me introduce you to what is perhaps his grandest piece of craftsmanship.

The First Universalist Church of Duanesburg was built between 1836 and 1838 in the little hamlet of Braman's Corners, a few miles west of Albany, New York. It stood fifty feet high to the tip of its belfry, its pediment and pilasters proudly recalling its classical inspiration. The cost of construction was recorded as $1,381.

Today the church is no longer in Duanesburg. Fifty miles away from its original setting, it dominates the village green at Eastfield. The second time around, it took roughly five years to build, starting in 1982, when Don Carpentier purchased it for $1,000.

Over the course of its history, the church has seen its share of events. It was used as a place of worship until the 1880s, when the shrinking congregation disbanded. Universalist authorities maintained the empty edifice until the 1920s, then it fell into disrepair. The abandoned church was sold in 1937 to a printer named Smith, who used it to store equipment.

During World War II, Smith moved his family into it. Until that time, the original configuration had remained. The interior was a large, open auditorium with a towering vaulted ceiling and a horseshoe-shaped balcony that lined the rear and side walls. The altar backed onto the vestibule at the front of the church.

Smith converted the church into a two-story home and print-shop. To do so, he added partitions and a second floor, removing the pews and taking down the elaborately grain-painted paneling around the balcony. A frugal man, he didn't throw anything away, stowing everything in the attic, down to minute, one-inch-square pieces of molding.

The Smiths lived there until 1961. Some years later Smith died, and in 1978 the contents of the abandoned structure were put up for auction.

Don Carpentier saw the announcement for the auction, an inconspicuous ad listing printer's supplies as the principal goods

In this circa 1920 photo, the First Universalist Church of Duanesburg appears much as Carpentier found it more than half a century later. *Eastfield Village*

for sale. Among the other structures at Eastfield Village is an 1840 printshop, which, at that time, Carpentier was filling with printing type and other equipment to complement both the building and his Columbia printing press, an 1876 version of a press originally patented in 1814.

Carpentier saw the old church for the first time when he attended the auction. It was then a rotting hulk, a rabbit warren of bedrooms and storage areas, complete with car parts, miscellaneous junk, and some remnants of its printshop days. The building spoke to Carpentier.

"I couldn't believe it," Carpentier recalled. "I went in and saw beautiful, original Federal staircases, all clean and crisp. There were grain-painted doors complete with original hardware."

When the auction got underway, Carpentier paid eleven dollars for the solar lamp that he later determined had stood on the pulpit. He bought doors and hardware for twenty-one dollars. Grain-painted columns cost him less than thirty. Somebody else bought a cupboard that had been at the rear of the church for forty-five dollars.

He returned home with his purchases. Second thoughts brought him back the next day to offer to buy the interior of the church for salvage. A friend along for the ride took one look at the imposing structure and said, "Don, you've got to have this church."

Carpentier remembers responding, "What're you nuts? It's huge!" He wasn't interested in big buildings at the time, and the owner refused Carpentier's offer to buy parts of the building for salvage. The church remained a decaying and forgotten structure in a town whose fortunes had faded.

Three years later, Carpentier's phone rang. He was offered another church that was to be demolished since a reservoir was shortly to flood its site. The price was right (the terms were essentially "Gimme a dollar and get it outta here"), but the church dated from the 1850s and wasn't consistent with the rest of the buildings at Eastfield. After some consideration, Carpentier said no, thanks.

"That call made me think," he later acknowledged. "I had to do something. I knew I couldn't go on running the school in a twenty-foot-square room." At the time, the largest room at Eastfield was the interior of a square meetinghouse, a composite structure made from a miscellany of old building parts, many of them from an old Shaker building a few miles from Eastfield. The workshops were becoming increasingly popular, but at that point Carpentier wasn't sure what his next move should be.

He considered other possibilities before he remembered the church at Braman's Corners. "Wouldn't it be a real quirk of fate?" he remembered asking himself. "They wouldn't sell it to me once, but I went to see if it was still standing."

He saw many more signs of deterioration and abuse than he remembered. The belfry roof was leaking; more windows were broken. But the First Universalist Church of Duanesburg was still there. And, of course, a variety of its original bits and pieces resided in a barn back at Eastfield.

He visited several more times. His collection then consisted of one- or two-room structures, vernacular buildings used for individual trades. Since he had never seriously considered purchasing so sizable a building before, he found himself having to rethink some long-held notions about Eastfield.

He inspected the church carefully. "I just could not believe the enormity of the giant beams and timbers. I'd never hired a crane before, but I knew I would need one to move the church. I'd never paid more than fifty dollars for a building either."

He decided he wanted it. He managed to contact Smith's widow, Eugenia. On a Sunday morning in April 1982, he went to visit her. She offered to sell him the building for $1,500. He told her he would restore it, and he described Eastfield. Eventually, she agreed to sell him the building for $1,000.

A contract was signed. "The day I bought it," recalled Carpentier, "I really thought I'd gone over the top."

It took Carpentier and his brother James ten weeks to clean, dismantle, and move the building piecemeal back to Eastfield.

Every morning they left home at six o'clock, traveling fifty miles and seventy minutes to Braman's Corners. They would work until dark, load the pickup, and drive home. Every piece had to be numbered and recorded to make reassembly possible. ("If you don't put them back the way you took them down, they don't fit.") Clapboards, timber frame, moldings, and other piles of pieces dotted the landscape at Eastfield. "By the second week of August, we'd got it all home."

Back in the Village, a spot in the onetime woodlot had to be cleared. September was devoted to removing the trees and to digging trenches for the foundation. The footings were poured on September 30. In October, foundation walls were built of new bluestone. In the original structure, the lowest members of the timber frame, the sills, had been rotted, but by early November, the foundation was lined with sills of fresh wood. The back wall was raised in one piece on November 5; by

Removed, restored, and repainted, the church at Eastfield Village in 1988.

December 31, the frame was completed and outdoor work was halted for the winter.

Not that complete idleness ensued until spring. Carpentier worked at restoring the church's badly rotted window sash. He also managed to uncover the church records in a state-owned library in Albany. They contained a wealth of information about the church and its history.

He learned that the builder, a carpenter named William Kellogg, had been hired in March 1836 to build the church. By September of that year the congregation amended its original plan, and the belfry was added to the design. The church records reported a second subscription of $133, on top of the original cost of $1,248.

In the spring of 1983, work resumed at Eastfield. By late May, the roof was on and the chimney built. The floor was in place in time for the first workshop of the year in June.

Work continued by fits and starts over the next several years. The last clapboard was nailed in place on Christmas Day 1983. In the winter of 1984, the balcony went up. In the summers of 1985 and 1986, portions of the building were plastered.

Carpentier's concerted labors have been enhanced by his ever observant eye. In dismantling the church, he saved a variety of parts that, at the time, he couldn't identify but that would later emerge as pieces of the puzzle. He found balcony bits, a curved wall that had been the facing of the first pew, and enough sections of the original marbleized pulpit so that he was able to reconstruct it.

One of his most serendipitous finds came in the summer of 1983. He was antiquing with a friend and stopped at a shop in western New York State. They got talking to another patron, and found themselves traveling a mile or two down the road to a converted chicken coop. They examined some salvaged house parts, but none interested Carpentier.

While waiting for his friend to complete his business, he spied some other goods in another section of the chicken coop. He recognized the graining on a pile of boards and realized they were the missing pews from his church. He found out who owned them—a woman who had planned to use them to make a floor in her kitchen—and bought the pew parts. One year to the day from the raising of the first elements of the church's frame at Eastfield, he brought them back to the Village.

Certainly the most momentous day in the recent history of the church was June 27, 1987. On that day, Carpentier and Denise Keegan Hartman were married there. It was the culmination of five years of work.

Taking a cue from the building, the bride wore a copy of an 1830 gown of plaid silk and a tortoise-shell mantilla hair comb. The groom wore a frock coat, neckcloth, and beaver stovepipe hat. The church, too, was dressed up for the occasion with a fresh coat of sky-blue paint on its vaulted ceiling twenty-two feet above the floor. A giant curtain of red wool was the backdrop at the altar, held in place by decorative brass tiebacks in rosette shapes.

The bride and groom, Denise and Donald Carpentier, emerging from the church at Eastfield on June 27, 1987. *Eastfield Village*

"I had to be married here," Carpentier said on his wedding day. "That church is very close to me, after having put all that time into it."

Carpentier tossed off that explanation, but there is a subtext to his words. As anyone who knows him can attest, Eastfield Village is his life. His words suggest an element beyond reason. An imperative is at work, one that I suspect he himself would be hard pressed to explain. It wasn't simply the church or the labor he had invested in it. Carpentier is of the past—and he acts as if he belongs there.

The church was standing by the time I first visited Don Carpentier, so I missed its raising. In recent years, however, Carpentier has raised other buildings in the Village, relying on the help of a group of volunteers.

These men and women have come to be known informally as the Eastfield Irregulars. After he completes the restoration of a dismantled building frame he has brought to the Village, Carpentier puts the word out, and thirty or more people come and spend the weekend. Some have been to more than a dozen raisings at Eastfield, but it isn't because they get paid. In fact, most of them have paid Carpentier to take part in Eastfield's workshops.

Eastfield is not a place for a lazy afternoon's diversion where, for the price of admission, you can flirt casually with a forgotten past but still be home in time for dinner. At Eastfield, most students come for a week at a time. They escape the twentieth century to live in some semblance of the medieval manner Lewis Mumford termed "Yankee Communism." They live, work, and stay at the Village. The outhouses scattered about aren't for show. Aside from the Carpentiers' personal dwelling, the Village has no indoor plumbing.

The students prepare their communal meals over an open fire in an early American fireplace. Their evenings are lit by the candles that they bring to pay for their room (ten white candles entitles a student to a week's stay on a rope bed with feather ticking). The experience isn't to be had elsewhere; it has its own chemistry, a camaraderie that develops between these sojourners who are curious about not only the trades and skills but also the life of pre-industrial America. It's part of why people keep coming back.

On one sunny weekend in the summer of 1985, the William Briggs tavern was raised at Eastfield, and watching it go up was an education. Much of its structure dates from 1793, but about a third of the gable-roofed building was an 1803 addition to one end. As work commenced that weekend, the 3,500 miscellaneous pieces of the building were stacked around the perimeter of the Village. The timber frame itself consisted of 600 pieces of oak, some as large as ten by twelve inches in section and more than forty feet in length. Following the usual pattern, the building had been disassembled over a period of several months and trucked to Eastfield from its original location in Hoosick, New York.

The education that weekend wasn't merely in timber frames and Federal architecture. There was also a lesson in the cooperation that is required to raise a building like the William Briggs tavern. The enormous structure (it's even larger than the church) has two parlors, a kitchen ell off the rear, and a second-floor ballroom with a vaulted ceiling. If it sounds big, then just imagine how it looked as the first wall went up, with nearly a ton of oak frame tilting upward immediately over the heads of a dozen members of the crew.

Carpentier's master carpenter for the weekend was his close friend William McMillen. Known to all as Billy, McMillen is restoration supervisor at the Richmondtown Restoration on Staten Island. During several weeks of the summer, he's also a fixture at Eastfield, as he teaches several courses there. His wife, Judy, teaches, too, her course being "Fireplace and Bake-Oven Cooking."

McMillen came to old-house restoration by birthright. His father founded Richmondtown, and McMillen figures that he

Today we would call the process of raising a timber frame "labor-intensive." "Dangerous" is another applicable word, considering the tremendous weight of the oak frame. Over the course of the 1985 weekend during which this photograph was taken, the frame of the William Briggs tavern was successfully (and safely) raised and the building now nears completion. *Eastfield Village*

probably wasn't yet on solid food the first time he visited the place. "By fourteen or fifteen, I was taking care of the gun and military collection," he remembers.

He went to work officially at Richmondtown at nineteen and has been there over twenty-five years. Old buildings are what he knows best. His idea of a vacation is to go someplace he hasn't been before and look at buildings. One year it was New Orleans. Another year it was the Netherlands, Dutch buildings being one of his specialties, thanks to their incidence on Staten Island.

McMillen, like Carpentier, is a combination of architectural historian and craftsman. He has restored or helped to restore virtually all of the nearly forty buildings at Richmondtown. He has come to understand windows, doors, moldings, and other house parts through taking them apart, fixing them, and copying them. When he doesn't have a model to go by, he finds other sources.

He has a substantial library for reference, but warns about relying on books. "There are lots of things books will not tell you. Lots of times you'll find a photograph of how it looks but not how to do it or why. Basically, only an old-timer who has done it could tell you, but they're mostly gone.

"By the end of the nineteenth century," McMillen continued, "they began doing books about the old ways, but they missed the reasons."

That's where people like McMillen and Carpentier come in. Hands-on craftsmen, they pass along the how-to-do-it skills they have resurrected.

"It's a magnificent piece of woodwork," Carpentier commented after the tavern's frame was up. "It'll last hundreds of years more with a decent roof." The work was by no means finished, however. As would have been the case two hundred years ago, the finish work was left to the individual owner or carpenter. A substantial skeleton stood in place, but it was devoid of its flesh of thousands of shingles, clapboards, and windows (over one hundred individual sashes, all of which had to be replicated from scratch, the originals having been long since replaced). Carpentier had years of work ahead of him.

The raising had taken three long days, and even then, as a sunset rain began to fall, only a handful of the rafters were in place. In 1793, it had probably taken a single day to raise the tavern.

"I think they knew more then than we do," Carpentier observed.

Some things are taught, others are learned. Carpentier and McMillen have taught me the names and shapes of many moldings, but it wasn't until a freak October snowstorm in 1987 that

I learned the powerful effect moldings can have on the visual imagination.

The snowstorm led to widespread power failures. The electricity was off for a week, and I found myself living in the age of candle power. A trio of kerosene lamps and a dozen or so candles lit the house.

I learned then how much brighter electric light is. Most of us are so profligate with our electricity that shadows are banished from our normal living spaces. But with the candles and oil lamps, shadows were suddenly everywhere. Walking around the house carrying a candle or kerosene lamp, I saw the shadows move, sliding along the floor or springing forth from chairs or other obstacles.

Even when at rest, candlelight is active. Any draft causes the flame to flicker and issue a plume of smoke. That flicker also translates into a delicate play of light on any nearby surface. A piece of furniture with curves or carvings suddenly has a darkness below and within and forward surfaces that offer themselves for inspection.

But it was the moldings that were truly transformed. I noticed the cornice molding at the joint of the wall and ceiling as if I'd never seen it before. Its several curves emerged as distinct shadings. Rather than being a piece of wood painted a glossy white, it was gray, and grayer, and almost black, and it moved with the candle flame. Its dentils proffered blocks defined by tiny voids on either side.

When the power returned, I had long since decided I was glad we don't live in an earlier century. But I see moldings differently now. I understand that the forms I've long known the names of have a dramatic capacity to give shape and subtlety to corners and wall surfaces. I suspect it wasn't a simple accident of technology that the advent of steady electric light coincided with the growing poverty of molding profiles and details.

At their simplest, moldings are transitions from one surface or material to another. A baseboard molding seems to join the floor to the wall, the cornice to connect the wall to the ceiling. Architrave moldings define the shape of doors or windows

This photograph of a column at the entry portico to an 1839 Greek Revival mansion suggests something of the play of shadows over the classical elements in the Ionic order. The ability to appreciate and to take advantage of the ever-changing qualities of light was once a given in studying and practicing architecture.

where they cut through walls. Chair rails both protect plaster walls and, when there is wainscoting, link it to the plaster above. Picture moldings provide a convenient place for paintings to be hung, but also visually bring down tall ceilings and give a room a different proportion.

Until the 1830s, all shaped wood was formed with hand tools. Rough-cut boards were smoothed with hand planes. These tools had slightly curved blades, so in hand-planed work, even beneath layers of paint, the slight waves made by the plane can be distinguished with a brush of the fingertips across the grain.

Moldings are, by definition, strips of wood, stone, or plaster that are used for finish or decorative purposes. They have regular channels or projections. In the handmade age of American houses, wooden moldings were worked using wooden planes fitted with iron blades, "plane irons." As with smoothing planes, the molding plane is repeatedly pushed along the length of a piece of wood. On each pass, shavings of wood are carved out. In the case of a simple molding profile, a few strokes produce a finished molding; with complicated combinations of curves, it takes more time and effort.

To the uninitiated, moldings can seem complex. However, in examining old houses, people like Don Carpentier read them like road signs. They are among the most useful indicators of age; they speak a comprehensible language of curves and straight lines in simple combinations, a language with into-nations as to the era and the craftsmanship employed.

Moldings offered an opportunity to the pre-industrial builder in a rough-hewn age to create soft lines and shapes. They were an exercise in decoration, one of the few in early, utilitarian structures. It was certainly labor-intensive, as a single doorway required shaping ten or more separate molding pieces.

Carpentier's collection of hand planes numbers in the hundreds. He uses them constantly in replicating missing moldings in his buildings. In his hands, the molding plane seems a fitting symbol for how different an age that was. Nothing was available off-the-shelf, and so much of the workmanship bespoke not only the time invested but a concern for shape and quality.

Walking around Eastfield Village, one encounters thousands
of pieces of moldings. Given the vintage of the buildings there,
all the original moldings were made by hand, and several restoration courses given at Eastfield teach students how to use
and maintain old-fashioned planes.

At Carpentier's personal village, the visitor can't help but
admire the hand of the craftsman on the range of buildings
assembled there. It's a historical exercise and a work in progress,
but it's more, too.

Most visitors find themselves amazed at what one man has
managed to create using a strong back and an enduring fascination with the old ways. Yet it is important to keep Eastfield
Village and its proprietor in perspective.

Some have called Don Carpentier "the Sage of Eastfield,"
but the title doesn't quite fit. Why it doesn't is illuminating.
He's too young, for one thing; for another, the knowledge he
dispenses isn't learning or wisdom of a profound sort. He isn't
a bookish man, really; in fact, he has periodic bouts with an
inner-ear ailment called Ménière's disease, which leaves him
dizzy after reading for any length of time. Yet Carpentier's
learning in his discipline is unparalleled.

He has accumulated knowledge, thanks to the unending passion he has for the handmade and the well crafted. He has
created for himself and visitors to his little village a microcosm
of the past. He has an insatiable desire to make things, to fix
things, to understand them and how they are made.

I like to think that Carpentier resembles the protagonist in
The Admirable Crichton. Crichton was the butler who, when
shipwrecked on a deserted island with the family he served,
became the de facto leader by virtue of his skills and practicality.
Wealth, social station, and the other intangibles of society were
suddenly without value. In the same way, Don Carpentier probably wouldn't mind half so much as the rest of us if, through
some cataclysm or natural disaster, the world were to find itself
deprived of electricity and other accoutrements of modernity.
He would have lessons to teach us about survival in an altered
world.

Carpentier spent more than a dozen years living in his village without a flush toilet and with no electricity. At first, perhaps, it was his way of demonstrating his independence, but gradually it became less of a game and more his personal commitment to recapturing something important that was being lost–that without him might have been lost forever.

The mysteries for Carpentier are the basic ones. He is less intrigued by how a computer can set type or how a fifty-ton printing press can produce ten thousand books an hour than in how a pair of human hands can position lead letters in a galley and in how the screw on the press is adjusted so the paper receives just the right amount of ink. It takes longer, the results aren't exactly interchangeable, but there is a notable humanity about it all.

Yet when it comes to applying the Carpentier model to others–ourselves or other restoration professionals–essentially none of us can invest the time Carpentier has in learning his crafts. Carpentier is entirely singular. He isn't a "homeowner," and he doesn't run a museum. He's not an academic or a philosopher.

Carpentier has pursued the handmade and the well made at a time when most people are largely desensitized to the pleasures of good craftsmanship. In dealing with any artifact that represents the past, we should never forget that the standards of that time (and Don Carpentier's standards) were (are) much different from those of today.

Today, almost everything is disposable. If you buy a new dresser at a department store for a few hundred dollars, you and the salesperson know full well that it is worth less the moment you uncrate it at your home than it was when the credit-card transaction was processed. Yet when you buy a nineteenth-century dresser at auction for the same price, you have made an investment in something that has already demonstrated a certain permanence. Its very survival is evidence of that timelessness. If it was made after 1850, it probably has next to no handmade parts, yet some years hence, it will be worth more than the price you paid, despite a few scratches and a drawer that perpetually sticks.

As the dominant mode of manufacture, the handmade has been dead for more than a century. Nothing short of a nuclear holocaust is likely to reverse that reality and perhaps that is as it should be. That doesn't mean, however, that there isn't room for a renaissance of tradesmen who can perform specialized tasks–both restoring the old and making the new–in the worlds of architecture, furniture, and hundreds of other crafts.

Ever since the birth of the industrial revolution, the loss of handcraft has been bemoaned in some quarters. Pockets of quality workmanship have survived, and some have even been born anew. Carpentier's workshops at Eastfield have certainly fostered the spread of such skills. Actually, fine craftsmanship isn't dead; it's just very difficult to find.

Carpentier's wish to conserve is intuitive and instinctual. The bottles, the buildings, and the thousands of artifacts that have caught his notice did so because his eye was attuned to perceive what was special about them. His name is Carpentier after all; chances are that further up his family tree there are other craftsmen, carpenters of an earlier age.

Carpentier is a peculiar admixture. The Creator's formula might well read something like: Take one part collector, one part teacher, and three parts craftsman. Mix well. But don't forget to add a dollop of extract of curiosity. Don, you see, got enough for a schoolhouseful of little children. His supply shows no sign of running out.

4
The Village Historian

_____

People will not look forward to posterity, who never look backward to their ancestors.
　　　　　　　　　　—*Edmund Burke,* Reflections on the
　　　　　　　　　　Revolution in France (*1790*)

"By the time that I was nearly through with my undergraduate work, I had concluded that I wanted to find some way in which I could earn a living doing history," John Obed Curtis recalled. Obed is a family surname, compliments of his maternal grandfather.

Sitting in his cluttered office, John Curtis wore suspenders, gray slacks, a button-down shirt, and a tie. His glasses were gold-rimmed. A solidly built man in his early fifties, Curtis looks quite capable of putting in a good day's physical labor.

He described to me a childhood trait that would prove useful in pursuing what eventually emerged as his life's work. It was his willingness to learn about old objects from the objects themselves.

"I had always been interested in old *things,*" he remembered. "In objects and in old houses."

I asked him what it was that attracted him about old things.

"I suppose I got it from my upbringing," he began. "I had grown up in an old house. Though there weren't very many

59

antiques in our family, I've always had a fascination with antiques and with old objects."

He stopped, seeming uncharacteristically at sea for a moment. Then he offered an example.

"When my friends were getting cars from the later 1930s to fix up, I got a 1912 Ford. My dad and I restored it. I was fifteen when I bought the car, and it took a couple of years.

"From my parents' perspective, that old Ford was a good thing because it channeled my interests to a car that, chances were, I wouldn't kill myself in. It just wouldn't go very fast."

He shrugged, then smiled and laughed softly to himself. I heard the relieved laugh of a father who has seen his own two sons make it to manhood.

"In retrospect, the car was also a very good investment. I have enjoyed it for many years and expect to enjoy it this summer, too." The practical man was speaking.

I asked him if there was anything special about the experience of working on something of a certain age. Even as a fifteen-year-old, was he conscious of the age of the vehicle having some significance?

"Definitely, yes, it had something to do with the age. All my classmates fixed up newer cars in different ways, hot rods and the like, and I enjoyed riding in their cars.

"But for me part of the enjoyment about the old car—and this is hard to articulate—was an element of romance about the fact that the car was then forty-some years old."

He stopped. "Forty-four years old," he corrected himself.

"It was a car that was made before World War I. It was an example of the automobile that had put this country on wheels and necessitated the creation of the roadway system. So there was a symbolic element to it, too, as the car was an important event in history. It was the Model T Ford, and when people characterize the most important cars in the history of motorcars, the Model T will be right up among them."

There were less intellectual pleasures, too. "It was and is an enjoyable car to work on because it's simple," he admitted. "It gave me as a novice mechanic of age fifteen or sixteen a great sense of accomplishment. I could not only put it together but also have it run and be able to drive it when I was through.

"So there was a sense of fulfillment. But that immediate link with the past was, I guess, 'romantic.'"

Would he use the same word to describe the appeal of old houses, the care and restoration of which became his career?

"I think that 'romance' certainly is a factor, but that's an association with the past on one level only. As I have become involved with more of a range of antique objects, I have found that many of those objects by their very nature can be identified as being the product of a person. That offers a whole new realm for historical research.

"When you're talking about a now eighty-year-old car that in its day was a pioneer of mass production, you can never know who made that car. Very likely, quite a number of people did. So the personalization ends at a certain point. But with a piece of furniture, one that is signed and perhaps even identified as to the town the craftsman worked in, you can learn a great deal more. The process of learning about it is much broader. You get to do research."

The practical realities facing a young college graduate in 1958 had little to do with such introspection. While Curtis had identified architecture as a principal area of interest, at that time there were no graduate programs in historic preservation in this country. (It wasn't until 1964 that the first graduate course was offered at Columbia University.) "So I wrote I don't know how many letters to museums all up and down the eastern seaboard soliciting a position," said Curtis.

He got one. It was a summer job at a seasonal museum. He was a combination curator and janitor at a 1750 fort in Augusta, Maine, that had been a stop on Arnold's march to Quebec during the French and Indian War. A brief stint in the Navy followed, but then it was back to old things again, this time working for the Society for the Preservation of New England Antiquities in Boston, the owner then and now of a superb collection of American buildings.

"I was there for almost a year, long enough to work at setting up what was the first architectural museum at SPNEA. It was a museum of the history of architecture as demonstrated through fragments of buildings. That was a good learning experience, as I got to work with Abbot Lowell Cummings." Then assistant director of SPNEA, Cummings subsequently became director, professor of history at Yale, and the author of notable publications on early American architecture.

But John Curtis is our subject here. On the first of September in 1960, he took a job at a place called Old Sturbridge Village.

He has been there ever since.

Old-fashioned historians have a fondness for drawing lines between points in time. The theory is that individual occurrences can sometimes serve to explain later trends or events. In this way, the invention of the longbow and the steam engine have been portrayed as frozen moments that forever changed the nature of warfare and manufacturing.

In our era, such after-the-fact speculations–and the good storytelling that often comes with them–may be regarded as less worthy than more objective findings of anthropological, archaeological, or other evidence. Even so, I've found that explanatory stories have always worked best in helping me reach first understandings of the past. Sometimes the narratives are a bit theoretical; perhaps too much can be read into them. But I'll take theatre over statistical analysis any day.

In 1877, one such little drama occurred. During that summer, four young men named McKim, Mead, White, and Bigelow went on a holiday trip to New England. They visited Colonial towns, including Marblehead, Newburyport, and Salem, Massachusetts, and Portsmouth, New Hampshire. In Mead's words, "all of us had a great interest in Colonial architecture . . . We made sketches and measured drawings of many of the important Colonial houses."

They might have been inspired by the *American Architect*. In March 1876, an editorial writer had, in the spirit of the Centennial year, advised young architects to study Colonial buildings, many of which were then in disrepair or being demolished. Perhaps the trip had been McKim's idea. For several years he had been writing about and drawing Colonial architecture for such publications as *The New-York Sketch Book of Architecture.*

The trip wasn't full of incident. The four bright young architects merely wandered through the coastline towns. But they took what they saw seriously.

They admired the symmetry of the early American houses, with their balanced arrangements of windows and simple roof shapes. They saw few of the complications of contemporary styles, like the Stick, Gothic Revival, and Queen Anne houses, which featured asymmetrical rooflines, a varied mix of windows, dormers, trusses, porches, wall surfaces, and even turrets and multiple chimneys.

Back at their drawing boards, they put what they had seen to use. Following that trip, the firm of Charles Follen McKim, William Rutherford Mead, and Stanford White drew together a variety of design and structural currents, past and present. In a house McKim built for his future wife, he used old mantels and woodwork salvaged from eighteenth-century American structures. His mining of the past was a physical as well as an aesthetic act.

These men led a move toward Americanization, a transition from the imported to the homegrown in American architecture. They were among the first to recognize that what was built here early on had some merit. Over the next several decades, they became perhaps the best-known proponents of the Colonial Revival style.

The line I'm drawing here—between McKim, Mead, and White and preservation today–is somewhat crooked. Despite the fact that they helped lead American popular architecture into the Colonial Revival, an era that in some areas of the United States has never ended, these men weren't preservationists per se. They were architects more interested in an expression of their own notions of good design than in preserving other people's.

In truth, there were but a handful of preservationists in nine-teenth-century America. Among the most prominent were the members of the Mount Vernon Ladies Association, which was founded in 1858 to save George Washington's home. That group is generally regarded as the first preservation organization in the United States, yet the Ladies began their private fund-raising efforts to save Mount Vernon not out of a concern for the architectural or even the cultural heritage of the house. Rather the impetus was to remember the man who lived there. The logic was that, since Mount Vernon had been built for the father of our country, it should be saved. Today we value the place for other reasons, too (its Banquet Hall is one of the first Adam-inspired interiors in the United States), but for the Mount Vernon Ladies, its appeal was its association.

Not until well after the turn of the twentieth century were buildings saved for their own sake in the United States; only in the 1920s and 1930s did preservation as we know it become a significant movement. During the 1920s, wealthy men like John D. Rockefeller, Jr., and Henry Ford, respectively, estab-lished the restoration at Williamsburg, Virginia, and the open-air museum called Greenfield Village in Dearborn, Michigan.

In the 1930s, there was a broader-based movement. The first local legislation establishing a historic district was passed in 1931 in Charleston, South Carolina. New Orleans and San Antonio followed later in the decade. In 1933, the Historic American Buildings Survey was established. The survey survives to this day, and continues to accumulate measured drawings, photographs, and written data on American architecture.

It was also in the 1930s that a well-to-do family named Wells decided to establish their own village in Massachusetts, in the town of Sturbridge. They hired architects associated with Wil-liamsburg to plan their village; they bought acreage and build-ings; they formed a nonprofit corporation. In 1936 they composed articles of organization which asserted that their purposes were:

> To establish, maintain, and operate a model village wherein shall be exhibited and carried on for the

educational benefit of the public specimens and
reproductions of New England architecture and
antiquities, the arts, crafts, trades, and callings,
commonly practiced in and about New England
villages prior to the period of industrial expansion in
New England.

The Wells family had founded the American Optical Company,
so they were able to draw upon their considerable financial
resources to launch and develop their project.

Their creation became what today is known as Old Sturbridge Village (OSV). McKim, Mead, and White never worked
at OSV but the linear connection is still there. It has only been
lost to the casual eye, like the spider's first silken thread in the
warp and weft of the web.

When listening to some people talk, do you ever get the feeling that they've lost their place? I can't conceive of that happening in a conversation with John Curtis.

He isn't the sort who will say, "The, uh, end of, well, I guess
it would be October." When asked the date of a forthcoming
seminar, he's more likely to respond, "Friday, October 28, Saturday, October 29, and Sunday, October 30."

I get the sense when talking with him that he learned a long
time ago that exact instructions offered with great courtesy are
more likely to be followed than those that leave room for interpretation. When precise, museum-quality restoration work is
your goal, there's little room for guesswork.

John Curtis is director of the curatorial department at OSV,
a post he has held since 1968. OSV is a "visitor's village"; its
underlying conceit is that the clock stopped there in the 1830s.

He described the goals there this way: "Here a conscious
ongoing effort has been made to try to re-create a hypothetical
and integrated (in the old-fashioned sense of the word) village
that would, through its architecture and its crafts and demonstrations, illustrate the interrelationship of people living in a
small, rural, inland New England community in the 1830s.

"We want to show who the craftsmen were, what their trading network was; who the agricultural people were, what they did, what their markets were; and who the intellectual and community leaders were. In other words, we're trying in our interpretation and in our selection of buildings to create something that knits together as a whole, as a cohesive community."

To put it yet another way, all the lines here lead to one imaginary place and one time, the fictitious hamlet established on OSV's two hundred and thirty acres in the 1930s. Except that the calendars there are to read 1830.

There are dwellings, mills, and trade, professional, and farm buildings. All have been brought from other locations around New England to form a composite community. Half a million or so annual visitors pay to visit OSV. Ticket fees provide the bulk of OSV's budget.

I've been there many times over the years, the first time at about seven years of age, but I still find the place a little disorienting. It just doesn't look like civilization as we know it today. Dirt roads intercut the landscape. Split-rail fences, fields of corn, pastures, woodlots, and a wide variety of buildings fill the spaces in between. In addition to the tourists, there are oxen, cows, chickens, horses, cats, and an appropriate variety of other animals.

About three hundred local residents are employed at OSV, many as "interpreters" dressed in period attire. They work the fields, make candles, cook pies, and do innumerable other chores as they would have been performed in the early nineteenth century. Great care has been taken to expunge all signs of the labor-saving devices we take for granted.

OSV shouldn't be confused with a real village. It's a very good stage set on which the curious visitor can be sparked into a series of bright historical epiphanies. As you stand there watching a meal being prepared, you suddenly find that your face is flushed because it's really quite hot immediately in front of the fireplace where the cooking is done. If you're tall, you find yourself aware of low ceilings and of how much smaller people must have been then. Indoors it's darker, too, and there's an absolute minimum of our modern conveniences, which means zero indoor plumbing and electricity. Inanimate power didn't appear as a factor in family life until the 1880s in the great cities, and in many rural areas not until well into the twentieth century.

As an architectural historian, John Curtis found the fictionalized aspect of the Village a bit awkward. "I have to admit that, at least at first, it was a little difficult for me to accept and to live with that. I felt there was a kind of intellectual dishonesty in playing down the buildings' own histories and geographical heritage. They were being subordinated to what I would characterize as a rationalized scenario, even though it was very well thought through.

"On the other hand, if a visitor comes up and asks, 'Where was this building built?' he'll be told where it's from. Our interpreters do have that historically accurate information, even though it doesn't always come through in their routine, day-to-day interpretation. Again, that's because we've decided those facts are less important than the character of the building, the nature of the people who populate it, and their relationship to the Village as a whole.

"To put it another way, the social-history component is number one. But number two . . . actually, there are lots of number twos. If you're interested in furniture, we can do furniture. And there's architecture, and paintings, and even the costume the interpreter is wearing, which tells you about dress, social station, and class. So it's a many-layered thing."

For the visitor, the effect of the game playing is considerable. In fact, it's possible to wax rather romantic about life as it would have been lived in OSV then, had it been a real village. Many people do, and it isn't a temptation or an experience that was invented at OSV.

Lewis Mumford and Oswald Spengler wrote about the appeal of the simple, rural existence before OSV was founded. Both expressed great admiration for the lifestyle of the sort of agricultural communities that OSV represents. That was a world much more to be desired than their own, they felt, and both envied the connection to the land and the simplicity of daily life. For them, the limits imposed by nature and by a close community were greater goods.

To Spengler, a world without the rootlessness, clutter, and competition of a more developed society was "organic." But I like Mumford's word better: he called it "medieval," a word that happens also to describe the origin of most of the buildings at OSV.

It may seem anachronistic to describe houses built after the European Renaissance as medieval, but Colonial American buildings had more in common with life in the Middle Ages than with Leonardo's world of advancing engineering. Average folk came to America, and they built what they knew, adjusting their designs, as necessary, to differences in climate. The result was seemingly artless American structures like the familiar Cape Cod design, inspired by the simple medieval dwellings the settlers had known back in England and the Netherlands.

Mumford and Spengler never visited a true "medieval" or "organic" society except in their imaginations. If they had, they probably wouldn't have had time to write letters back; that's how tired they would have been after finishing their daily chores in that labor-intensive world. We can learn such lessons at Sturbridge watching the women cook and clean and the men do their chores. (Conversely, a visitor from a medieval village would surely think it a little strange that we strive to avoid physical work in almost every aspect of our lives, then go out and burn as many calories as possible running in circles or lifting weights for no apparent purpose. All this, the medieval visitor might observe, you futurists do while dressed in short pants.)

We can't invite that imaginary medieval visitor to our century. In the same way, we shouldn't confuse a visit to OSV or any restored Colonial or early American setting as a true visit to another era. Yet wandering the lanes and hallways of a restoration like Sturbridge can allow us a glimpse of an earlier time. The tableaux at OSV cannot help but make us see our own era a bit more clearly.

Curtis summarized the lessons of Old Sturbridge Village this way: "Knowledge is an enrichment of one's life, and I think that that is really the role of the Village. There are people who come to the Village because they are interested in antiques, and they learn about them here. There are some people who come to the Village because they are interested in social history, and they learn about that. Others are interested in architecture, animal husbandry, plants, gardens, women's history, or handcrafts.

"There are also some people who come here without any real formed interest other than that they've been told by somebody, 'You really ought to see Sturbridge.' Then there are some people who come here, get off the bus, and sit on the grass. They won't go in any houses and don't walk around. They like the blue sky and the grass and birds and flowers and they may not really gather any knowledge. But they might come away feeling renewed and refreshed.

"The Village may or may not be a learning experience, but it still may be a renewal, a spiritual renewal in that very basic, elemental way. But I like to think that most people come away from the Village having really learned something about history."

During his tenure at the Village, Curtis has put his continuing fascination with old things to practical professional use. He has played a key role in enlarging the collection of buildings. The Village opened in 1946 with five; today, there are more than forty. He has also written a book on moving houses, *Moving Historic Buildings*.

The most recent relocated structure to open to the public at OSV is the Emerson Bixby house. While the Bixby house doesn't have Curtis's fingerprints in the paint or plaster, he supervised its move to Sturbridge, as well as its restoration. The story of the house, both in the early nineteenth century and in its more recent incarnation at Old Sturbridge Village, suggests the kind of work done by Curtis and his colleagues.

I've visited the 1807 Bixby house several times, but not because I couldn't see it all the first time. The original structure has but three simple rooms downstairs and an unfinished attic (the latter isn't open to the general public). The configuration of the Bixby house, like so many plain dwellings of its era, is so simple as to make the term "floor plan" seem pedantic. You don't need a map to get a fix on its arrangement.

A large room with a cooking fireplace and a bake oven runs the length of the north elevation. All the functions of today's kitchen, family room, and dining room were originally performed in this hall, or "keeping room." On the south side are the two remaining rooms, each of which is slightly more formal than the kitchen.

The "sitting room" was the small room in which much of the work of the household was done, a combination workshop, sewing room, and home office. In those days of self-sufficiency, homework included the manufacture of many consumer goods we buy off-the-shelf and take for granted. The manufacture of clothing alone was a necessary and time-consuming task for any wife and mother.

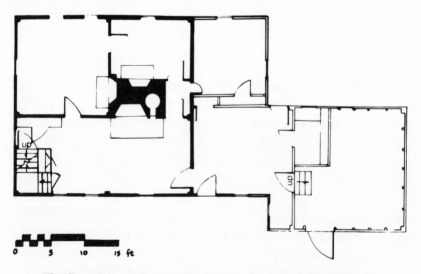

The floor plan of the original three-room Bixby house (at left), complete with later additions, including an ell and woodshed. *Myron O. Stachiw/Old Sturbridge Village*

The third room was the parlor, or "best room." In the parlor, one entertained guests and kept heirlooms or treasures from ancestors or even the old country. The parlor was also the master bedroom, since room-by-room inventories from the time generally listed the bedstead as belonging there.

The children slept upstairs, sharing the attic with barrels, grain, yarn, and other goods. The cellar below, a New World innovation, was little more than a hole used for storage. As reconstructed at OSV, the Bixby house also has an added bed chamber and a small unfinished storage area and a shed which had been added onto one end of the house perhaps ten years after its original construction.

Most of the old houses you will encounter in these pages get their names from their original owners. Not so with the Bixby house, whose builder and first resident was named Nathan Hemenway. Today the dwelling is known as the Bixby house because, in keeping with Sturbridge's "stopped clock," it is presented as it might have looked in the 1830s. During that decade, Emerson Bixby lived in the house with his wife and three daughters.

John Curtis showed me the building in March 1988, before it was entirely restored and open to the public. I've also had an opportunity to see the photos of the work as it progressed. In looking at the restored house and the earlier pictures, what struck me was how much of the original house was intact. Prior to its move to Sturbridge, neither plumbing nor central heating had ever been installed in the house. The electricity was limited to a bare bulb in the center of each downstairs room and several outlets.

While the sills and some other parts of the wooden structure required replacement, as did a number of the clapboards, much of the rest of the house was original, or at least as it was when the Bixby family made it their home. The house, which was moved from the hamlet of Four Corners in Barre, Massachusetts, was still in the hands of Bixby descendants when OSV acquired it in 1985.

Archaeological digs on the original site produced enough

The Bixby house dates from the turn of the nineteenth century. But the juxtaposition of the newfangled pram out front says much about the world it has survived into and from which its visitors come to look back to the Bixbys.

ceramic shards so that the cupboard in the sitting room today is stocked with plates and other kitchenware that match what the Bixbys themselves used. As is often the case in rural settings, the broken tableware was literally "thrown out," so the diggers found a fanlike pattern of household ceramic shards buried outside the door of the parlor.

A detailed knowledge of how the site had been used for

agricultural and other purposes also emerged from the exca-
vation. Patterns of use were identified, so it has been possible
to replicate, for purposes of OSV's demonstrations, the move-
ments of the Bixbys to and from the barn, well, privy, and sheds.
Other clues suggest that the labors of their maturing daughters
enabled Emerson Bixby and his wife to add to their income.
The daughters did piecework, weaving straw hats and sewing
uppers for the shoemaker whose shop was nearby. In that era,
women sewed the uppers, while the shoemaker shaped the soles
and assembled the shoes. On a return visit I made after the
official opening of the Bixby house, the interpreters there were
weaving straw and acting out the daily rituals, much as the
Bixbys did in their lifetimes.

Documentary sources also provided valuable evidence.
Emerson Bixby's account books were found in the American
Antiquarian Society Library in nearby Worcester, Massachusetts. The first American historical society, founded in 1812, it
has an unequaled collection of Colonial and early American
books, newspapers, maps, broadsides, and other material.

Among countless useful finds, the Bixby records offered
researchers the dates and quantities of plaster purchases. By
comparing the recorded weights of the purchases with calculations made on-site of the quantities of plaster required to
finish individual rooms, it was possible to determine in which
years plastering had been done in the house. Drawing on all
of these sources, a surprisingly complete picture of the Bixbys'
life in the house emerged.

In studying any old house, physical findings are best understood when they are related to what is known of the historical
context. Consider the covering on the plastered walls downstairs in the Bixby house. (The Bixbys would have known it as
"paper hangings"; we call it wallpaper.) Early inspections had
led Curtis and company to conclude that the Bixby house had
only two layers of wallpaper. In some houses of its vintage, the
buildup consists of twenty layers of paper or more, since the

practice of steaming or scraping off wallpaper is relatively new (a change in renovation practice that can make the restorer's job today more difficult). However, the finding of but two layers of wallpaper was consistent with the generally unrenovated state of the house.

The two layers of paper found on the Bixby walls almost certainly postdated 1837, the patent year for a steam-powered machine that manufactured wallpaper (by the 1840s the option of relatively inexpensive decoration was available to most people). Thus, the OSV restorers assumed that the walls were bare prior to that era. Yet when the wallpaper at the Bixby house was being stripped off during restoration, small remnants of a third layer were found beneath.

That third and earliest layer of paper at the Bixby house was a wallpaper with a drapery-and-vine pattern printed in black and white on a blue-colored sheet. OSV investigators discovered that it had been made by a Boston manufacturer before 1817, making it almost surely the wall surface with which Bixby and his wife had lived. The paper was replicated and is to be seen on the parlor walls of the house today.

Preservationists frequently use the term "fabric" to describe the physical materials that compose the structure of a building. It implies that the various component materials are "interwoven" to form a historic as well as a physical presence.

Because it retained so much of its original fabric, the Bixby house was a rare treasure. It lent itself to a detailed restoration to its circa 1830 appearance, although the process did require certain compromises and presented some unusual problems.

In keeping with OSV's notion of the calendar that stopped in the 1830s, the house has been restored without a modern kitchen or even a flush toilet. After all, the house is really an oversized exhibit in an open-air museum. On the other hand, the Bixby house now sits in an entirely new context, though one not dissimilar from its original circumstances.

Bixby was a blacksmith. As was the norm for most rural

The reproduction drapery–and–vine wallpaper on the walls of the Bixby house loses little of its visual impact, despite the absence of its brilliant blue background in this black and white photograph of the sitting room interior. The original paper was attributed to Moses Grant, Jr., of Boston, circa 1811–1817. *Henry E. Peach/Old Sturbridge Village*

Americans at the time, he and his family also ran a small farm. In its new setting, the Bixby house has a blacksmith's shop for its most immediate neighbor. Documentary research revealed that Bixby purchased a small parcel of land down the street from his home for his shop. Today, the proximity of the OSV blacksmith shop mimics the original setting of the house in Barre Four Corners.

The OSV blacksmith shop isn't Bixby's, since his original blacksmith shop was gone when OSV acquired his house. But archaeological investigations in and around the remaining foundation revealed much about the technical details of blacksmithing as Bixby practiced it, and his trade closely resembled the blacksmithing operations performed today in the shop across from his house. That smithy was moved from Bolton, Massachusetts, a few miles east of Barre Four Corners.

The barn, garden, adjacent fields, pig lot, and even the privy at the Bixby complex are much like those the Bixbys would have had on their family farm. But the Bixby family buildings are also part of a larger context, in what Curtis calls the "Mill Neighborhood." This includes the Freeman Farm, an 1801 farmhouse along with its barn and several agricultural buildings, and three mill buildings.

This subset of structures reflects the developmental patterns of the era. When a band of families arrived in a new region in that pre-industrial age, the spot chosen for settlement would have had a source of power, typically a stream. By creating dams and sluiceways, the water would be harnessed to power a sawmill. The logical sequence continued with trees being cleared (for fields) and then sawed into timber and boards (for buildings).

The construction of access roads to the sawmill and the watercourse that powered it would have allowed for other uses. Thus, millers and tradesmen, like blacksmith Emerson Bixby and the proprietors of the neighboring grist and carding mills, would likely have established themselves nearby.

Such a mill neighborhood, though assembled for convenience at OSV only a short walk from the village green, would in its time have been more remote from a town. The intention at OSV is to represent life as it would have been in a more isolated setting, a clear contrast to the so-called Center Village. There, a church (meetinghouse), a tavern, a law office, several trade shops, and a number of dwellings make up a more densely populated town.

In comparison, an isolated mill neighborhood afforded much less exposure to the parson and other neighbors. Unlike denizens of the Center Village, the Bixbys and their handful of rural neighbors would also have been less influenced by current social and material notions. Thus, Curtis pointed out, certain aspects of the Bixby house design are *retardataire* (an art-history term meaning backward-looking), including Georgian-inspired paneling on the fireplace wall in the parlor that no up-to-date householder in a coastal Massachusetts town would have had constructed as late as the turn of the nineteenth century.

Despite its accuracy, certain aspects of the Bixby house restoration have proved to be confusing to visitors. In one study done to determine how the house was being perceived, a questionnaire asked visitors how well-to-do they thought the Bixbys would have been. The majority of people responded that the Bixbys must have been quite well off.

Yet that was simply not the case. The Bixbys lived simple lives, in a challenging rural environment that made enormous physical demands. They lived in a house that was small even by the standards of the day, and one that offered few amenities. So why the confusion? John Curtis suggested several possible explanations.

The exhibit opened recently (April 1988), so the paint and finish are still new and neat. Another possible source of misunderstanding is the four-poster bed in the parlor with its handsome cloth canopy. Today we think of such pieces as a sign of wealth, but in 1830 it would have been regarded as rather out of fashion (or, to use Curtis's term, a bit *retardataire*). And then there's the wallpaper. In its day, that American-made paper was probably inferior to its imported equivalent, which would have been regarded as more stylish and certainly would have cost more. Yet its bold patterns do strike our eyes as impressive.

Even in the rarefied air of a world-class restoration like OSV, modernity made conflicting demands upon Curtis and his crews as they restored the Bixby house. While all the buildings at OSV resemble the originals as closely as possible, the different uses the buildings serve today demand compromises. They usually are disguised, but they're there.

The Bixby house will accommodate millions of visitors in the years to come, all of whom will, at least during the early spring, track in their share of mud from the dirt paths outside. (As all New Englanders know, the region has five seasons: spring, summer, fall, winter, and mud season.) To deal with such everyday problems of museum maintenance, a central vacuum-cleaning system was installed. The chimney, which is used frequently (as it would have been during the Bixbys' residence), required a solution that was safe, relatively maintenance-free, yet invisible. The choice was an insulated, stainless-steel flue lining, an option that was clearly not available to Emerson Bixby in 1830.

A key criterion each of the compromises had to meet was that they be "reversible." That's a word that, these days, tumbles frequently from the lips of preservationists. As John Curtis put it: "There is a new, broadly accepted awareness of the responsibility of the owner of a historic building to conserve the original." He wasn't talking only about buildings in museum villages.

Curtis has seen the changes in his years working in Sturbridge. Until recently, "restoring" a house was thought to be a matter of expunging what had been added in order to return to the original. "The tendency," he said, "was to inflict your own personal taste. But those were *personal perceptions.*"

Today, the conscientious restorer doesn't obliterate all the early evidence in order to re-create his or her best guess of what was there. "If you can conserve at the same time as you strip," said Curtis, "the generations to come can use their own judgment." That's why beneath the reproduction drapery-and-vine wallpaper are the remaining vestiges of the original, carefully protected from wallpaper paste by a layer of chemically inert acrylic resin and paper. That's also why nothing irreversible was done to the building's structure.

Most visitors don't appreciate Old Sturbridge Village for its implied consciousness of such issues as *retardataire* architectural elements and reversibility. Rather, they see it as an example of "living history."

OSV is a museum. By definition, it is a place where objects of permanent value are kept. But the experience of visiting can be both more transitory and more transcendent than a trip to a traditional museum with glass cases and detailed labels.

On one of my recent visits, I listened to the blacksmith answering questions. A boy of perhaps thirteen stood next to me. He wore both a vapid expression and a portable radio with earphones.

I didn't think he could hear what was being said, but apparently he could. He laughed softly at something the blacksmith said and removed his earphones.

In a polite and, I thought, a bit embarrassed tone, he asked, "What's a *horse*shoe?"

John Curtis showed me not only the Bixby house at Old Sturbridge Village but also his own eighteenth-century wood-frame home in nearby Brimfield, Massachusetts. In Curtis's words: "It's a full two stories, with center chimney–a classic colonial."

He and his wife, Susan, bought their house in 1966 and have brought up their two sons there as they have gone about restoring the place. The younger one painted the house three summers ago; the older son, a former marine, is in coliege in California.

The house has been more than a home for him and his family. It's also a busman's holiday for Curtis, an opportunity for him to experiment on his own with restoration technology. The dwelling testifies to his willingness to spend countless hours both serving history and making the house better serve his family's needs.

"My job has kept me fairly current with the literature. That has suggested different avenues for technological exploration in restoring the building.

"I've used the house as a little bit of a laboratory for trying things that I probably would not have known about were it not for my work. For instance, I've tested out epoxy resins in filling rotted timbers."

I asked for another example of such experimentation.

"Some years ago a tree fell against one side of the house and I had to take off the asbestos siding. Then I discovered why they had put the siding on. The clapboards were badly deteriorated. When I took them off, I saw that the sheathing was also deteriorated. But they were the eighteenth-century clapboards, and I wanted to keep them.

"The problem was that many of them had rotted out at the junctures where the nails held them to the studs. So I cut those sections out and pieced in little pieces. It took a bit of figuring, but I undercut all of them so the pieces were mechanically locked in place as well as held by the epoxy adhesive. That was done ten years ago and they've lasted very well."

In short, Curtis had cut, *by hand,* hundreds of little chunks of wood to fit into hundreds of little hand-cut holes in the ancient clapboards. He glued the bits to the boards and nailed them back on.

"That must have been quite a job."

"Oh, it was all summer long," he replied, his Massachusetts accent substituting "sum-ma" for "summer". "A lot of the things I've done are things that nobody could afford to pay someone else to do."

His tone was matter-of-fact. Like many serious students of preservation, he derives his greatest satisfaction from the unique jobs he does. The result achieved is important, but that isn't the real reward. Having to spend a great amount of time performing a task is equally beside the point. I think what chal-

John Curtis calls the house "a classic Colonial," though to some knowledgeable neighbors in Brimfield, Massachusetts, the place is also known as the Elmtree house. The automobile is a 1912 Ford Model T. In different ways, both the car and the dwelling have provided John Curtis with what he terms an "immediate link to the past." *John O. Curtis*

lenges John Curtis and other people who tithe a piece of their lives to old houses is the jolt of the unfamiliar. It's finding a new way to save valuable vestiges which time and the elements would, if unopposed, simply destroy.

The front elevation of Curtis's house features ten window and door openings. The door at the center is flanked by two pairs of windows on the first story. Aligned above on the upper floor are five windows. Each of three main downstairs rooms and the two main bedchambers upstairs has a fireplace.

The massive central stack into which the fireplaces feed has six flues, one each for the fireplaces and another for the bake oven in the kitchen. Built of brick, the chimney is bonded with a mortar of local clay. More expensive (and stronger) lime mortar was used only in the fireboxes and on the portion of the chimney exposed to the elements above the roofline. Yet Curtis still uses several of the fireplaces in the house.

If the house had been constructed in the South, the fireplaces would have been built into chimneys located on the end walls. Often in southern states, chimneys stand apart from the gable ends of the house. That way, they radiate unwanted heat in warm weather away from the living spaces. The end-wall chimney location also meant that the center hall was open, which increased cooling ventilation.

That process of adaptation to climate has continued in Curtis's years in the house. "When I first moved in, the house was largely uninsulated," he recalled. "I was told then that I could get away with three inches of glass wool, so I marked the floorboards in the attic and took them up. This was in the late 1960s. I vacuumed and shoveled out the rat and squirrel nests—they were ten inches deep in places—and put in the insulation. Then I replaced the boards in their original positions.

"When the energy crunch came along in the early 1970s, I realized it wasn't enough. So I took the floor up *again* and put in more. I've got eight or ten inches up there now." While he hasn't insulated all the side walls ("It would necessitate destruction of a lot of original fabric"), events like the tree falling against the house, the need to do some sill work on another wall, and other repairs have given him the opportunity to insulate some portions of the house while other necessary repairs were underway.

How old is the house?

"It was here at least from the 1790s and possibly prior to that." While Curtis admits he hasn't a single date he can confidently offer, he can suggest a litany of reasons why it could be as early as 1749 (among them a deed, some early paneling, and a characteristic staircase design). On the other hand, he has another body of evidence that argues that the house was constructed several decades later. He cites the absence of large boxed beams, called summer beams, bisecting the ceiling of major downstairs rooms and other construction details.

"The date continues to be something of an enigma," said Curtis. Perhaps I imagined it, but the very imprecision of it seemed to give him a certain perverse satisfaction. It's his own house, after all, and he doesn't have tens of thousands of tourists tramping through looking for pat answers.

He may not know the date, but what he does know about the house far outweighs what he doesn't. Consider, for example, a peculiarity of its design.

Before an ell was added sometime after 1798, the back of the house had only two windows, one over the other at the center of the building (unlike the ten openings on the front). This would have been rather unusual, since that is the east façade of the house and thus the source of morning light.

"It's curious," said Curtis. "I've not seen that before and I've looked at a lot of old houses."

He has, however, come up with a reasonable explanation. "There are references in the paperwork to a leather shop on the property." That trade involved tanning the hides first, and indeed the earliest existing deed to the property refers to "Tan Vats and a Bark Mill." Oak bark and animal urine would have been used in the tanning process, producing waste materials that were about as close as Colonial America came to toxic waste. All in all, Curtis concluded, "a good argument for not having a whole lot of ventilation on that side of the house."

Despite the presence of the tannery and tax records showing that its earliest owners kept horses, cows, sheep, oxen, and goats, Curtis's is an in-town house. Located on a side street in Brimfield, the house has always had neighboring dwellings. The livestock and land in cultivation were most likely used for family needs rather than for sale.

The house was quite literally regarded as a mansion in its time, as, in another of the deeds, it is described as a "mansion house." While such an identification is consistent with a two-story building, the name may also imply a fancier house more impressive than most. Indeed, there are aspects of the finish and design that make the term "mansion" particularly appropriate.

Inside, the house has two parlors at the front, on either side of a small stairway to the second floor which stands immediately in front of the center chimney. Across the back of the first story is the kitchen, flanked by two small rooms at the ends, one a pantry, the other a small bedroom. The same five-room configuration is maintained upstairs (with stairs and the two principal bedchambers at the front and three smaller rooms at the rear). Upstairs, the room at the middle of the back was left unfinished, apparently for storage.

This configuration was not in itself remarkable. ("It is," said Curtis, "one of the most common New England house forms.") But some aspects of the house set it apart from dozens of others of its vintage that I have visited and studied in recent years. One is a domed room; another is the extensive use of decorative painting schemes.

Curtis admitted as he directed the tour, "This is the room I had to buy the house for." The room is at the front of the house on the second floor, immediately to the left of the stairway. Its ceiling rises from all four walls to form a tall dome roughly hemispherical in shape. The effect is stunning. Walking from the small hallway through the low door, even the twentieth-century visitor is struck by the sudden reach of the ceiling. The peak of the dome is fourteen feet above the floor and seems even higher because, at about fifteen-foot square, the room itself isn't large. Curtis's investigations have revealed much about the room, both factual and conjectural. First, the facts.

Seen from the attic above, the dome is a great protuberance dominating one corner of the large attic space. Close examination reveals that its structure, a tepee-like framework of boards with the profile of the dome cut into them and with plaster and lath attached, was fastened directly to the chestnut frame of the house. Curtis found no indications that an earlier attic floor was removed to accommodate the addition of the dome. Thus, he concluded, the dome was original to the house and was not added after its construction.

The guesswork is more intriguing. The most significant historical figure associated with the house was a congregational minister named Clark Brown. Ordained in Boston in 1795 and having been a pastor in what was then the province of Maine, he moved to Brimfield and bought the house in 1798. He resided there until 1803, when he was dismissed from his post and moved on to Montpelier, Vermont.

Local legend has it that the Reverend Brown practiced his sermons in the domed room. No doubt the acoustics of its tall ceiling more nearly resembled those of his church than did the other, more rectilinear rooms in the house.

Another local tradition asserts that the town's Masons met there. In studying the records, Curtis found that the membership of the Humanity Lodge of the Most Worshipful Grand Lodge had met in Brimfield between 1813 and 1828. One member of the Humanity Lodge, Elijah Tarbill, Jr., purchased the house in 1813. At the very least, the chronology provides a convenient correlation.

In an attempt to verify that the Masons did meet in the domed room, Curtis has studied the plastered walls for signs of Masonic decoration. He uncovered no Masonic symbols, but did find faint and fragile freehand floral decorations. They apparently weren't stenciled, but are delicately modeled, giving the design a three-dimensional quality.

It is such decorative painting that, along with the domed room, sets Curtis's house apart from similar dwellings of its era. Virtually every room in the house features ornamental paintwork of the sort that came into vogue in the eighteenth century. During that era and after, inexpensive woods were given the appearance of more expensive ones (pine could be "grained" to look like mahogany or figured maple), and wooden mantels were painted to look like stone ("marbleized").

The process involved a base layer of one color, which was allowed to dry. Then a second layer of paint of a darker color was applied but partially wiped off before drying. The tools and techniques with which it was removed accounted for the patterns of the grain or the veining of the faux wood or marble. In some cases third and fourth colors were added to suggest veining or variations in the grain. These techniques, along with stenciling, were widely used during and after the Revolution and remained popular for much of the next century.

In Curtis's house there are decorative friezes in another upstairs bedroom and in the stair hall; the latter features swags and tiny flowers. "The swag motif," said Curtis, "suggests a late-eighteenth- or early-nineteenth-century origin. Freehand work in general precedes the stenciled decorative work, which is more characteristic of the 1820s and 1830s."

John Curtis doesn't leave his passion for precision and accuracy at the office. The documentation he is assembling on his house reflects the methodical way in which he has approached its restoration.

At present, he has three large ring binders for recording what he has done to and learned about his house. Two are full, bursting with carefully organized typescript, photographs, Xeroxes, and other material describing the history and restoration of the house.

The third three-inch-thick binder is being filled gradually, as it awaits ensuing events in the process.

Every step is recounted, beginning with a meticulous description of the as-found condition of the house. Photos document what was there, how it was changed, and the present appearance of each element. Single-spaced text describes the work invested. The attention to detail is such that even the number of hours of labor required for each task is recorded. Dates, materials, observations, sources of supplies, rejected solutions, problems encountered–they're all there.

It's impossible to summarize Curtis's labors on his house in these few pages. He's restored the original twelve-over-twelve windows (in the nineteenth century, two-over-two windows had been installed). He discovered wood that had originally been part of a kitchen partition but later was reused upstairs. Countless objects have been found inside and out, ranging from barn hinges and bottles to wrought-iron lady's hair curlers.

I inquired how the process of restoring his house is different from supervising the work on the Bixby and other buildings at Old Sturbridge Village.

"The criteria, the game plan, the rules vary if you are living in the building. For instance, the downstairs bathroom in my house was the pantry until indoor plumbing was brought into the building after World War II (though there had been water in the house, a pump, much earlier).

"I didn't choose to restore that back pantry because there would be very little to be gained by that. But I remodeled it as a bathroom and replaced the plasterboard with lath and plaster. And I remade an appropriate early-nineteenth-century window frame (the kitchen ell went on sometime after 1797). And I reboxed the corner post with beaded boxing.

"I attempted to do it in character with that part of the house. But it *is* a bathroom.

"There are changes that you have to make in order to live in the house and be comfortable. Each situation is different, and you just have to think it through. That's one of the classic differences about your own house. At home I can afford to experiment, to try and see if things can be done."

There's another difference, too, of course. While Curtis aims to preserve his house and to restore aspects of it to its original appearance insofar as he can ascertain it, he isn't required to pretend that the clock stopped at any time in the near or distant past. At home, he doesn't have to pretend to be living history. He lives there with his family, he brings home today's paper to read, he owns a TV and a radio or two, he is concerned with our time as well as the past.

John Curtis has elected to treat "old things" on his own time with the same degree of care and attention to detail that he does in his official role at Old Sturbridge Village. "My interest in objects concerns more than just research and acquisition," he said. "Another important realization is that the object needs to be protected and preserved if it is to be passed along. Although my role continues to be that of acquisitor, gathering in for the museum and sometimes for myself, it's also increasingly as care-taker for the *future*. I may not be here, but the things will be here because I was responsible for their safekeeping."

Why are they worth keeping?

"The artifacts are a catalyst or the focus of a learning experience," he replied.

He was quick to add that, especially at the Village, the interpretation is an essential component, too. "You still have to have people, whether they are passive, as with the person who wrote the label but is not on the scene, or whether the person is there as an interactive one-on-one interpreter who tells you about these artifacts.

"Now, if you were to ask me if I think that all the people who see these artifacts have their lives changed, the answer would have to be no, I'm sure they haven't. A lot of people come to the Village, zip through in two hours, buy a postcard, and they're off. People visit us at home in Brimfield and come and go in the same way.

"On the other hand, there's clearly a lasting impression made on some people. We get quite a lot of letters and calls from people who want to learn more or to emulate what we have at the Village. There's definitely that kind of germination and growth of knowledge. That I'm sure of. I'm not directly involved with the gardening program, the animal program, the farming or cooking demonstrations in the Village, but I know that if you talk with people in the demonstration department they would say very much the same thing."

So the Village is a learning resource for lots of people on lots of different levels. Is the process the same for John Curtis at home and an interpreter at OSV? Does the artifact remain secondary to the bigger picture?

"The artifact is the means whereby the picture is explained."

In the nineteenth century, art critics in general and John Ruskin in particular believed that the term "architecture" referred to the great monuments, works of the classical and Gothic past. By their lights, classical temples and Gothic cathedrals were the fit subject of the lofty pursuit termed "architecture." In contrast, mere houses built in vernacular styles were just buildings.

The definition of architecture has broadened greatly, and today most of us recognize the Bixby house as worthy of study, preservation, and perhaps even a certain reverence. In countless other ways, we see this kind of human expression–that produced by simple craftsmen as well as by artists of the first rank–can inform and stimulate us. By that logic, simple buildings have become architecture.

With one or two exceptions, the medieval village that is OSV features no buildings that Ruskin would have thought of as architecture. One of its basic premises was to avoid having impressive, Renaissance-style houses in the Village. The goal was to remain consistent with the notion of re-creating a rural New England village and the sort of structures that were to be expected there–Cape Cods, Saltbox-style houses, and other medieval-inspired dwellings.

Not that there haven't been opportunities to broaden the focus. As early as 1937, Perry, Shaw & Hepburn, an architectural firm that could cite Colonial Williamsburg among its clients, proposed a brick Mansion House for the Village. Curtis said in horror of their design, "They were talking about building one out of whole cloth!" It was never built, but the Village does own a high-style eighteenth-century house from Portsmouth, New Hampshire, and an elegant 1836 Greek Revival mansion from downtown Worcester, Massachusetts.

Fortunately, the basic philosophical guidelines established right from the inception of the museum precluded the integration of these impressive Greek- and Roman-inspired buildings into the Village. They have been put to other uses outside the confines of the Village itself.

The mission at Old Sturbridge Village is clear and consistent. Preservation is the first priority, but always with a goal in mind, to offer today's visitors an opportunity to get a sense of the society as it existed in rural New England in 1830.

For Curtis, his urge to conserve is more complicated. It followed a certain sequence, beginning with what he called a romantic connection to another time that, in turn, matured into a complex series of decisions.

Today, as a man with more than thirty years' professional experience with old things, he admits, "As much fun as it may be to acquire, catalogue, and research an object, until you put it before the public as a statement of one sort or another, you're not really fulfilling your mission. So that's another component of my one-on-one relationship with history. I'm constantly challenged to think about how we are to display an object, how will we interpret it, what role it will play in the presentation before the public."

The very notion of OSV and of Curtis's work is dependent upon an implied confidence in our ability to try to understand another era. The attempts to do so certainly rely upon architectural, sociological, and archaeological facts as they are analyzed today by increasingly scientific methods. In a sense, however, what John Curtis and his colleagues do is more closely tied to old-fashioned notions of history.

The "living history" at Old Sturbridge Village is at once intuitive and emotional. It functions, in part, according to the geometric model, in which an assemblage of lines has been drawn, a series of connections made, in order to offer images representative of another time. Using his gifts for recognizing, restoring, and understanding old things, Curtis the historian has helped re-create what might best be termed an "immersion" experience. No one, Curtis included, would argue that the 1830s are truly recaptured at OSV. At the same time, the experience of the place is vivid, surprising, and remarkably real. John Obed Curtis, the Village historian, helps us to look into and to consider our past.

In the next chapter, we will see a different approach to a distinctly different kind of village. At the University of Virginia, the clock hasn't been stopped, but the buildings have survived, in all their classical and Renaissance glory, at Thomas Jefferson's "Academical Village."

5
The Epochal Carrier

———

Whenever it is proposed to prepare plans . . . I should prefer the adoption of some one of the models of antiquity, which have had the approbation of thousands of years.
—Thomas Jefferson

"**I** keep coming back to this question: A hundred years from now, what will they think of our efforts at preservation?" John Mesick was talking. Like Curtis, he's a man in his fifties and bespectacled.

"Will technological change have so overtaken things that it will not be possible to live in the buildings we are restoring today? I'm certainly not predisposed to think so. I think the things that touch us about the older dwellings are almost eternal."

His voice swelled—it often does as he talks of the old buildings he admires. "I would guess that even a hundred years from now they would be perceived as something wonderful."

After a pause, he continued.

"The modest house of average scope is not a great deal different today from a house that we found habitable two hundred years ago. You know, three or four bedrooms, a couple of living spaces. I would imagine that need or the feeling for it won't become obsolete." I thought he was finished, but, as is his way, a pause was followed by another rush of words.

91

"I like to say it's like the fishworm. Architecture is, I mean. You know, you come out in the morning after a dewy night, and you see all these little heaps the fishworms have left on the soil. The fishworm doing it probably doesn't realize he's leaving behind these little monuments to his activity.

"Essentially, architecture is that little heap that we leave behind us. Except that subsequent generations can look back at architecture and say yes, this was thus and so at this time because of this or that."

He looked up to see if I were following him.

"Only we can't do that. We're still underground burrowing, leaving our little heaps behind us."

Some of Mesick's burrowing in recent years has taken place in Charlottesville, Virginia.

On the day I first visited in March 1989, the daffodils announced the arrival of spring. Mother Nature had been assisted by Thomas Jefferson, since the curved brick walls he incorporated into his landscape design created heat pockets, forcing the flowers to bloom even earlier than usual.

For a man who died in 1826, Jefferson still exercises an astonishing influence at the University of Virginia. His is a welcome ghost, in Charlottesville and elsewhere. Jefferson, like few others in any era, looked intently at the past but always tried to anticipate the future. Nowhere is this more in evidence than at the school's architectural focus, what Jefferson himself called the Academical Village.

The cold spring rain that fell that morning had little effect on the spirits of the students or the sightseers on campus (some 400,000 people visit annually). I listened for a few minutes to an undergraduate guide leading a tour of prospective students and other visitors. His description of the buildings was smooth and practiced, yet I sensed an added reverence in his manner and in the expressions of his listeners when he spoke of "Mr. Jefferson." His somber tone lightened when he talked of the victory the previous evening. The University of Virginia bas-

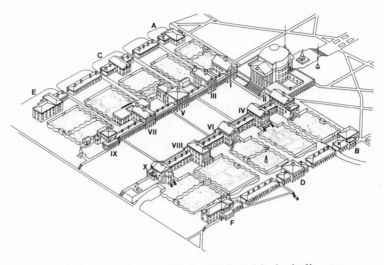

The Academical Village as Jefferson designed it, including ten
Pavilions (I through X) connected by colonnades; the Rotunda at
one end (the other was originally open); and the hotels outside,
three on either side (A through F). The Lawn at center measures 740
feet in length and 192 feet in width. *Mesick, Cohen & Waite*

ketball team, the Cavaliers, had upset highly ranked Oklahoma
to advance to the final eight in the National Collegiate Athletic
Association basketball tournament.

Instead of constructing one large building, Jefferson had
believed it "infinitely better to erect a small and separate lodge
for each separate professorship." He saw educational content
and the buildings as inseparable, and tried to create at his
university a place for scholarship. The result was and is hardly
humble, as his inspiration, as well as the architectural style and
detailing, was drawn directly from a range of earlier, high-style
European models.

Standing on the main common at the Academical Village, a
terraced series of open, grassy lawns surrounded by brick buildings, I couldn't help but be struck by the scale of the place.
The common—it's known as "the Lawn"—is enclosed on either
side by columns, a pair of facing colonnades. The two-story-
tall columns at the front of the buildings are large in cross-
section, like great whitewashed oak trees. The place has a feeling

of grandeur, in part due to its size. Yet the architectural elements are only big, not so enormous as to seem all out of human proportion.

It's easy to see how Ralph Sampson, a Cavalier basketball star a few years ago, could choose to live in one of the student rooms that open onto the Lawn. He's seven feet four inches tall, but amid Jefferson's forest of classical columns, he probably felt–for one rare moment–as if he were designed to scale.

One of the appeals of old buildings is that they are rarely incomprehensibly large. The introduction of the passenger elevator in the 1850s and the transition to steel buildings toward the end of the century did allow for taller buildings, a dozen or more stories high. But even those buildings can be taken in from the street. Something of the details at the top as well as at the bottom can be identified.

At, say, forty stories, that is rarely so. A giant glass wall that tall doesn't fit in the human eye, so it can't have the same immediate meaning a smaller building does. In theory, one can view the skyscraper from afar, but in practice it's rarely possible. The irony is that most office and apartment towers are tall because they can't be short. They're squeezed onto small plots and their neighbors are shoulder to shoulder with them.

This isn't to say we can for a moment deny the need and appropriateness of the skyscraper; overbuilt as some cities have become, the consolidation made possible by stretching buildings upward was and still is a practical necessity. A few of them are surprisingly pleasing to the eye, too. On the other hand, it isn't solely an accident of chronology that Jefferson's Village doesn't reach beyond three stories, and that upon first and repeat viewing it still conveys a sense of majesty that eludes most larger buildings. That's one of the lessons of buildings built before we were able to defy gravity: they look good for earthbound people as well as birds flying south.

The University of Virginia was Jefferson's brainchild. He conceived the notion of a state-supported university, then he devised the curriculum and designed the original buildings. Sitting atop a hill, they enclose that terraced common. The schema includes a main building at one end, the Rotunda. It's flanked by ten Pavilions, five on each side of the Lawn. Two rows of lesser buildings lie parallel to and outside of the aligned Pavilions. These latter buildings, originally used as student rooms and eating facilities, now act as a buffer between Jefferson's Village and the rest of the University and the city of Charlottesville. When originally laid out, the end of the Lawn opposite the Rotunda was open, looking south into a long valley. Using his telescope, Jefferson was able to follow the progress of construction at the school from Monticello, his home several miles to the east.

While the Rotunda was designed as a public building to house the library, the Pavilions were to be lived in, professors' domiciles though with classroom space on the first floor. Construction began in 1817, and by 1822 all ten had been completed. The Rotunda was constructed between 1823 and 1826.

The Pavilions were intended to be models for the young men who came to the University of Virginia to be educated. Judging by much of the domestic architecture that was constructed for gentlemen graduates of the University in ensuing decades, at least the architectural lessons were absorbed. Like much of the South, the state of Virginia is filled with houses that greet the visitor with columned façades which also feature the geometry of Greek and Roman architecture, including triangular pediments, boxlike volumes, and curvilinear moldings.

On that spring day, I met my tour guide, James Murray Howard, inside the Rotunda. Murray Howard's presence at the University speaks for the metamorphosis in the last few years in the way Americans regard their historic structures.

There's an old joke about Virginians: How many does it take to change a light bulb? Three, says the punch line. One to change it and two to reminisce about what a good light bulb the old one was. Despite their reputation for being proud of their past, however, generations of Virginians ignored the monumental Village, though it lay at the University's physical and philosophical center. For a very long time, as Murray Howard noted, "there was no one at the helm."

That has changed recently, at the University of Virginia as in so many other places. In 1981, a restoration program was begun under the dean of the architecture school, Jaquelin T. Robertson. In 1983, Howard's post as Architect for the Historic Buildings and Grounds was created and he was hired to fill it. The next year, the Jeffersonian Restoration Advisory Board was established, with an imposing membership that includes the likes of architect Philip Johnson, architectural historian James Marston Fitch, and University of Virginia professor Frederick D. Nichols, an early advocate for preservation of the Village.

"The Advisory Board," Howard said, "is responsible for, first, raising money. Second, the board is to give some direction or comment on a philosophical and executive role." The fund-raising efforts have been very successful, and the first ten-million-dollar goal has nearly been met.

The second task is a bit more complicated. As one would expect in the politically charged atmosphere of a state university, running the Academical Village has its bureaucratic aspects. However, the potential obstacles implied by that bureaucracy seem to have been kept at a minimum. In Howard's words: "It's not that we've been extracted from the state and made a foundation. We are still within the state yet we've been given a way to do our job comfortably."

For me, among the most interesting aspects of the work of the Advisory Board is what it doesn't do, what it has delegated to Howard and to others, some from outside the University. Particularly intriguing is the task that John Mesick and his partners have been assigned. Unlike most people in the architectural profession, they share with Thomas Jefferson a recognition that the architectural past is a living force for the present. They have found at the University of Virginia an opportunity to act upon it.

My chance introduction to John Mesick in Essex, New York, led me to interview him several years ago at his office in Albany. Since then we've talked many times, but I discovered early on that the commissions he and his firm get arouse envy in every ambitious American architect concerned with preservation and restoration.

The Mesick, Cohen & Waite job list includes several state capitol buildings (in New York, Pennsylvania, and Tennessee), Blair House (the presidential guesthouse in Washington), George and Martha Washington's Mount Vernon, more than a few house museums (including Montgomery Place in New York and Homewood House at Johns Hopkins University), and a range of other famed American buildings from the eighteenth and nineteenth centuries. Then there are the diamonds of this particular setting, which include not only the Academical Village but Ashlawn, a nearby house Jefferson designed for his friend James Monroe, and Monticello.

Mesick is one of the good talkers of this world. A conversation with him ranges widely as he describes a building. He moves through time, mingling the pictures he has in his mind of the edifice at different moments. Talk of particular structures is rich with references to others, past and present.

Located in downtown Albany, the firm's base is in a converted nineteenth-century warehouse. The offices themselves are not a showplace. The simple wood-and-brick superstructure of the building is exposed, the large spaces partitioned off, and the floors carpeted.

On the other hand, a visit to Mesick's office is always an opportunity for show and tell. There are usually bits and pieces of what is officially called "physical evidence," a bushel basket of a term for any actual piece of a building. On my first visit, a carpet sample from the Tennessee State House, bits of molding, even chunks of the original tin roof from a Jeffersonian building littered his office floor.

"I had a grandfather who should have been an architect," John I Mesick told me then. (No, that's not a typo; there is no period after his middle initial. It's a family tradition, signifying no middle name.) Even though that grandfather was a Methodist preacher rather than a builder or designer, he managed to instill in his grandson an enduring attachment to buildings.

"When I was a teenager, we had a debate about whether the portico on the Pantheon was original," Mesick recalled with obvious warmth. From such precocious enthusiasms, he moved on to the Pratt Institute in New York, where he studied architecture. Not, to his surprise, classical buildings, but how to build new buildings in our century.

Initially disappointed at the lack of historical curiosity in evidence at architecture school, he adapted quickly. After graduation, he went to Copenhagen on a Fulbright scholarship. He then worked for Eero Saarinen for two years in Michigan, but after Saarinen's sudden death, he took a job closer to home at an architectural firm in Albany. He still works for that same firm more than twenty-five years later, though its name has changed as partners have come and gone.

For much of his early career, Mesick concerned himself with new buildings. Experiences with the new afforded him a clearer way of approaching the old structures he had learned to admire as a very young man. As he explained it, before approaching old buildings "it's very good for an architect to build new." That way, he added, you work through "all that confusion about letting your ego manifest itself in the building and let the building speak for itself."

Mesick's firm has evolved along with him. Two of the three principals in the firm today, Mesick and James Cohen, have been working together since 1972. John G. Waite joined them in 1974. They estimate that over the years they have worked on more than five hundred preservation projects.

Along the way, they have developed a distinctive approach to historic structures. Unlike many people confronted with an old house, they think before they act. In approaching any building, they study, research, inspect, and try to understand as completely as possible every detail of the structure and its history—*before* making any recommendations as to its preservation, restoration, or renovation.

This detailed study is often embodied in something called a Historic Structure Report. In conversation, it shortly becomes HSR. Mesick's firm has done more than sixty such reports over the years for various restoration projects. He and his partners do them so well that the National Park Service reprinted one report as a prototype for other firms to follow in carrying out similar studies.

The research involves tracing ownership (if it is or was a privately owned building) and researching the lives of the people who lived or worked there. A detailed study of the site is done, as is an investigation of both the property immediately surrounding the building and the neighborhood, town, and region to identify broader historical patterns of agricultural use, the evolution of transportation systems, and other factors. The study of the structure involves an inch-by-inch inspection, a room-by-room description, and innumerable photographs and drawings. The whole process, says Mesick, is a kind of "architectural quarrying."

The Historic Structure Reports done at Mesick's firm are immense tasks. Preparation of such reports usually involves the work of roughly a dozen people, ranging from the partner-in-charge to artists, designers, architectural historians, and even historic landscape consultants.

Theirs is investigative work of an order far beyond the means and abilities of most people. But the difference is more than a matter of affordability. Mesick makes a distinction between his usual clients and homeowners. He rarely works on historic structures for individuals. He explained it this way:

"Frustrating as it can be to work for a committee, if they've gotten so far as to hire an architect to restore their building, the desire to restore has already manifested itself. That means there is a committee member or two who has been able to bring the rest of that committee along. You still have the dynamics of a group, but our experience is that the group will work out its differences.

"Ultimately, even those members who are afraid of raising taxes or are otherwise resistant to the restoration will go along out of a latent patriotism or some other instinct. It may be dormant, but there's something nudging at them that says the building is part of their community and it should be saved.

An 1856 print by F. Sachse and Company of the Jeffersonian Precinct and surroundings. Note that the Rotunda is distinctly out of scale and that Monticello is barely to be seen at the horizon line, just right of center, alone on its hilltop. *The Rector and Visitors of the University of Virginia*

Every vote along the way may be a cliff-hanger, but usually the committee will respect the advice of the professional.

"On the other hand, when you work on a private house, logic and objectivity will not generally convince the home-owner. The home is the realization of some sort of dream world. More often than not, the homeowners don't want to read the evidence of history or of usage in their house but want to impose some fantasy notion drawn from other sources, like childhood recollections or books or magazines."

The firm's work at Mr. Jefferson's Academical Village (a commission they received in 1985) led to the Monticello commission in 1988. Both are jobs that, in a sense, Mesick has worked toward his whole life. Thomas Jefferson was an early idol of his and he recalls drawing floor plans of Monticello as a teenager. With a characteristic passion for accuracy, he also pointed out that "at that time, there were only two books that had floor plans of Monticello. And they were *both* wrong."

The opportunity to work on buildings of Jefferson's is the fulfillment of some childhood wish that perhaps only he and his grandfather can understand.

Occasionally a special preservation opportunity offers itself. The work at the Academical Village is just such a one. After all, Jefferson's Lawn is one of a small number of obligatory stops on the consensus tour of Great American Buildings. The conservation process is progressing, but funds are still limited and each Pavilion can be studied and restored only between tenancies. It's a one-or-two-at-a-time process that will take perhaps fifteen years.

Even when "finished," the job won't be truly complete. The buildings will grow older and will require continuing care and attention. But the careful restoration work that is being done, along with the accumulation of research, will offer future caretakers a framework for making maintenance and other decisions that suit both past and present.

Thus, the assignment given Murray Howard and John Mesick's firm is more complicated than for most house renovations. Their principal obligation is not to the academics who will reside in the Pavilions, although the comfort of those scholars or administrators and their families is a part of the charge, too. Nor, in some sense, is the firm's client the Rector and Visitors of the University of Virginia or even the august group that meets as the Jeffersonian Restoration Advisory Board.

The long-term plans must consider the fact that these buildings are artifacts that are destined to outlast not only this generation of residents and guardians but even their working systems. In a very real sense, the goal is to serve the best interests of that abstract time and place called posterity.

Is the cause of Great Architecture also to be served? Many architectural critics have been less than kind in rating Jefferson's contribution to world architecture. I have come away from reading assessments of his architectural work with the feeling that he is most often regarded as rather like a privileged child with an immense collection of well-crafted tin soldiers. He set out to design his Village with prefabricated armies from his toy chest. Jefferson used designs, the façades and the detailing, from pattern books of the eighteenth century. No matter how creatively he deployed these troops, however, some critics would dismiss him as an amateur.

From the perspective of history, it really doesn't matter if, to the architectural scholar, the Village gives the sense that there was a whole lot of borrowing going on. It is an extraordinarily successful architectural adventure that, against great odds, got built and has lasted on a rural Virginia hilltop.

To my eye, Jefferson's Academical Village is a monument for reasons of its architectural quality, as are his Virginia state capitol and the imaginative Monticello. Even to the architectural purist, its historical importance must be apparent, not least because of its uniqueness in America.

Just as Mount Vernon is a historical monument because George Washington slept there, the Village is monumental in part because of its association with Jefferson. Jefferson was, after all, a framer of the Constitution, a President and ambassador, and, for his time and ours, a sage and grand old man of politics, the law, and other fields. But we now recognize that his buildings have a merit of their own quite apart from the roles they have played in the life of a famous and powerful man.

In dealing with the multi-dimensional Jeffersonian legacy, Mesick sees the nature of his task as a constant balancing act. For him, the buildings are "cultural artifacts" that must be integrated into the modern world. "The greatest decisions in dealing with a historic building are about how to do what's asked of us in a way that won't diminish its cultural integrity."

That involves keeping a tradition alive, a tradition that fell into disuse and disfavor decades ago. As he designed the buildings around the Lawn, Jefferson aimed to endow them with the ambience, seriousness, and historical depth that he sensed were present in the models he admired. He had an advantage we do not. He was working, by force of historical circumstance as well as choice, within the context of a long-established tradition.

Yet the tradition within which Jefferson toiled and that today is being preserved is peculiarly American as well as European. Through the labors of Mesick and the others, we can better understand how Jefferson's technical imagination, as well as his knowledge of architectural history, allowed him to adjust to his own time and locale while employing his sense of history.

A building is to be seen in the present. Yet, like a single frame in a motion picture, that one moment must be regarded as little more than a glimpse, a passing flash of light. Buildings are undergoing constant change, so they must be regarded with the past and future, as well as today, in mind.

In order to consider the labors of Mesick and Jefferson, it is necessary to bounce around a bit on civilization's time line. In this case, the destinations are Colonial America and Renaissance Italy.

Aside from a handful of wealthy plantation owners in the Virginia colony, the early European settlers constructed simple and practical buildings. They relied upon their learned skills and good sense to meet their immediate need for shelter. A few generations later an instinct for innovation and a reverence for the ancient monuments emerged, but much of the housing stock built in the seventeenth and eighteenth centuries, in Virginia as in the New England represented at Sturbridge, conformed to the same basic configurations with only minor modifications.

By the eighteenth century into which Jefferson was born, the population and productivity of North America had developed to the degree that it was both a market for British products and a provider of raw materials. One result of this growth was the emergence of the commercial town, which joined what had been an almost exclusively agricultural economy. Hand in hand came significant class differences and a desire for more elaborate housing. Simple shelter was no longer sufficient for a minority of moneyed and privileged Americans, especially in cultural centers like Boston and Philadelphia.

The fancy eighteenth-century dwelling required more public space. From almost any angle, the new Georgian-style houses were larger and more elaborately decorated. The front entry was a statement, with adornments of classical orders of full columns or pilasters with triangular pediments above. The windows were multi-light and double-hung, typically twelve-over-twelves or twelve-over-eights. The cornice (the projecting portion of the roof) had molded shapes. The corners of the building had pilasters or quoins, large stones or wood shaped to resemble blocks of stone.

Inside, the ceilings were taller, and the rooms carefully proportioned and detailed. In structural terms little had changed, as the framing, the masonry, the walling, and other structural details remained much the same. There was just more of each. If the medieval houses proclaimed, "Live in me," the Georgian house called out, "Look at me!"

In some high-style examples, a classical Palladian or Venetian window was located at the center of the façade above the door. (Recall that the front elevation of the Georgian-style Hascall house in Essex features a Palladian window.) While the Palladian window is more prevalent in the later Federal style, it is a key puzzle piece in understanding the stately eighteenth-century American house and the tradition within which Jefferson worked. It is not that all Georgian dwellings had Palladian windows or that they were used only in those years. The link is both more subtle and more obvious than that.

Though new to the Americas, Palladian windows weren't truly new, as there was a demonstrable historicalness about them, even when they first entered the American architectural vocabulary in the second half of the eighteenth century. The Palladian window evolved from careful study of ancient Roman buildings, as interpreted in Renaissance Italy, and was reproduced in books published and in buildings erected in the intervening two centuries. It was less a departure from what came before than a borrowing and a modification.

The thread of the story reaches back to Italy, to the second quarter of the sixteenth century, and to an Italian hat maker's son named Andrea di Pietro. Having lived his entire life in Italy in the sixteenth century, he may seem an odd choice for a role in a book about conserving American houses. But he was (and is) a conduit between the classical past and every educated builder who came after him, including Messrs. Jefferson and Mesick.

Di Pietro (his dates are 1508–80) apprenticed as a stonemason at thirteen, and was working as a carver of architectural stonework when good fortune (his and ours) knocked on his door in the person of Count Giangiorgio Trissino. A poet, antiquarian, and dramatist, Trissino saw great potential in the young Andrea, who was then in his mid-twenties. Trissino recognized that the young man had it in him to be much more than a stone carver and he offered him an education in things Roman—architecture, engineering, and topography. He also gave his disciple a new name, Andrea Palladio.

Trissino took him to Rome to study the ancient monuments. Palladio not only visited the Roman buildings but made measured drawings of them. He came to understand through this discipline the shape and proportion of the buildings and their ornamentation. He wasn't the first architect to scrutinize old buildings, but his understanding and interpretation of the lessons of classical structures are unique.

Palladio has often been termed the most influential architect who ever lived. He was certainly a prolific designer of beautiful and practical buildings. That a great many of his designs have survived also enhances his reputation, as does the fact that his mentor helped him secure many important commissions, for public and private buildings, both religious and secular. Of paramount import, however, is the fact that unlike so many gifted designers of his and earlier eras, he built many *houses*—villas and palaces, perhaps, but places for people to live. Palladio's villas and palaces are his most enduring and influential contribution to architecture.

Much of his creative energy came to be invested in homes rather than in churches or public buildings since, as he himself put it, the houses came first, "because one ought to believe that those first gave rise to public edifices." He conceived the theory that the simple house of man had produced the House of God. Thus, he argued, wasn't it reasonable to combine the elements of the sacred with the domestic, as he did by using a temple façade on his villas and palaces. Palladio may have started by designing houses because of the circumstances of his humble birth and the contacts of his patron, but he made the house a fit subject for great architecture.

Another key reason for his enduring influence is that he not only designed buildings but wrote books about his designs and his philosophy. His *I quattro libri dell'architettura (The Four Books of Architecture)* was published in Venice in 1570, and has been reprinted ever since in Italy and in translation in Spain (1625), France (1650), and England (first in 1721 and later in 1738 in the now classic Isaac Ware edition). His popularity didn't stop there, as even into our century new translations have appeared, notably in Warsaw in 1955.

Palladio's houses are recognizable as the progenitors of what is colloquially known as the English country-house style. His book defined the classical orders of columns and architectural decorations, examined ancient models, spelled out construction methods using both text and woodcut illustrations, and presented Palladio's own designs.

The villas and palaces he designed for the Italian countryside were suited to the agrarian needs of their owners. Typically, a central rectangular block was linked to subsidiary wings. The master and his family lived front and center, on the main floor elevated off the ground. The animals, servants, and farm equipment were set apart in order that, according to Palladio, "the one may not be any impediment to the other."

Palladio's buildings were strictly symmetrical, with temple fronts on their façades. Countless other designs, including those at the Academical Village, are copies or imitations of Palladio's villas. But as common as the direct visual echoes of Palladio's work are in later buildings, even more influential were Palladio's most basic notions about design.

"I gave myself up in my most early years to the study of architecture," he wrote in the preface to *The Four Books*. "I began very minutely with the utmost diligence to measure every one of the [ancient edifice's] parts . . . [to] comprehend what the whole had been, and reduce it to design.

"Whereupon perceiving how much the common use of building was different from the observations I had made upon the said edifices . . . it seemed to me a thing worthy of a man . . . to publish the designs of those edifices . . . and concisely to set

From Palladio's *Four Books*, Plate 42 illustrates a country villa near Venice, one that features a temple front with pedimented façade, Ionic and Corinthian columns, and a distinctly Palladian grace and symmetry.

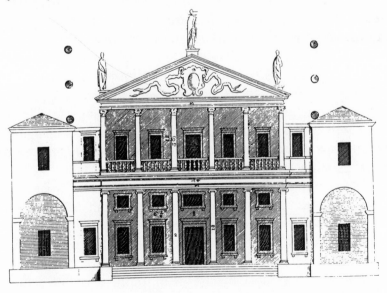

down whatever in them appeared to me more worthy of consideration; and moreover, those rules of which I have observed and now observe, in building."

Palladio was convinced there was a correct way to design a building. His examination of ancient Roman buildings had demonstrated to him that, with study and careful application, one could learn the vocabulary of architecture developed in ancient Rome. He concluded that, by employing the vocabulary properly, one would produce beautiful buildings. Arithmetical calculations could be used to achieve architectural harmony. His book sought, in short, to *"reduce it to design."*

Palladio had his age's confidence in general rules. He believed in dos and don'ts, and assured himself and his readers that if he provided prescriptive guidelines to solving architectural problems, beautiful buildings would be produced. His rules were softened by the heirs to his tradition (the English Adam brothers, in particular, moved to a freer interpretation from classical sources in the mid-eighteenth century), but his influence was overwhelming for more than two centuries.

In our time, the import of Palladio's approach is difficult to understand. His age believed that learning required repetition, memorization, and other authoritarian approaches. In the twentieth century, thanks to the educational philosopher John Dewey and others, we don't teach our children that way. Dewey's notion of instrumentalism held that man must develop flexible instruments to solve problems rather than master specific bodies of knowledge; he believed that since the problems are forever changing, the instruments must change, too. Today's Dewey-inspired progressive curriculum teaches "language arts" rather than "English"; repetitive teaching techniques and rote memorization have been rendered irrelevant.

This isn't the place for a debate about learning processes, of course. Yet the terrible loss of style in American domestic architecture—a loss that is apparent upon visiting almost any suburb built after World War II—is in part the result of a failure to learn about what came before.

More has been lost by the abandonment of old teaching methods than a few lines from Longfellow, a staple of elementary education only two generations ago. Prescriptive learning allows for the transmission of many kinds of information, some of which disappear without it. Architecture is a case in point. There are no magic formulas or fixed proportions that, when learned, deliver guaranteed results. But architecture practiced in a historical vacuum, without reference to or knowledge of what came before, is most often an architecture in which taste is eclipsed by ego; for much of the postwar era, architects have not been required to study the stylistic history of architecture.

Palladio's by-the-numbers approach is fundamental to his wide influence. Inigo Jones, the great English architect of the early seventeenth century, acquired a copy of the Italian edition of *The Four Books* on his travels and brought some of Palladio's own drawings back to England on his return from Italy in 1614. Jones's annotated copy of the book still exists, and it suggests how important Palladio was to Jones's work and that Jones almost single-handedly, via Palladio, brought high Renaissance architecture to England.

The first volume of Palladio's masterwork was published in England in 1663 by Godfrey Richards. Devoted to the orders of classical columns and decorations, it was a crude translation from an earlier Dutch version, to which Richards added materials about doors, roofs, and other subjects of interest to builders, offering specific, how-to advice. While it didn't accurately represent *The Four Books,* Richards's adaptation of Palladio was the first builder's handbook published in English. If the term "best-seller" had been in use in that era, it might well have been applicable, as Richards's adaptation of Palladio saw a remarkable twelve editions over the next several decades.

The complete *Four Books* didn't appear in English until 1721, in an edition published by an itinerant Italian architect named Giacomo Leoni. Although riddled with inaccuracies, Leoni's *Four Books* was immensely popular, and within months Palladianism was *the* style in English architecture.

In the years that followed, numerous books were published in England filled with Palladian-inspired designs. Some were large and expensive folio editions like today's coffee-table books, adornments for the drawing room of the informed, up-to-date man of taste. The classic *Works in Architecture* (1773) by Robert and James Adam (about which more in a later chapter) sold for more than ten pounds in Great Britain, a princely sum in the eighteenth century. Smaller and cheaper editions (typically costing only a few shillings), "pattern books" for the artisan, were even more influential. One such volume, titled *Practical Architecture* and written by a prolific producer of pattern books, William Halfpenny, was a manual of rules. Moving from the five orders (according to Palladio), and including details borrowed from Inigo Jones's and other Palladian-influenced buildings, Halfpenny went on to set out tables of proportions. The result was a standardized method of balancing the proportional widths and heights of columns and cornices and other shapes in a design. Halfpenny's pocket-sized volume saw seven editions by midcentury, and Halfpenny would write twenty other books.

Halfpenny was joined by Batty Langley, Abraham Swan, and other authors in the bookselling sweepstakes with highbrow volumes and pattern books alike, as many as a dozen a year for the next few decades. The key to their success was the practicality of their offerings.

Many architectural historians have traced specific architectural elements in existing houses back to the pattern books of that era. Houses in Virginia have doorways that are exact copies of plates in *Palladio Londinensis,* an English pattern book by William Salmon (1734). In Newport, Rhode Island, another major city of that era, the Redwood Library (1749) is a virtual copy of a building reproduced in one of the plates in Palladio's *Four Books* (as well as in a more likely source, Isaac Ware's *Designs from Inigo Jones*).

The transmission of Palladio's stylistic notions and, more importantly, his prescriptive rules in published materials seem strangely anachronistic in our age. Today building codes are established to assure the safety and suitability of new or remodeled structures. Those codes, like so much of the law, have evolved not to enhance our world but to prevent abuses; sadly,

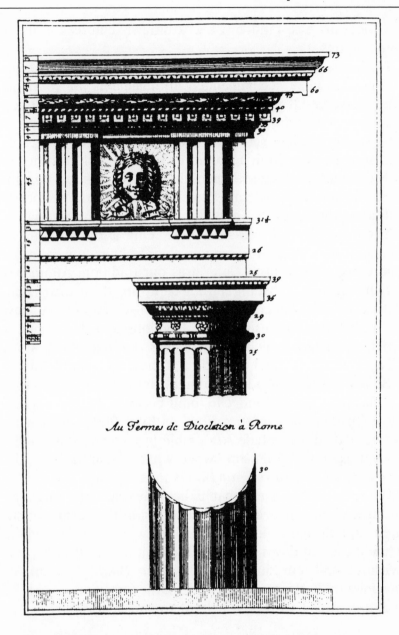

Au Termes de Diocletion à Rome

The classical source of the decorations on the entablature of
Pavilion I (and the inspiration for much of the building) was the
Roman Baths of Diocletian, as Jefferson knew them from his library,
in a 1766 edition of *Parallèle de l'architecture antique avec la
moderne,* by Roland Fréart de Chambray.

the codes are also randomly and arbitrarily enforced in many communities.

No formal rules to regulate style, no mandated schemes for ornamentation or recommended arrangements are routinely followed today. Nor should it be so. I for one find the notion of anyone telling me my new garage requires this or that decoration unacceptable. Yet I can't help but believe that being able to distinguish the Gothic from the Greek in architecture can only enhance our appreciation of the buildings we see. It might even educate us away from the characterless and needlessly utilitarian dwellings that now dominate new construction.

There are, in fact, pleasures here. One is the pleasure of recognition: being able to see ourselves as heirs to what came before, with the right to claim it as our tradition. Another is enrichment: just as shading can add depth and detail to a sketch, experience can deepen our appreciation of architecture, new and old. When he designed his Pavilions and drew upon a variety of ancient models, Jefferson was working to offer at his Village an architectural education of the most tangible kind.

Before we leave Andrea Palladio, let it be recorded that Thomas Jefferson's Monticello, built between 1771 and 1782, has a façade from *I quattro libri*. As John Mesick succinctly put it: "Palladio was Jefferson's bible in matters of building." Legend has it that Jefferson owned what was, at the time, the only copy of Palladio's *Four Books* in America.

While research suggests that his actually wasn't the only copy on these shores, it is certain that Jefferson the cosmopolitan knew and elected to imitate Palladio's work. His Rotunda is actually a scaled-down version of the Pantheon as Palladio had measured and reproduced it in his *Four Books*. The line of transmission is clear, as is the fact that Jefferson advanced the tradition. Today, Mesick is helping to conserve it.

The first occupant of Pavilion I was John Patton Emmet. As professor of natural history, Emmet was one of the eight original faculty members at the University of Virginia. Professor Emmet married several years later, but initially he shared his house with a variety of animals, among them a white owl, a brown bear, and some snakes. All in the interests of science, no doubt.

When I first talked with John Mesick, he was immersed in learning everything he could about Pavilion I, including who and what had lived there. He and other members of his firm were preparing a Historic Structure Report on the house, the first of a planned series of HSRs on each of the buildings in the Village.

The report covers the entire history of the Pavilion. It reveals that James Oldham was the carpenter-joiner in charge of constructing Pavilion I and that Oldham had previously worked for Jefferson on Monticello. The research uncovered revealing correspondence. In 1804 Oldham had borrowed Jefferson's personal copy of the first volume of Palladio's *Four Books*. Other letters recounted a disagreement about Oldham's bills that later led the carpenter to sue the University.

Every construction job, past or present, involves changes of mind, unforeseen complexities, and design mistakes, for which allowances have to be made. According to the HSR, Jefferson's problems were greater than average. He was trying to adapt centuries-old designs, inspired by great classical stone monuments, to the New World. But the reality was that in America the carpenter-joiner was the principal building tradesman, not the stonemason. Jefferson found himself having to make adjustments both in design and in the manner of execution.

The isolation of his work site exacerbated his problems. The materials in rural Virginia differed from those in Europe. Bricks rather than dressed stone were basic building blocks at the Academical Village; wood carving, stucco, and "burnt composition" (terra cotta) had to be used in place of marble and limestone ornamentation.

Highly skilled laborers of any kind were difficult to find. Initially, Jefferson imported tradesmen from Philadelphia (he termed them "the chepest, and generally the most steady & correct workmen in the US"), but the location of the construction forced him to rely on craftsmen from Virginia cities.

Jefferson wanted to use but also improve upon the best of the old by integrating the technological advances of his day. His preoccupation with new solutions to old problems created yet another series of complications. The roofing he devised for the Pavilions, which has been rediscovered and explained for the first time by Mesick, Cohen & Waite, has only enhanced Jefferson's reputation as an architectural innovator. It has presented a range of peculiar problems since the time of construction.

Evidence of the original roof at Pavilion I was gone by the time Mesick's firm arrived because an 1886 fire had required complete replacement of the roof surface and supporting structure. However, while he was in Charlottesville examining Pavilion I, Mesick's partner Jack Waite was asked to examine a leaking portion of the roof on Pavilion X.

The top surface at Pavilion X was slate, a covering known to have been a later addition. The mystery was what lay under it. In investigating the leak, Waite removed a few slate shingles and, to everyone's surprise, uncovered a rusted roof surface. The removal of more of the slate revealed a pattern of folded, tin-plated shingles.

An entirely new investigation ensued, one that involved scrutiny of Jefferson's notes and correspondence. It emerged that Jefferson had, while living in Europe, seen metal roofing. Upon his return to America, he had conducted experiments, both at Monticello and at the University of Virginia, in the use of metal for roofing surfaces.

He tried sheet iron but found that it rusted, then experimented with other metals, including copper and zinc. After a long search for an American foundry that could fabricate the material to his specifications (he found one in Philadelphia), the solution finally settled upon was sheets of iron plated with tin. The material had significant advantages over the wooden shingles that were commonplace at the time. It was light, resistant to fire, and, according to Jefferson, long-lasting. He estimated it would last one hundred years.

Jefferson had to devise a method whereby the novel roofing

surface could be installed by workmen with rudimentary skills. His solution involved a system of interlocking folds, which meant that a journeyman carpenter, rather than a highly skilled tinsmith, could install the shingles. The solution wasn't quite perfect, as there were continuing problems with the tradesmen.

When the tin-plate roof of Pavilion X was being replicated in 1988, the architects met with the same obstacles. As Waite told the story: "We had quite a few problems teaching the craftsmen how to lay this replica of Jefferson's roof. But when you read Jefferson's correspondence, you realize that he had exactly the same problems with his craftsmen one hundred and seventy years ago."

The restoration of the roof demonstrates the careful approach to these historic structures. The original tin plate was first uncovered. Then plywood was affixed on top, protecting the original. Next another touch of modernity was added, a membrane of neoprene, a synthetic rubber, because it was determined that the original tin plate hadn't been quite so weatherproof as Jefferson had wished (Professor Emmet wrote copious complaints about his leaking roof only a few years after its installation). If the 1988 tin plate fails, the neoprene will prevent leaks. The tin plate itself, fabricated of stainless steel with a metallic coating that is sixty percent tin and forty percent lead, was cut to individual ten by seven inch shingles. The result is a practical, durable solution that replicates the appearance Jefferson had in mind, both in texture and in color, as the new surface will darken in time to a pewter-colored patina.

Back at Pavilion I, the roof surface that had survived into the 1980s was radically changed, but much of the rest of the building's fabric was found to have remained more or less intact. Though the care it and the rest of the Pavilions had been given was less than vigilant prior to the recent restoration efforts, the buildings had not been subjected to wholesale renovations. The solidity and the quality of the original construction also helped assure the survival of the structures. Yet, as with all buildings of such vintage, there were a multitude of minor problems.

Typical were deterioration of some exterior wood surfaces,

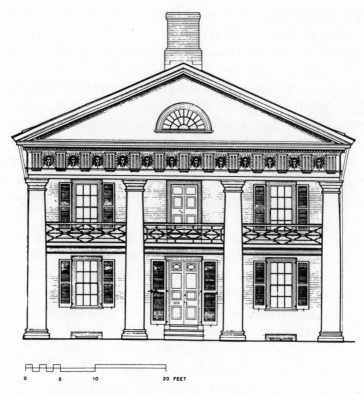

An architectural rendering of the front elevation of Pavilion I.
Mesick, Cohen & Waite

minor masonry cracking, and flaking paint. Certain changes
made by the human hand had introduced unsightly intrusions,
like the heating pipes that were run in front of basement windows and the eclectic range of light fixtures added throughout.

The Historic Structure Report on Pavilion I summarized the
vast research effort conducted by Mesick and his firm, but it
also made expansive recommendations for how to deal with
the building. One goal was to retain the original shape and
configuration of the rooms. In the bathrooms, the report recommended, the sinks were not to be set into cabinets and the
storage areas were to be confined to antique cupboards or
chests. Modern materials like vinyl, plastic laminates, and
ceramic tile were frowned upon. The plan focused on stabilizing

the structure and adapting it to contemporary demands while preserving as much of Jefferson's vision as possible. Where changes were deemed necessary, materials compatible with the original were to be used.

When I visited Pavilion I, the restoration had been completed. On my tour I felt that had I not been familiar with the changes, I wouldn't have been able to distinguish them. The process had left few footprints and succeeded in erasing a few left by previous renovations.

A new heating, ventilation, and air-conditioning system had been installed. This allowed for the removal of the old steam pipes and radiators. The new vents are almost invisible and most of the mechanical systems are hidden in the tall attic space. The kitchen finish relies upon simple, hand-planed paneled doors and muted colors.

Where possible, the changes were made according to evidence found within the structure itself. According to Murray Howard: "We didn't want to rely on a generalized understanding of Jefferson. Some years ago in the Rotunda restoration there was a willingness to borrow evidence from other sites. For example, the door graining from Monticello was borrowed, though it might or might not have been used here originally." Instead, at Pavilion I, clear evidence was found of the style and coloring of the mahogany graining, and it was carefully replicated.

One innovative solution was devised for the tall window openings at what at the time of construction had been the rear of Pavilion I. An 1850 addition had put two of the four openings to use as doorways; the others became niches with shelves. In the restoration process, the shelving was replaced with window sashes. Since they were to be windows to nowhere, the glass was mirrored, using silvered glass made in West Germany. Jefferson himself had written about the technique in his notebooks. The visitor now gets a clearer sense of the original appearance of the rooms.

Pavilion I was formally reopened in September 1988. The restoration and renovation had cost some $900,000, another indication of how serious the caretakers are about the Academical Village. "When I first came here," said Murray Howard, "pieces of the cornice from Pavilion III were dropping to the ground. It took two years to convince the University that it was a problem in need of funding. The amount we would have spent on Pavilion I five years ago would probably have been around $100,000."

Upon its completion, the University's vice president for health sciences, Dr. Don E. Detmer, and his wife, Mary Helen, moved in. Unlike the original occupant of Pavilion I, natural history professor Emmet, the Detmers don't own an owl, a bear, or even any snakes. But they did bring along their large and friendly dog, Nikko.

There's another lesson here. The Romans, Andrea Palladio, the authors of the pattern books, and Thomas Jefferson all believed that the builders who came before had lessons to share. Each amended and improved upon the notions they inherited, but all felt it entirely appropriate to use established parameters to create habitable and handsome buildings.

In contrast, traditional architecture is only recently returning to the curriculum of architecture schools. For decades, to teach yesterday's design styles was considered reactionary, and the atmosphere has been decidedly uncongenial to ideas that predated modernism. Our own context, it seems, was quite sufficient in and of itself; there was no need to use or even regard the older traditions of Western architecture. As John Mesick told me: "Certainly, when I was introduced to architecture, traditional architecture was just not considered."

Though the bulk of Mesick's practice today involves restoration, he continues to design new buildings. I asked how the diverse elements of his practice, the restoration of the old and the building of the new, informed one another.

"I am a *carrier*," he said with a certain emphasis. "What I'm confronted with now is what's endlessly, repetitiously in the past. I gain greater insight by understanding that process working backwards from my time. I see the traditional building not as the manifestation of just a lot of ornaments that you attach names to but to know they took the shape they took because that's the shape of life at any given time.

"It's the sum total of materials available, the ability to work those materials, it's the technology, it's transportation, economy, it has to do with the development of skills, the guilds, can they do metal as well as stone and wood. You can read the forces that were running rampant or being controlled at a given time, just as I suppose a botanist would from a fossil.

"Hence, when you look back to the past there's almost nothing you look at that a contemporary architect wouldn't be involved in today. It's still a question of how to keep the rain out. That gives rise to an investigation that tells you a lot about any one time. It might also illumine your next new building when you sit down at the board tomorrow and try to do a new building. That's at the more practical application level. I think almost as an ideal, metaphysical situation, it is the thing that sort of unites humanity for all time, just a flow."

I asked him if, with the newfound concern for restoration and preservation, he thought there was a chance that new buildings might reflect more of the qualities of the old.

"I don't believe in progress—each generation has to enter the lists anew. But if you are alive to learning, you'll be alive to good architecture. Still, the odds of your wanting good architecture, even if you are alive to many things, are much less today than they would have been back in the period before the industrial revolution. Then, other than having a good library, better clothes and furnishings, that was practically the only thing a man could do to manifest physically that spirit of being alive."

Are more people alive in that sense today?

He paused. "I would certainly have to say that there are more people alive to the values of historic buildings today. Our own practice manifests that. But then there are more people of all kinds, both interested and indifferent. Do you think the ratio ever really changes? I don't know. Look at the new buildings around now."

He paused, perhaps for effect, then answered the question again.

"I think the answer is no."

Restoration today is quite different from that practiced a century ago when an early wave of preservation fever was to be seen in the United States. A key figure in that movement was New York architect Stanford White, he of the coastal New England wandering in 1877.

Perhaps the best-known architect of his day, White was hired to restore both the White House and Jefferson's Rotunda at the turn of the century. Following an 1895 fire at the Rotunda, he chose to "restore" it in the Beaux-Arts style. At the White House, he supervised the 1902 installation of Colonial Revival paneling and detailing. In both instances his renovations have subsequently been almost entirely erased, in 1948 in Washington, in 1976 in Charlottesville; in each case, White had installed what he thought was right and proper, an admittedly handsome interior that paid virtually no heed to what had originally been there. His "restoration" approach contrasts starkly with today's.

In attempting to characterize the larger role that John Mesick and his partners, Murray Howard, and other restoration architects play, I keep coming back to Mesick's notion of the "carrier." In medical terminology, a carrier is a person who harbors a specific organism and who is capable of spreading it to others. In an architectural context, the carrier metaphor helps distinguish the restoration architect from other architects (today and in White's time). The carrier isn't entirely passive, as he must do more than merely pass on or preserve what he finds. He or she has an overwhelming desire to understand and interpret in order to preserve or restore. Yet the complete exercise must not be principally a creative act.

The restoration architect today must be satisfied that he or she isn't smarter or better than his or her antecedents. There must be a sublimation of ego in order to preserve the expression of the original designer.

I think a maxim of Mesick's is fitting. "At our best restorations," he observed, "you should not know we were there."

6
The Victorian Merchant

_____

The backward glance transforms and regenerates.
        —*Henry Hope Reed,* The Golden City (*1959*)

"**I**t was really this house that created the *Old House Journal.*"

Clem Labine gazed around the room with its high Victorian decoration. We sat at a great heavy dining table, surrounded by such architectural features as elaborately painted borders, a pair of tall, Eastlake-style walnut pocket doors, a deep plaster cornice, and leaded-glass windows.

(And, no, once more for the record, he's another Clem Labine, not the Brooklyn and Los Angeles Dodger pitcher of the 1950s. No relation.)

"We bought the house in 1967. Actually, my wife got me into it because it came wrapped around those Victorian tiles." He gestured at the fireplace surround with its border of decorated tiles. "It's an *Idylls of the King* series, and my wife is a Tennyson freak." The purchase price for the house (and tiles) was $25,000.

"Anyway, we piddled around with the house, interacting both with it and with people in the neighborhood about their houses. Some of them were really into architectural history, which I was not at the time."

By training, Labine is a chemical engineer. Upon graduating from Yale in 1957, he went to work for the publishing giant McGraw-Hill and spent the next fifteen years there editing *Chemical Engineering* magazine. But he knew a publishing opportunity when he saw one.

When he left McGraw-Hill, in November 1972, he had a plan. Eleven months later, the first twelve-page issue of the *Old House Journal* appeared.

Clem Labine lives in the Victorian neighborhood of Park Slope, on a street called Berkeley Place, in Brooklyn, New York. His four-story row house, constructed in 1883, was built of quarried brown stone (thus the generic name for such houses, so common in New York City, "brownstones"). Labine described the house as an example of the "Levittown housing of that era," an assertion that is supported by the fact there are twelve nearly identical houses on the same block that were built by the same developer.

"It's cookie-cutter stuff," said Labine, "just machine-made, industrial revolution materials that were available to the middle class. But then they still had good craftsmen to assemble them." By that era, the pattern book had been replaced by the manufacturer's trade catalogue from which factory-made hardware, decorative elements, and other goods were ordered.

"The house was a rooming house when we got it, though it wasn't originally. There had been a lot of damage to the building, with three apartments on this floor alone. You can see on the doors where they added locks. That alcove"—he indicated a long, narrow niche dominated by a large carved sideboard— "was a bathroom. There were Sheetrock partitions, and they practically destroyed the floor . . ." His voice faded, as if he were pained by the recollection.

"We had little partitions all over," he resumed. "There were sinks in the corners. There were little stoves. It was painted boardinghouse green . . ." Another fade. "I mean, it was a mess, it was a wreck. A physical and aesthetic wreck."

Over a period of years, the Labine family—Clem, his wife, Claire, and their three children—performed the demolition

Clem Labine's row house on Berkeley Place in Brooklyn, New York, one of hundreds like it built in the 1880s. Despite its apparent similarity to its neighbors, however, the house's interior bears the individual imprint of its owner.

tasks, removing flimsy partitions and restoring the original floor plan. "What we did was certainly not a historic restoration, because I could find little evidence of what had been here in 1883," Labine explained. "The house had gone through too many transitions.

"Instead we did a Victorian fantasy re-creation, doing things that *might* have been done in 1883, but weren't ever done in this house." It seemed like an issue he had talked about before, one about which he had been challenged. Perhaps a purist or two had suggested that he should have remained more strictly within the bounds of what had been there, but Labine seemed happy with the result.

"It's sympathetic to the spirit and character of the house, it's totally reversible, which is the key. We preserved the essential character of the house. But it isn't *historical*."

Now, more than twenty years later, would he do things differently?

"Not a hell of a lot differently, just because of limitations of time and budget. I mean, this is not a museum house, it's a real-world question. If I was redoing this today, I'd probably use a lot more reproduction wallpaper, for example. We did all the decorations in paint and stencils because when we did it we had no choice. Today, I'd probably use paper because it's easier and faster and cheaper. I'm not unhappy with any of the things that I did, but the house does reflect where I was at the time."

Does he plan to take on another house?

"Absolutely not," he replied quickly. His response was accompanied by a sound I couldn't quite identify. It seemed a crossbreed, half laugh and half exclamation.

"There are two kinds of old-house people," he went on. "There is the kind that just adores the process. They've got so much energy that as soon as they get through with one they've got to sell and move on to another. Then there's the second group—and I think it's roughly fifty-fifty—where one's enough. I'm in the latter category."

He laughed his nervous laugh, as if the prospect of taking on another project was a bit overwhelming.

Labine is a tall man of medium build. His hairline has receded to reveal more of his high forehead, but it is his mustache that leaves the strongest impression. If you were to take a photograph of him and process it in sepia tones, Labine, with his handlebar-shaped, waxed mustache, could easily pass for a prosperous Victorian merchant.

In an odd way, he actually is something of a Victorian merchant. His living has always been made selling magazines, first as an editor and sales promotion specialist at McGraw-Hill. Then he became a publisher himself, and his chosen subject was Victorian houses.

He started the *Old House Journal* (*OHJ*) on an $8,000 savings account. "It was literally a kitchen-table start-up," he recalled, "one made easier by my family. We have three children, but of course it always helps to have a working wife. She was able to get us over the financial gaps, and some of them were quite significant."

Mrs. Claire Wood Labine co-wrote and co-produced, among other projects, the Emmy-winning soap opera *Ryan's Hope.* In the early days of *OHJ*, its staff shared the house with the writers of that television show, and all work stopped at 2 p.m. to watch and critique the day's episode.

The newsletter started with five paid subscribers, although some 2,000 copies of the first issue were given away. Most went to fellow Brooklynites at flea markets, a few to newspapers and other publications. Labine was a desktop publisher long before the term was coined, as the type for *OHJ* was set on Labine's own IBM Selectric. His office was on the ground floor of the house that had initiated Labine into the world of old houses.

"One of our first missions," he said of *OHJ*, "was to raise the consciousness of the American home-buying public to the intrinsic value of the nineteenth-century house. We eventually moved on to the early twentieth century, any house more than fifty years old, really. But we started out crusading on the Victorians because they [constituted] a very large area of architectural housing stock that was totally undervalued and underappreciated."

The strong Victorian bent of *OHJ* almost immediately met with a warm reception. Within two years, the magazine was profitable. Within four years, the paid circulation had grown to 20,000 subscribers representing all fifty states. At first, many of the articles were born of Labine's and his neighbors' experiences, but gradually a larger network of contributors evolved, including contractors and restoration professionals.

The staff grew, too. An editor was added, and a circulation director, an assistant and then two. One day in 1979 a subscriber named Patricia Poore knocked at the door and offered her services, asserting that she could write better articles than those the magazine was featuring. She made good on the promise and Labine shortly made her a partner and the magazine's editor-in-chief.

In a period of fifteen years, *OHJ* went from a twelve-page newsletter to more than one hundred pages. Charming but workmanlike line drawings gave way to photographs; the cover now features a glossy, four-color photo. How-to articles were supplemented by more features and articles on architectural history. It was a success, to say the least. Even a purist and museum professional like John Curtis expresses his admiration for *OHJ*. "Its success," he suggested, "is attributable to people's interest in doing things right."

In 1986, the decision was made to accept advertising. "The basic editorial focus didn't change," said Labine, "but the packaging and business concept did. One of the things that make the *Old House Journal* relatively unique is that it has a very concrete philosophical point of view, very specific, oriented to restoration and historical integrity. Unlike most of the house magazines, where it's about the style of the month or the fad of the month, *OHJ* has always presented a fairly coherent philosophy."

Another key to its success was that it filled a void. "At the start," Labine said, "it was totally seat-of-the-pants, while now there's an incredible reservoir of practical, how-to knowledge. A few years ago you might spend an awful lot of time worrying about how to keep the plaster from falling. Today there are a lot of proven techniques for doing that.

"A lot of it now gets into living history. It's like doing your own Sturbridge Village. You dress up and do the whole thing, and maybe you're more concerned with where to get high-button shoes to wear to a costume ball on Saturday night.

"I feel I now know a great deal about nineteenth-century cultural and social history, but in school, as a chemical engineer, I was not exposed to a lot of it. I was up there in the lab worrying about thermodynamics experiments."

Labine obviously feels more comfortable with the hands-on than with the dressing-up. Perhaps that's why, as of January 1, 1988, he sold his interest in *OHJ* and went off to start a new magazine.

"The preservation-restoration movement is entering a new phase," Labine explained. "It has already influenced America and our opinions about our houses in ways that really hadn't been anticipated in 1973 when we started *OHJ*.

"One major way is in the professional end. Right now architects and builders are constructing neo-historical houses. That was totally unheard of in 1973. If you wanted historic architecture then, you had to buy and fix up something old."

Labine's answer to this trend is his new magazine, *Clem Labine's Traditional Building*.

"I liken the restoration movement to the medieval monasteries. They kept the light of learning lit during the Dark Ages and then helped foster the Renaissance. All accumulated knowledge suddenly spilled out when mankind was ready to use it again.

"The preservation-restoration movement sort of nurtured the craft and ornamental traditions through another Dark Age.

Suddenly a few years ago a lot of the craft skills and products that had been developed for the restoration market began leaking into new construction. Many architectural firms were backing into historic work just because that's where the money was—they had no real understanding or passion or training in that area. So I aimed to focus in on this professional market as an area that wasn't being very well served by the existing professional publications, none of which had any real background or interest in historicism."

"Historicism" is a favorite word of Labine's. For him, the term implies a sensitivity to history, "to give people a sense that, hey, you're not really the first ones." Therein, said Labine, lies "the underlying message of historic preservation. Properly, it teaches human values. It's a great object lesson that makes human values tangible, so you can see and touch and feel them."

In the first issue of *Traditional Building* he offered two other coinages he favors. For Labine, "neo-traditionalism" is "new design that uses historic forms for inspiration in a sensitive and intelligent way, without necessarily copying the past. Neo-traditional buildings refer to their historic antecedents in a respectful and loving manner."

In contrast, there's "architorture," which is "a brutal, mocking, uninformed, or absurd handling of historic forms, either in restoration or in new construction."

In his speech, Labine often uses these and other terms, including "façadism," a term that describes the recent trend to preserve the shell of a building for outward appearances but make little or no effort to retain the original interior. Labine is, however, an eminently practical man: "Actually I don't denounce façadism as vehemently as do a lot of purists in preservation. I think it's better than nothing, and if we can preserve the rhythm of the façade while building something in back of it, at least the streetscape benefits."

Part of the appeal of Labine's publications is his willingness to preach to the converted. His readers already believe in the restoration gospel; they find comfort in these terms. For years,

a fixture of *OHJ*'s back cover was the "Remuddling of th
Month," which offered two photos of an older structure. On
revealed the house more or less as it began life, the other it
appearance after "a brutal, mocking, uninformed, or absurd'
remodeling ("remuddling"). To many people, the photos wer
entertaining and at the same time appealed to their moral cer
tainty about the rightness of restoration.

The subject of *Traditional Building* isn't language, of course
but rather the business of traditional building, from working
on older structures to building new ones with an eye to the
past. There are feature articles on specific restoration projects
and on distinguished professionals (John Mesick and his part
ners were the subject of a piece in one early issue) and occasional
technical articles. But the publication's subtitle expresses its
intentions most clearly: "Historical Products for Today's Pro
fessional." *Traditional Building* includes many advertisements
for such goods and much editorial copy about lighting fixtures,
hardware, glass, millwork, and other materials.

Launched in the fall of 1988, the publication found an immediate market. As Labine told me in the spring of 1990: "It's
actually one of those wonderful accidents where things are going
according to plan. At first it was more a suspicion on my part
that there was an unfilled niche in the design-building field.
Now that seems to have been the case, given the acceptance
among readers and advertisers." The percentage of paid circulation (as opposed to the giveaways, or "controlled circulation" in magazine-ese) is gradually increasing.

This time around, Labine's market is, unlike that for *OHJ*,
a professional one. Rather than the homeowner, Labine aims
to reach the contractors, the craftsmen, and the architects, those
concerned with restoration as well as those involved in new
construction in revival-style buildings. "The products and a lot
of the craft skills are the same as for *OHJ*," Labine said. "But
Traditional Building is not a how-to publication. It's a resource
publication for suppliers and, to a lesser extent, craft people
who do historically related work."

Labine sees this venture as a reflection of a change in the architectural climate. He cited the transformation in the practice of restoration architecture.

"I had a line I used in the early days of *OHJ:* 'Architects are the worst enemies of old houses.' That was because they viewed them as a blank canvas on which to make bold personal statements. Some architects still treat old buildings dreadfully, but I think they are almost becoming a minority.

"You even see politicians lining up behind preservation projects. That would never have occurred a few years ago. Today, the concept of preservation has a lot of political capital inherent in it."

The New York Times once termed Labine "the guru of old-house restoration." Given his role as something of a locus of activity in what he calls "the Movement," Labine's concerns about his own neighborhood are illuminating.

"When we moved here in 1967, it was"—there was a mid-sentence pause while a silent word search took place—"it was *colorful.* Definitely not a yuppie neighborhood."

As it is today, I observed. But was the change good or bad?

"Well, it's fifty-fifty. It's good for property values and it's certainly a safer neighborhood than it was. We don't hear so many beer bottles breaking out on the curb, so it's a little easier to sleep at night.

"But there is less of a spirit. One of the things that made this neighborhood quite wonderful was whenever there were 'new folks' moving in, it was news. All the recent arrivals knew each other and we sort of banded together for comfort and support. There isn't any need for that anymore." I looked at him carefully. He didn't look the least bit misty-eyed; faintly sad, perhaps, but mostly matter-of-fact.

He added: "Certainly, the type of housing we think of as premium housing stock has changed. Now, people with discretionary income choose to spend money in older neighbor-

hoods with good-quality housing stock. That wouldn't have been true fifteen years ago.

"Older buildings have something to say about the human condition. The striving for excellence and trying to do the best kind of work you can—I think that ennobles us all, unlike the temporary, the disposable. I think that slapdash mentality really diminishes us in very fundamental ways.

"But another of the funny transitions that have taken place in this neighborhood is that it's now so bloody expensive that the people who can afford these houses have to go out and work full-time just to make the mortgage payments. It's no longer a do-it-yourself process. They're two-lawyer families, and everything from changing a light bulb on, they've got to get somebody to do it. When we first came, it was a big do-it-yourself information exchange. Every Saturday night we spent our time exchanging paint-stripping tips.

"It's a very different process, you know. If you buy a place and turn it over to an architect and general contractor, I don't think you get as much out of it personally."

Labine said his engineering training was a bonus in understanding materials and solving restoration problems. "On the other hand," he added with a laugh, "one of the fine points of chemistry I never really thought through was spontaneous combustion." Then he told a story.

He and his children had worked together refinishing a cabinet. It had been painted, so they had laboriously stripped it. When they were finally ready, they spent one entire Saturday putting the finish on with linseed oil. They applied the oil with paper towels.

The task itself wasn't complicated—or dangerous—but the garbage was. That night, Labine thought his wife had put it out for collection. Claire thought he had. Instead of being dispatched to curbside, the bagged towels sat by the kitchen door.

On Sunday morning, Labine awoke at six o'clock and thought

he smelled fire. He looked down the dark stairwell and saw a cloud of dense smoke.

His wife called the fire department while he raced around looking for the source. He couldn't find any flames, but did observe that the choking smoke was heaviest in the kitchen. He opened some windows to clear the air only to see an unplanned demonstration of that elusive concept, spontaneous combustion. The oil-soaked paper burst into flame.

"Fortunately," Labine recalled, "I had a fire extinguisher around."

The house was saved, of course, and that was probably very good news for many concerned with old buildings. As Labine told me: "This house—and the things that have spun out from the house—it has literally changed my life. It's the single most important thing that has happened to me, other than marrying my bride. And it was my bride who led me to this house. I guess it was all connected."

Clem Labine's influence, like Don Carpentier's, is as transmitter. Through his publications, he has reached millions of Americans.

His magazines are not slick. They are professionally edited and packaged but with a minimum of posing. Aside from the underlying philosophy—"We all care about old buildings, right, gang?"—there is actually very little passion. The reader rarely gets the feeling of being manipulated or sold a bill of goods.

I asked Labine about publishing versus preservation. Having spent twenty-odd years editing a trade magazine, what led him to go out on his own and found *OHJ*? Did it have to do with homes or old things or was it just a good entrepreneurial opportunity?

Even before the last syllable was out of my mouth, Labine interrupted. "It has to do with old things, because, well, just because of the person I am.

"I am *not* a generic publisher. I sold one publication in the historical field and have started another one in another part of the historical field."

"But you started out at *Chemical Engineering.*"

"That's right. But I would not remotely consider doing an offshoot publication in, say, chemistry. Anything that I'm going to do businesswise is going to be related in some way to preservation, historical building, or this basic field.

"The house crystallized it for me, but it goes back, I think, to my upbringing. My father is something of an antiquarian. I grew up in Springfield, Massachusetts, in a turn-of-the-century house which we didn't think of as an especially architectural thing. It was just a place to live.

"But my father has a great sense of family tradition that is reinforced as he gets older. I think it was his interest that got me attuned to antiquarian things."

He's a collector?

"Of everything," he said with a resigned laugh. "Actually, his is an antiquarian interest tempered very much with technology. My father is a mechanical engineer, or was until he retired. But he's always building machines, so he's still very much a scientific person.

"One facet of that is his interest in things of the past. That's generated to a large extent by a profound respect for the skills and crafts of the past. There were many skills that were commonplace a hundred or a hundred and fifty years ago that are no longer commonplace today."

I asked if Labine's father collected tools.

"He collects, but not as a collector. He collects tools to work with. I guess the things he comes closest to collecting are clocks, but mainly because he likes to make them work again."

He paused.

"We had a friend here in town who acquired a segmental clock. I'd never even seen one before. It was made in China, probably in the 1830s or '40s, something like that."

Labine's hands came to life, sculpting the air between us. "It doesn't have a round dial. It has a segment of a circle that's about this much." His gesture circumscribed a curve roughly a quarter of the circumference of a large dinner plate. "You know, an arc. The minute hand goes like this to the end." He swung his right hand, wrist up and fingers down, pendulumlike, back and forth over the open palm of his left hand.

"And then it goes *whap*," he said with emphasis, "swinging back to the beginning.

"You can imagine, mechanically, that's quite a thing. The clock didn't work when he got it, and our friend couldn't get anybody in town to fix it. I thought, 'Well, my dad might find it intriguing.'

"He approached it very warily." Labine assumed a gravelly voice, imitating his father's reluctant tone. " 'I've never seen anything like this. I don't know if I can do anything with it.' "

Labine suggested he think about it.

"Inside of a week he was taking it apart. He discovered that somebody had tried to repair it sometime in the past and had really botched it up. My father has a lathe and he machined a couple of new parts, so pretty soon he had the sucker working."

I thought I recognized a certain filial pride in Labine's expression.

Labine calls Queen Victoria's husband, Prince Albert, his "personal icon." He lives in a Victorian house, and the first magazine he published had a principal focus on things Victorian. Given his posture as a man of another time as well as of his own, Labine's perspective on the past and present differs from the average person's.

I asked him about the notion of progress, in the nineteenth century and today.

"It was *the* Victorian theme," he began.

"But I think you have to make a distinction between progress as the passage of time and progress as improvement. In the nineteenth century there was an assumption that tomorrow will be better than today, therefore the passage of time, ipso facto, means improvement. That persisted pretty much up through World War II.

"We used to believe in the theme of progress and the march of mankind into the future. But since the sixties the theme that the future is by definition better than the present has certainly been muted. There's a growing realization of what has happened to our planet, the population pressures, and what is being done to our ecosystem. I think we're getting much more humble, much more careful about how we get behind progress."

Is there a connection between such environmental concerns and preservation?

"There definitely is. For example, there's the trend toward trying to identify building materials and practices that are harmful to the environment. I think that's a wonderful area to explore.

"It would be difficult, but I think it can all be tied into the market. The economy can control some of these things if you have full cost accounting."

In other words, you should be paying tomorrow's costs today?

"That's right. Part of the problem with, say, disposable plastic things is that the cost of production and the cost we pay sort of ends at the plant fence. The discharge of effluents has been basically free. Stuff is thrown into the air, into the streams, or buried in the ground, degrading the environment.

"There's a real long-term cost to you and me associated with that in terms of having to live in a crappier world. And we're not paying for it in the price of the plastic we're buying. While I'm not a big-government guy by a long shot, I do think government has to create a level playing field. So if restrictions and environmental regulations and controls were such that we had to pay the full cost of what we do, then preservation and conservation would happen a lot more automatically.

"You know, the building boom of the fifties and sixties that demolished a lot of fine old buildings was caused by quirks in the tax laws that encouraged new building. It gave you a very rapid write-off of your construction costs, so there was an artificial stimulation on the building side that had a very negative impact on old buildings. That skewed the true economics.

"Actually, Charlie Howell, a contractor turned environmentalist, talked even then about 'embodied energy.' " Howell, an occasional contributor to *Traditional Building,* is president of the Cumberland Science Museums of Nashville, Tennessee, and past president of the Trust for the Future, a nonprofit organization devoted to finding and using environmentally sensitive construction methods and materials.

"At the time of the energy crisis Howell was the first one to say, 'For heaven's sake, these old buildings are tremendous packages of energy.' You know, all the energy it took to produce the materials, to bring them to the site, and to put a structure up—there is a tremendous amount of energy that either is going to be lost or has to be replaced when we just thoughtlessly demolish a building. That's not even considering the historic preservation aspect, that's just talking about practical economics.

"So a lot of these broader-scale preservation, conservation kinds of things do tie in closely if you cast your net widely enough. Preservation is basically good for the environment; the damage to the environment has already been done in creating them. To maintain them is basically labor-intensive. It takes a lot of little patty-caking by hand to repair and maintain, but it's basically very low-impact on the environment."

Labine's words and his manner put me in mind of a notion I've heard bandied about a few times in idle conversation. It's a kind of cocktail-party approach to slotting people into categories. Not on the basis of race or age or sex, but on more philosophical grounds. It's a five-and-ten-cent-store approach to understanding intellectual history.

According to this "theory," everybody's a poet or an engineer. You *think* or you *do.* You consider the world around you, or you build or change or somehow transform that world in a physical sense. For purposes of this easy division, historians and politicians and lawyers and psychologists are "poets," while construction workers and mechanics and computer technicians are "engineers."

I've bounced back and forth in my characterization of Labine. Not everyone fits neatly in one or the other category, of course. But it seems appropriate to categorize Labine as an engineer, literally and otherwise.

"By my lights, process is all," Labine has said. "It's the doing that is what living is about. It's the process, not the having. Whether or not it's ever done doesn't matter as long as what you're doing you do to the best of your abilities and you're always striving to improve your skills, and to pass on those skills to other people."

Words like "process," "skills," and "doing" all make him sound engineerish. Yet his sentiments seem rather philosophical for a nuts-and-bolts type. I explain that to myself by recalling that Labine is in a real sense imbued with the spirit of another time, one in which not all knowledge was so compartmentalized and specialized.

Perhaps the directness of that age is part of the appeal of the Victorian era to Labine. Certainly his willingness to think of it as a living presence today helps explain his personal appeal and that of his magazines.

After all, the nineteenth century was a time when an engineer could be a poet and a publisher could speak, as Labine does, like a poetic engineer.

7
The Artist's Collector

It is only an auctioneer who can equally and impartially admire all schools of art.

—*Oscar Wilde*

Growing up in rural New England, I was given to understand that an "old house" was at least a hundred and fifty years of age. A building dating from 1830 or before would have been built before machine cutting tools were widely used. It would still be likely to feature elements shaped by hand, like decorative moldings and a timber frame.

For more than a few old Yankees, however, even the century-and-a-half parameter doesn't work. To them, houses that don't predate the Revolution or, at least, Washington's presidency aren't truly old. For those willful conservatives, if it's not eighteenth century, it's not worthy.

I've gradually unlearned such inbred prejudices. The Victorian revival we've seen in the last decade or so has exposed and educated many of us to the appeal of that later age of decorative (if machine-made) excesses, the breed of houses that Clem Labine came to love and celebrate. But my personal march of architectural time has only recently introduced me to the twentieth century. Specifically, I have gone about learning something of the man who seemed the most obvious spokesperson for modern American architecture, Frank Lloyd Wright.

In 1887, when Wright left the University of Wisconsin to seek work in Chicago, he had never seen electric light. When he died in 1959, he was the notorious designer of the new and controversial Guggenheim Museum in New York. In the intervening years, he made himself an undeniable presence in the modernist landscape of the first half of the twentieth century.

Wright is both the best and the worst of choices as an exemplar of things modern. His life was filled with drama, to which volumes have already been devoted. Among the most memorable events was his 1909 abandonment of his first wife and six children to travel to Europe with the wife of a client, Mamah Borthwick Cheney. In doing so he scandalized his friends and neighbors in Oak Park, Illinois. Wright married three times, but Mrs. Cheney was not destined to be among his wives. The love of Wright's life, she was murdered by an arsonist in 1911 before the necessary divorce proceedings had been completed.

In more than seven decades of work, Wright experienced the ebb and flow of fame. Both financial success and failure were familiar to him. Despite the distractions of a personal life filled with incident and no small investment of time in devising a peculiar mythology about himself, Wright managed to produce a body of work of unparalleled innovation, one characterized by technical as well as stylistic invention.

For all of these reasons, his renown in the United States (and abroad) is unequaled by any other American architect. Thomas Jefferson may be familiar to more people, but not entirely for his buildings. Henry Hobson Richardson probably had the greatest international influence of any American architect; after all, no other American designer had a style named after him, as with "Richardsonian Romanesque." Nevertheless, as American architects go, Frank Lloyd Wright's is *the* name to reckon with.

Therein also lies the problem with using Wright as a paradigm for twentieth-century American architecture. Wright was unquestionably a magician, and the experience of almost any Wright building is dramatic. The problem is that, as any magician will tell you, the conjurer must never explain his tricks.

In his fashion, Wright obeyed that code. His "tricks" (an unfair characterization of his work, of course) remained his secret. The notable absence of significant buildings inspired by Wright's work, designed by either his contemporaries or subsequent architects, is convincing evidence of that.

The explanation for this doesn't lie in any attempt by Wright to keep his work a secret. Unlike Coca-Cola, no undisclosed Wrightian formula is locked away in a vault in Atlanta (or even at Taliesin or Taliesin West, Wright's homes and communities in Spring Green, Wisconsin, and Scottsdale, Arizona, the latter the repository for his archives). It's just that Wright's highly individualized buildings don't seem to be reproducible. You can copy them, but no self-respecting architect wants merely to copy. And variations on a theme by Wright, unlike those based on Palladio or Mansard or Richardson, just don't appear on many lists of all-time great buildings.

Nevertheless, this chapter is about Wright. And it's about a contemporary cultural conservator of a rather unusual sort who has associated his own name with Wright's—namely, Thomas Monaghan, the founder of Domino's Pizza.

Monaghan is the Mr. Moneybags who has made front-page news for collecting Wrightiana—chairs, tables, windows, architectural elements, drawings, letters, anything of Wright's (including, at different times, several of his houses). Almost single-handedly he created a bull market, and introduced a whole new set of ethical questions for preservationists to argue about. We will look at some of them in this chapter.

About 450 of Wright's designs were actually constructed. Among them were a handful of office buildings, factories, a bookstore, a fountain or two, a hotel in Tokyo, numerous places of worship, and a considerable miscellany of other structures. But Wright is probably best remembered for his hundreds of house designs.

No doubt Wright's best-known house is Fallingwater. Located in the Pennsylvania hills sixty miles from Pittsburgh, that famous house, along with its surrounding 1,750 acres, has been in the public trust since 1963. Despite its isolated setting in the hamlet of Mill Run, the house draws more than 100,000 visitors annually.

Built for a Pittsburgh department store magnate, Edgar Kaufmann, in 1936 and 1937, the house leaves an indelible mind print, even on those who have seen it only in photographs. Its elongated, horizontal concrete tiers seem to be suspended atop the gush of water. If it wasn't cantilevered over a waterfall, the house would no doubt still be much admired. Yet it is its placement—not, as the client requested, with a view of the waterfall, but actually *in* the waterfall—that has to stand as Wright's best-known epiphany.

Fallingwater was something of a fulcrum in Wright's career, positioned as it was between a long fallow period (he saw only two of his designs built between 1928 and 1935) and the intensely busy and productive twenty years that followed (at his death, his practice was more active than ever). The house was perhaps his greatest act of prestidigitation.

One of his apprentices at the time, Edgar Tafel, recounted the circumstances of its design. One fall morning in 1935, Kaufmann called Mr. Wright (among Wright's acolytes, it's an obligatory affectation to refer to him as "Mr. Wright") to announce that he was coming to see the plans for his country home.

According to Tafel, not so much as a preliminary sketch of the house was on paper. Unperturbed, Wright took a seat at a drafting table. He began to draw, rapidly, and stayed at it for two and a half hours. When Kaufmann arrived for lunch, there were floor plans, elevations, sections, and detail drawings. The name, Fallingwater, was written boldly across the bottom of one of the drawings in Wright's own hand.

Other sources recount the story differently. According to one, Wright had several days' rather than several hours' notice. Another claims there were some preliminary drawings in advance of the intense drawing session. And surely Wright had imagined the house in considerable detail well in advance of the phone call, as it seems unlikely that even he could conceive

The wondrous Fallingwater, designed when Wright was sixty-nine, in which the reinforced-concrete house is set literally into a mountain stream. *Harold Corsini/Fallingwater*

the design so completely in one sitting. Yet the anecdote reinforces the architect-as-conjurer image of Wright. As built, the basic design is the same as that shown in those first sketches.

Wright himself and Tafel and countless others who have attached themselves to Wright's legacy have done little to demystify the man. One biographer, Brendan Gill, at the close of his suggestively titled book, *Many Masks,* addresses Wright as "old scamp, old teller of lies, old maker of wonders!" For Wright, not even his own life was free from Wrightian trickery, since he lied about his age and distorted many aspects of his life and work in his public pronouncements.

Fallingwater has already been the subject of at least one book and discussions of it fill important portions of numerous others. In addition, that house never saw a dark day. It has always been given attentive care by, first, the Kaufmann family and, second, the Western Pennsylvania Conservancy, its present caretaker.

The key building in this chapter will be another important but less well-known Wright residence. Built in 1904 in Buffalo, New York, it has been badly mistreated for more than fifty years and has yet to be restored. It presents an opportunity to look at an extraordinary house, at a range of people concerned with its preservation, and at the unusually complex restoration challenges it presents. And it allows us to take some sidelong glances at a pair of men who share a certain strange kinship, Frank Lloyd Wright and Thomas Monaghan.

The quiet, residential neighborhood of Parkside in Buffalo was planned by Frederick Law Olmsted and is on the National Register of Historic Places. Yet it is the Darwin D. Martin house that stands out today amid the collection of late Victorian and early-twentieth-century houses. It speaks in its designer's own, original manner.

Most of Wright's Prairie-style designs were constructed prior to World War I; his later work offers a more diverse array of buildings. There was the Usonian period, which gets its name from the coinage "Usonia" of Samuel Butler, the British Victorian-era author of *Erewhon*. Usonia means "United States" and, in Wright's usage, alludes to his democratic, everyman houses aimed at people with moderate incomes. Later, Wright built "textile block" houses, which used precast, textured concrete blocks, as well as a range of idiosyncratic buildings such as the Guggenheim Museum in New York City and office, municipal, and residential structures in a variety of modes. But for most people, it is Fallingwater or the Prairie-style dwellings like the Martin house that come to mind at the mention of Wright's work.

Wright's designs forever surprise the eye, and the Martin house is no exception. Outside, the rooflines and deep overhangs of the two-story home hover long and low like the prairies, after which the style was named and for which it was created. Inside, the main focus is a seventy-foot-long room that serves as a combination library, dining, and living area. Wright's cove lighting and almost unbroken rows of windows give the interior an openness, and the changing ceiling heights distinguish the different areas.

Upon visiting the Martin house, I was struck first by its emptiness. With only a few pieces of furniture scattered about, some of them designed by Wright specifically for the house, the place had the lonesome quality of an abandoned mansion. That my guide didn't know where all the light switches were added to the effect, as did the fact that the house needed a thorough sweeping.

This house has been called a white elephant over the years and the cliché fits. In scale, the Martin house is certainly elephantine, with about ten thousand square feet of living space. Because of its reinforced-concrete construction and finishes of russet brick and oak the house also needs rather special care and feeding. Its inherent rarity as a work of Wright's gives it an added exotic appeal.

The man for whom the house was built, Darwin D. Martin, was manager of the Larkin Company, a mail-order concern in Buffalo. Martin was no ordinary client, as the Martin-Larkin connection was responsible for commissioning no fewer than a dozen Wright buildings. While the man who held his position at the Larkin Company before him, Elbert Hubbard, hadn't used Wright's services, he had left to found the Roycrofters, the arts-and-crafts community in East Aurora, New York. Among other goods, they produced handcrafted furniture, some of which is nearly indistinguishable from certain of Wright's work.

Martin admired Wright's work on the Larkin Company administration building. One of his landmark designs, the 1903 building (demolished in 1950) was notable for the use of plate glass, metal furniture, and air conditioning, all innovative at the time. The air conditioning used ice as the cooling medium, with air circulated from the ice room throughout the building.

Martin asked Wright to design a house for him in 1903. The commission was an unusual one in that the budget was unlim-

Pictured in this 1904 photograph is the just-completed Darwin D. Martin house in Buffalo, New York. *The Buffalo and Erie County Historical Society*

ited. Wright proceeded to design not only the house but also its furniture, including the first version of the familiar barrel chair, and a variety of elaborate decorative details (among them gold leaf in masonry joints and several mosaics). In addition to the main house, Wright designed several other structures on the two-acre property. These included a smaller house for Martin's sister, Mrs. George Barton; a gardener's cottage; and a long pergola that connected the main house to a garage and conservatory. Wright even designed stone birdhouses for the exterior. They are, of course, "Martin" houses.

Among the memorable details in the Martin house are the art-glass windows, about half of which remain in the house. Some feature a geometric pattern of muted green and yellow glass, representing Wright's "tree of life" design. The windows act like his own lenses, filtering and shaping the world without. They effectively symbolize something of Wright's approach. The finish is emphatically modern, its sharply defined geometry of straight lines a product of a machine age. Yet the allusion is to nature, to a tree, to an essentially organic image of growth and life.

Too much analysis of his work doesn't pay dividends, judging by the copious literature about Wright. His spell seems to have had its strongest effect on those who write about him. Few other artists and perhaps no other architect have spawned a literature so full of vague thematic maunderings. In Wright's case, he started it, as he himself composed a considerable body of theoretical musings, most often addressing the organic qualities and the interplay of nature and architecture in his work.

At least to me, the narrative of the house is more interesting. Martin lived there until his death in 1935, despite the fact that his wife never liked it. It was a masculine house with strong right angles and dark coloring.

Like many of Wright's designs, it was also quite inflexible. When he could, Wright built client-proof houses. A given space was designed for a purpose, then filled with furniture designed specifically for it. In the case of the Martin house, he even selected the artwork to be hung on the walls (mostly Japanese prints). Mrs. Martin found the place quite uncongenial to her family heirlooms and even the daily routines of her life.

Since Darwin Martin's death, the house has been more often empty than inhabited (Mrs. Martin moved out two years after her husband died). Its great size is one factor, no doubt, since few people require a house with floor space equivalent to more than two basketball courts. Fewer still would be willing to bear the not inconsiderable costs of heating and maintaining such a house in Buffalo's challenging climate.

The Martin house had been unoccupied for several years when the city of Buffalo seized the property for unpaid taxes in 1946. In 1951, the Catholic Diocese of Buffalo purchased it, but plans for making the house a summer retreat were never put into effect. In 1953, a Buffalo-based architect bought it and installed his office in the basement. Subsequently, he divided

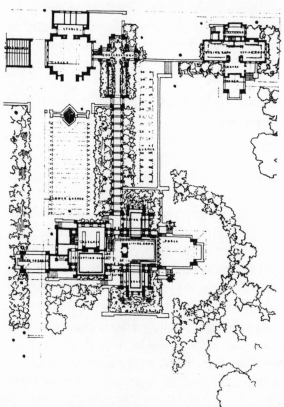

Before and after, the Martin house site: with the pergola and all structures intact (left) and after the demolition of the pergola and the construction of the apartment house. *Edgar Tafel*

the house into apartments. Still later, the pergola and conservatory were demolished and the property subdivided to subsidize repair costs. Three plain, box-shaped apartment houses were then constructed, separating the Martin house from the surviving Wright structures at the north end of the property.

In 1966, a change in fortune seemed imminent. At the the behest of its president, Martin Meyerson, the State University of New York at Buffalo purchased the property. It was to be the president's house. Its architectural significance and sheer size made it seem the perfect structure to suit the presidential needs for both a home and a large entertainment space for impressing alumni and potential donors.

The next move was also promising. Edgar Tafel, who had studied under Wright for nine years, was hired to design and supervise renovations. Who better than someone who had

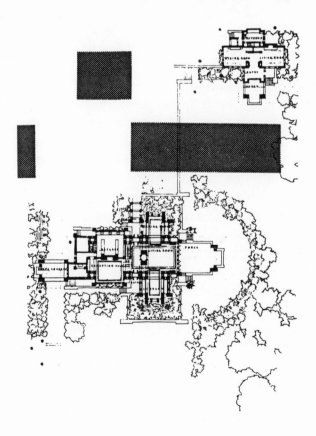

trained with Mr. Wright? Tafel had even visited the Martin house with Wright while the Martins were still in residence.

So much for good omens. The university purchased the house for $60,000, but committed only a limited sum for renovation and restoration costs. As Tafel told me: "I was engaged to do the first restoration–rather, to make it livable–at $30,000. . . . It hardly did the kitchen, clean it up, install a needed skylight, some paint, etc." The new owner and the architect proved unable to return the Martin house to some semblance of its impressive past. The appearance of the house today attests to that failure.

The principal work Tafel did for Mr. and Mrs. Meyerson was to remodel the kitchen. With its yellow Formica counters, the space can be most charitably described as sixties functional. It's of a time, certainly, but it is graceless and entirely unsympathetic to Wright's original design.

It wasn't long before the house was empty again. Several prominent architectural critics, including Ada Louise Huxtable of *The New York Times*, have written scathingly of how little the university has done to preserve the house. In 1982, the School of Architecture and Planning was given responsibility for it and, in 1983, as an apparent act of appeasement to its critics, the university hired a part-time curator, John O'Hern.

As he recalled it: "I went in there with absolutely nothing. The mandate was sort of 'Here, do something with it.' "

When he left to become director of the Arnot Art Museum in Elmira, New York, in the summer of 1989, he had assembled a substantial body of materials about the house. There's a collection of photos, notebooks, and account books from the Martins; the correspondence between Wright and Martin will probably prove invaluable. Some of the building's structural problems had also been resolved. Thanks to repairs and the replacement of gutters and downspouts, the roof no longer leaked. Exterior wood trim had also been painted.

Yet there still had been virtually no restoration, only a renewed understanding that it would be a staggering job. Inside, wall and ceiling moldings would have to be replicated, lost mosaics re-created, and leather floor tiles fabricated. O'Hern and some graduate students studied the building and learned much of what once had been there but no longer was. Among the losses are most of the original Wright furniture. Tom Monaghan, among others, owns elements from the Martin house.

An auspicious event occurred in 1989. The house was awarded the then annual Domino's Pizza Preservation Grant (it was not awarded in 1990). That $25,000, which the university matched, has been used for badly needed structural and restoration work on the second-floor terrace, its glass floor, and the art-glass skylight that illuminates the living room beneath.

"There was an emergency need, plus the university and community are finally starting to take an interest in the house," said Sara-Ann Briggs, a member of the selection committee. At the time, she was also the executive director of the Domino's Center for Architecture and Design in Ann Arbor, Michigan.

But are they really interested? So far, the commitment extends only to fixing the terrace and a further grant from the university to fund a detailed study of the house. "The Historic Structure Report," says O'Hern, "will give us a dollar figure, and at that point the university will decide what to do."

When investigating old houses, talk of original construction costs versus contemporary restoration prices rarely makes much sense. It's like comparing apples and oranges. In the case of the Martin house, however, the monetary mix is illuminating.

The original construction cost of the house was in excess of $100,000, perhaps totaling as much as $300,000. How extraordinary a sum that must have been in 1904 is suggested by the 1966 purchase price of the house for $60,000. The university then invested another $30,000.

Another irony bears closer investigation. The grant–welcome as it no doubt was, important as the work was that it financed– covered only a fraction of the restoration work required. Edgar Tafel described the grant as "a measly $25,000." But it did garner Tom Monaghan and his Domino's Center publicity they couldn't have purchased for a far greater sum. A sad paradox presents itself, as the reacquisition of the original Martin house

furniture would surely cost millions, in part because of the
inflation in the marketplace produced by Monaghan and other
collectors. A Wright-designed dining-room set now sells for
$1,600,000 and a table lamp for $705,000.

In the world of Frank Lloyd Wright, the name of Thomas
Monaghan cropped up a great deal in the 1980s. Some people
have a strong dislike for him. Others think him a great pop-
ularizer who has done much to remind a forgetful public of an
American architectural genius. He certainly represents both bad
and good news as far as the Martin house is concerned.

Frank Lloyd Wright was a master at manipulating the public.
He wanted the world's attention, and adjusting a few factual
details here and there hardly mattered. Perhaps Wright's invention of himself explains part of his appeal to Thomas Stephen
Monaghan.

Monaghan's story has brought joy to the hearts of more than
a few writers and editors. *Time, Gentlemen's Quarterly,* and
many other publications have recounted a childhood that bears
more than a passing resemblance to David Copperfield's.

Monaghan remembers a close attachment to his truck driver
father, who died at twenty-nine when Monaghan was four years
old. In his autobiography, *Pizza Tiger* (Monaghan owns the
Detroit Tigers baseball team as well as a controlling interest in
Domino's Pizza), he tells the story of the funeral. He remembers
jumping into the open casket, hugging his father's corpse, and
crying, "Wake up, Daddy!".

Like Dickens's protagonist, Monaghan found himself an
unwanted child, moving from one foster home to another. He
spent six years in an orphanage, St. Joseph's Home for Boys,
in Jackson, Michigan. His mother actually lived down the street
for some of that time. "I went there," Monaghan wrote, "but
only when she came to get me."

Like the rest of the orphans at St. Joe's, Monaghan was
assigned an eighteen-inch-square cubicle in which to store his

possessions. For the two-bit psychologists among us, the symbolism here is transparent. His privation was such that his accumulated possessions totaled little more than a few writing utensils, a deck of cards, and a box of marbles. Little wonder that, once success came his way, Monaghan, now fifty-four, became a demon acquirer.

Monaghan's life, unlike David Copperfield's, is archetypal American. He's Horatio Alger. He traded up, leaving behind his impoverished childhood for a net worth that *Forbes* has estimated at more than half a billion dollars. In 1983 he bought the Detroit Tigers for a purchase price of $53 million. He has assembled a collection of 300 classic automobiles, among them a Bugatti Royale, Ettore Bugatti's personal car, for which Monaghan paid over $8 million. Monaghan himself doesn't drive, having let his license expire years ago.

Consistent with Monaghan's poor-boy-becomes-patron style, bicycles are intermingled with the Duesenbergs, Mercedeses, and one-of-a-kind Detroit prototypes in his car collection. They're just like the plain old bikes an average paper boy would have ridden three or four decades ago, plebeian Rosses, Schwinns, and Columbias. Monaghan also owns his own jet and a substantial array of homes, a schooner, and thousands of acres of real estate. And in a few short years, starting in 1985, he assembled the world's largest collection of Frank Lloyd Wright decorative objects.

He made his millions selling pizza, starting at age twenty-three with a $500 investment in a single pizzeria in Ypsilanti, Michigan. Over the next thirty years, he established a chain of 5,000 shops guided by the slogan: "Hot pizza delivered to your door in thirty minutes or less, or your pizza is free." Among purveyors of pizza, only Pizza Hut is larger than Domino's.

Monaghan's image is carefully crafted. Press releases from Domino's Pizza, Inc., recount events from his orphanage childhood. His is a real-life storybook and no small part of the credit for its telling must go to the man himself.

He makes himself available for interviews and, if my meeting with him is typical, it's difficult not to like Monaghan. He's five-ten, with a full head of curly hair and aviator glasses. He's a bit deaf, so he cocks his head oddly when he listens.

I found him to be the most unassuming rich man I've ever met, and I don't think for a moment it's a ruse. Wright purists who dismissed him at first had come to treat him with respect and courtesy. Even his critics stopped questioning the sincerity of his passion for Wright; they'd never doubted his flair for the public eye.

Monaghan has often told of first learning of Frank Lloyd Wright in a library book at the age of twelve. "The first time I was ever in a public library, I took out a book about Wright," Monaghan remembered. "I saw pictures of the Robie House, Fallingwater, and the Johnson Wax Tower, all by the same architect. Who could not admire him?" At twenty-two, as a Marine stationed in Japan, he spent his weekends studying Wright's Imperial Hotel in Tokyo. He's been a convert ever since, and has said, "Wright is the equal if not the superior of Michelangelo."

Monaghan's personal wealth and corporate control of Domino's have allowed him to exercise his passion for Wright in several ways. In 1986, the National Center for the Study of Frank Lloyd Wright was founded. In 1989, it was renamed the Domino's Center for Architecture and Design. It stemmed originally from a simple whim: Sara-Ann Briggs, executive director of the Center, remembered Monaghan coming to her one day and saying simply, "I want a museum."

He got it. Today, the Center administers Monaghan's collection of Wright's designs, both in traveling exhibitions and at the Ann Arbor headquarters. There's also an archive open to scholars; for four years, it sponsored an annual Frank Lloyd Wright Symposium which brought several hundred Wright scholars, homeowners, and interested others to Ann Arbor; and the Domino's 30 architects program, which annually identifies the thirty most outstanding architects in the world. The Domino's 30 program is also associated with a planned community Monaghan is developing on a 550-acre tract in Ann Arbor called the Settlement. Fay Jones, who apprenticed with Wright in the 1950s, is designing a Prairie-style house for Monaghan, the first house to be built on the property. All the other houses must be designed by architects who, like Jones, are on the Domino's 30 list.

One purchase for Monaghan's Wright collection was a disassembled model Usonian house, for which he paid $117,500 at a call-in PBS auction. Only after its purchase did close examination reveal that barely ten percent of the plywood structure existed and much of what was there was rotted. Sara-Ann Briggs shrugged with a certain resignation when asked about the purchase, and cited its considerable publicity value. This attitude is no doubt a reflection of Monaghan's own, a position that one Domino's executive characterized this way: "Tom has an approach to marketing that few people have. He feels that any time his name is in print, it sells pizzas. He uses himself as a sacrifice."

Shortly after the debacle with the Usonian model, Monaghan hired David Hanks, a New York decorative arts consultant and expert on Wright. Monaghan has since paid more than $3,000,000 for a set of thirty-four original Wright windows from the Coonley playhouse, a kindergarten of Wright's design constructed in Riverside, Illinois, in 1912. The sums add up quickly: $198,000 for a dining chair from the 1901 Willits house in Highland Park, Illinois; $1,600,000 for a dining table and eight chairs from the 1899 Joseph W. Husser house in Chicago; $264,000 for a nine-drawer chest designed for the 1902 Little house in Peoria, Illinois. He owns the still-to-be-reassembled bedroom wing from the demolished Francis W. Little house (1912) in Deephaven, Minnesota (its living room is on permanent exhibit at the Metropolitan Museum of Art in New York City). There are some 5,000 Wright drawings and uncounted models and letters in the archives. But the furniture and the architectural elements–more than 300 of them–distinguish this from all other collections of Wrightiana.

The value of the objects has been variously estimated. If it were to be sold today, supposing there are enough Tom

Monaghans out there to pay top-of-the-market prices, the gross might well be in excess of $30 million.

After his tenure as curator of the Martin house, John O'Hern said, "It's awful to walk out of there after six years and have it right back to where it was when you started. The Martin house still needs to be restored, properly and accurately."

O'Hern is a verbal man, precise and careful in his emphases. "The essence of a Wright house is that it was done 'Wright'– this house wasn't done 'Martin.' At best, the client got Wright's version of his client's vision. Here, we've got to restore the house to what it was, not to someone's approximation of what it was."

This presents a range of problems, not unlike those seen with earlier houses in previous chapters. To cite but one example, a time must be selected. O'Hern suggests that it makes sense to incorporate some of the Martins' minor changes–they lived there for decades, it was their house in a material sense. But where is the right point on the time line? Before 1920, most changes made were approved first by Wright; in contrast Mrs. Martin found the house dark and harsh, so when her husband died (in 1935) she repainted much of the interior beige. Turning the clock back to a time prior to that painting would seem logical (the beige certainly contravened Wright's vision, to which at least Mr. Martin acceded). But how far back should the clock be turned?

The dean of the SUNY-Buffalo School of Architecture and Planning, Bruno B. Freschi, raised another key issue. "I think everybody wants to see it preserved and kept and developed," he began. "But there's a schizophrenia here, too. The university doesn't have a mandate to raise money for this." At present, there isn't really enough money to seek out decisions, let alone carry them out. It's not clear whether the house should be strictly a museum or whether it should be put to some other purposes as well.

There's a corollary question that must also be resolved: Is

the restoration to be limited to the existing house or should an attempt be made to reconstruct the entire complex?

Dean Freschi said, "It's painfully obvious that you should recapture all the buildings and rebuild the pergola, which was the access to the back of the property. Without that, you've just got a couple of good Frank Lloyd Wright pieces." Accomplishing that, however, would require acquisition and demolition of the apartment building behind the main house, the purchase of the two surviving structures at the north end of the property, and the reconstruction of the pergola, conservatory, and garage.

Freschi's ballpark estimate of the cost for restoring the existing house is $3 million. Restoring all six structures might well cost $10 million. But a complete reconstruction could be done, said O'Hern. "There are drawings at Taliesin for all of it. It would not be too conjectural."

One potential participant in the restoration is the New York State Office of Parks, Recreation, and Historic Preservation in Albany. At the request of the university, that office has been involved in the physical investigation of the house.

When I asked Deputy Commissioner Julia Stokes what approach she favored, she said, "If we're going to afford anything, we are going to have to refrain from grandiose ideas." She added, "Realistically, in light of the state's current fiscal condition, it might be advisable to begin to work just on the property we have rather than to take on the whole thing." It is her office that commissioned the Historic Structure Report.

At present, the house is used only occasionally for faculty meetings and receptions and for preservation courses. It is open to the public on Saturdays and Sundays for guided tours. But its future is, obviously, undetermined.

It's not your typical house. I found one of its many eccentricities slightly irritating. Despite its expansive floor plan, many of the ceiling surfaces hang low. As a tall man, I felt I had to duck, not only at doorways but beneath soffits within individual rooms when Wright changed ceiling heights for dramatic effect. I realize it probably didn't matter to Wright or the Martins

(Wright was five-eight, while Mr. and Mrs. Martin were five-seven and five-one, respectively). But it does suggest the unending individuality of the design.

On the other hand, steeped as I have been in the qualities and character of much older houses, I immediately recognized that the Martin house was of a vintage and quality that, while not well known to me, compels kind and appropriate treatment. Wright's houses are less documents of a time than they are demonstrations of his idiosyncratic artistry. But in the continuum of American houses, Thomas Monaghan and even Frank Lloyd Wright have important contemporary roles to play. There is little doubt that it is houses of the vintage of the Martin house that will present us with perhaps the greatest preservation and restoration challenges in the immediate future.

Monaghan is not a polished public speaker. Though deep, his voice is nasal, making him difficult to understand. He's not particularly articulate. He's a college dropout and he's, well, sort of a regular guy who calls out "How ya doin'?" to employees passing in the halls.

He exhibits a stolid reliance upon a limited range of fixed ideas for orientation in dealing with issues. His coordinates are his faith, his work, his family, and the passions of his childhood.

On the subject of Catholicism, he said, "The most flattering thing anybody can say about me is that I'm a good Catholic." He goes to mass daily. About his work ethic, he has remarked, "I find it very hard to believe that anyone who wants to work can't get work" and "I was born to work." On the subject of family he is equally assured. He and his wife of twenty-seven years have four daughters; of Wright he says, "Walking away from his family was unpardonable."

Then there are the passions from his childhood, and he indulges himself in them as only a stupendously wealthy adult can, including his baseball team (he remembers looking forward to the annual orphanage outing, a trip to Tiger Stadium); the car collection; and architecture, initially the work of Wright.

Monaghan has picked up more than a little architectural jargon. In explaining why he liked a certain building, he told me, without any of the hesitations in his speech that are usually the rule, "I think it's the strong horizontal lines, the overall composition. The massing is right." Yet when asked if he had ever considered pursuing his fascination with buildings by going to architecture school, he said quickly, "I'd rather be a client."

Monaghan pretends to no particular intellectual bent. When advised that a symposium he sponsored wouldn't be written up by a local newspaper, he inquired why. He was told that the subject of the meeting was "too esoteric."

His response was an unabashed question. "What's 'esoteric' mean?"

He is, as *Time* reported, "almost achingly ingenuous." Yet he has studied Wright and is familiar with much of his work. Upon meeting a waitress from Buffalo at baseball spring training in Florida a few years ago, he immediately asked her if she'd seen the Martin house. "She had never heard of it," he recalled. "Never heard of Frank Lloyd Wright!" He was a bit stunned and outraged at her ignorance.

He met with me in a small room adjacent to his main office. The larger space is as long as a bowling alley and nearly as wide, some 2,800 square feet in area. It seems to daunt him, and well it might, given its leather floor tiles, African mahogany walls, and a bathroom that features a vaulted ceiling decorated with gold leaf and a floor-to-ceiling marble urinal.

Prairie House, the headquarters building in which it is located, is commensurately disproportional. From a distance, it echoes the lines of Wright's Prairie style. When finished, the brick-walled and copper-roofed structure situated amid 320 acres of onetime farmland in Ann Arbor, Michigan, is to be a half mile long (2,700 feet).

During my time with Monaghan, I couldn't help but think of the other architectural conservators in this book. They have all had some influence on the practice of restoration and preservation in this country. Millions of people have visited the buildings John Curtis and John Mesick have worked to restore;

hundreds of craftsmen have come from virtually every state and abroad to learn skills from Don Carpentier. It's difficult to estimate the considerable impact the *Old House Journal* has had.

Yet none of these people has the fame of Monaghan. More important, perhaps, none has broken the same ethical ground and none faces the same ethical complications that Tom Monaghan does.

Money does strange things to people, whether by commission or omission (my surmise is that Monaghan belongs in the latter category). His wealth apparently hasn't changed him a great deal. He has remained married to the same woman with whom he shared a trailer in earlier, poorer times. He's proud of having maintained his standards, too, his faith and work ethic.

Monaghan has an unwritten code to live by, for himself and his employees. Reportedly he has fired subordinates for philandering and requires workers to cultivate a certain appearance; haircuts are mandatory. Monaghan cites his stint in the Marine Corps as a formative influence in his life. He joined in error (he thought he was enlisting in the Army) but found that "they break everybody down to nothing. . . . They're experts at harassment. No mercy. The greatest organization in the world." He contributes to a variety of Catholic organizations and charities. The anti-abortion movement is a particular favorite of his for donations.

At the same time, however, this self-consciously moral man has found himself widely criticized on ethical grounds within the worlds of art and preservation. Prices for original art escalated in recent years, but nothing in the marketplace has seen so spectacular an increase as has Wrightiana. One result of this is that in both the short and the long run Wright's chief works, the buildings he designed, will be continually diluted or even destroyed.

To make it personal, assume for a moment you're a Wright homeowner. Yours is a lovely Wright home, but it isn't Fallingwater, and the cardinal rule of real estate still applies: Its value is determined by location, location, and location. All right, maybe location, location, Wright, and location, but the place still can't be worth much more than the most valuable house in the neighborhood. For purposes of our little ethical paradigm, let's agree that the most valuable neighboring dwelling recently sold for $500,000.

Now, let's say that your house has ten Frank Lloyd Wright art-glass windows. And you were lucky enough to inherit a couple of chairs, an urn, and some other original Wright-designed furniture and decorative arts when that ancient, cranky aunt of yours left you the house and its contents in her will. You're thinking about moving to Florida to escape the snowy winters, but you feel a sense of conflict. Should you sell the house? And what about the furniture?

You've heard the arguments. Wright designed the windows and the other objects for your house. They belong there. They were specifically designed to be an organic part of the whole. In preservationist parlance, it's a contextual matter.

But the pieces can also stand on their own. In fact, they could have put your kids through Harvard all by themselves. Today, $100,000 is not an atypical price for a Wright-designed art-glass window. Your house, which probably has problems, as any house of a certain age does, has a value of half a million dollars more or less. But a mere station-wagonload of its furniture is almost certainly worth two or three times as much. In short, the value of the house would be greater if it were carved up and sold to a series of bidders than if it were kept as an integral whole.

Consider a variation on the scenario. You caught the Wrightian bug and just bought that same Wright house. Now you want to buy back the original furniture that Wright designed for it. Can you afford to pay six-figure sums for individual chairs and windows?

Chicago architect John Eifler, who has directed the restoration of several Wright houses, said some years ago, "[The owners of Wright homes] can't keep up with the prices. Because of people like Monaghan, the furniture becomes an investment." In his defense, Monaghan has made his collection available to architects and scholars, which the Frank Lloyd Wright Foundation at Taliesin, until recent years, had resolutely refused to do with their holdings.

Can we blame the predicament on Monaghan and his competitors, which include the likes of Barbra Streisand, a frequent underbidder to Monaghan? Monaghan has said with evident pride, "I've raised the value of Wright's work." When pressed, however, he defends his actions, observing that prices were escalating before he entered the market.

Public pressures led him to agree to forgo buying Wright's decorative arts directly from owners of houses. Yet many purchases he made subsequent to that promise were made at the New York galleries of Christie's, the auction house, whose policy is not to release the names of sellers. Almost certainly, some of the objects did come from owners of Wright houses.

Christie's, too, has been the subject of criticism. Its response has been: If we don't sell it, somebody else will and perhaps the objects will disappear into the netherworld of private collections, never to be available to the public again. The publicity associated with the major purchases has fueled other activities, including the reproduction of original Wright designs. While Wright might have frowned upon what he regarded as location-specific designs being used in thousands of different settings, he might well have approved of a more general distribution of good (to be read: Wright) designs.

One strategy Monaghan has used to combat his negative image as nouveau riche salvage king has been to offer the Domino's Pizza Preservation Grant. That brings us back to the Martin house.

Essentially none of the challenges of the Martin house have yet been met, even with the Domino's money. Its continued existence periodically provokes little flurries of concern and discussion, but thus far to no particular end. True, the house survives, but it is hardly intact, as its original configuration has been defaced by a combination of renovations and demolition.

Like most Wright houses, it will always defy true restoration. Contrary to the rule of geometry that the whole is equal to the sum of its parts, the parts of a Wright house are worth more than the house can be worth. Thus, reassembling a house's furniture, windows, and other architectural and decorative elements has become too expensive a proposition for any but the wealthiest of benefactors.

One obvious notion in this context would be for Monaghan to devote some of his financial resources to such preservation efforts, in Buffalo or elsewhere. He has bought individual houses in the past, but has usually resold them. Again, an individual Wright house isn't the best investment, with inherent financial limitations as to its liquidity and upside potential. However, as of 1990, Monaghan withdrew most of the funding for Wright-related activities at the Center.

To be fair, Monaghan is clearly a man of good intentions. He has no wish to do architecture in general or Wright in particular anything but good, and most of his activities did serve to increase people's awareness of and the availability of Wright's works. Yet when considering Monaghan as a cultural conservator, I can't help but think of a moment in a 1944 movie, *The Big Sleep*, based upon a Raymond Chandler novel of the same title.

Humphrey Bogart starred as Chandler's gumshoe, Philip Marlowe. In the opening scene, Marlowe visits a new client, General Sternwood. The wizened old man, confined to a wheelchair, receives Marlowe in an overheated greenhouse. Though rich and influential, Sternwood has been reduced to vicarious pleasures, in this case watching the likes of Marlowe enjoy a whiskey and a smoke.

In some ways, Monaghan reminds me of General Sternwood. For one, they share the desire to do good. Unfortunately, they also have a similar, bemused inability to control events around them, despite their wealth and power.

8
The Man Who
Sells History

The present in New York is so powerful that the past is lost.
                                        —John Henry Chapman

A friend of mine describes himself as a "business junkie." It's not the vagaries of the Dow Jones stock average or even _The Wall Street Journal_ that gives him his high. For Matthew, the perfect day is one during which he learns of a new business, a unique and imaginative new venture born of plain old entrepreurship. His personal pantheon of all-time greats includes an unlikely range of people, from Ted Turner and his round-the-clock news station to the man who invented the pet rock.

I made Matthew's day when I told him about the Office for Metropolitan History. Despite its official-sounding name, the OMH isn't a CIA front or even some city agency. Rather, the "Office" consists of the mind and archive of one Christopher Gray, both put to entrepreneurial use.

Gray is a youthful-looking man just into his forties, tall and trim, clean-shaven with a full head of hair. His clothes are shabby prep, no doubt a lifelong habit born of a patrician upbringing in Kansas City and Manhattan. His education was at private schools and Columbia College.

Like others of our cultural conservators, Gray turned his

167

passion for buildings into a business. He is an architectural historian, a title that fits a good many other people. Some of them write books, others teach classes, but none that I know of have spent their entire adult lives transforming building genealogy into commerce.

He doesn't have a degree in architecture. "I'm not really an academic," he told me in his office one winter day in 1989. "I barely escaped school with a bachelor's degree—which I expect them to recall at any moment. I never went to graduate school."

What he does have is an encyclopedic knowledge of the architecture of New York City. His spacious office is decorated in the early storeroom style, packed with books and long rows of four-drawer filing cabinets. On top of a beat-up oak desk are loose-leaf binders, files, photos, and a multitude of loose papers. This mass of material constitutes his immense personal collection of printed and photographic documents about things architectural in New York.

It's also his livelihood. "I run a retail business operation with a businesslike turnaround." His manner was businesslike. "We don't do any grant-funded projects. I don't do public education, no teaching, none of that stuff.

"I try to be a market-related, private-sector type of operation. Law firms, individuals, corporations come to me. I don't care who."

It isn't a business that is going to make him rich. "A while back," he observed, "I hoped to at least make an investment banker's salary." The short pause that followed suggested that perhaps that hadn't been a reasonable expectation.

On the other hand, his is a livelihood rich in history and anecdote. As Gray himself described his business: "In a city as dense as New York, each structure forms its own little table of contents to the history of that site. Or can, as there are almost certainly gaps. My mission is to understand and explain all that." In the background, the aural life of the city was unmistakable, horns and sirens and noise of all kinds.

"That's not the same thing as making a living, but that's what

I became interested in. Being a willful and undisciplined and self-indulgent person, I decided to set about making a living by what I enjoyed."

Gray will research any building in New York, but his specialty is Manhattan, in particular buildings constructed between the Civil War and World War II. If he is able to supply the customer with the needed pictures or information—and he can with remarkable frequency—then he negotiates a fee.

What the customer does with the material he or she purchases is that person's affair. "I'm not married to one side or the other," Gray commented. Two jobs Christopher Gray did for two different clients in years past suggest something of the dynamic of his business.

The Unification Church of America (UCA) is the American wing of Korean churchman Sun Myung Moon and his acolytes, the so-called Moonies. The UCA has substantial Manhattan real estate holdings, including apartment and office buildings, a hotel, and other structures. It also has a building it calls the Unification Church.

To understand the assistance the UCA wanted from Gray, a little background about the peculiarities of preservation in the city of New York is necessary. New York City has a unique watchdog organization, a city agency called the Landmarks Preservation Commission, created in 1964.

The Commission is charged with identifying buildings and other structures and locations that are thirty or more years of age, located in New York, and worthy of preservation. Its staff considers candidates for designation (including individual buildings and even entire neighborhoods) and then makes recommendations to the commissioners. This board then formally designates its selections as landmarks, or historic districts in the case of neighborhoods.

A certain prestige comes with a landmark designation, as it means the building has been deemed by the Commission to be of historic, architectural, or cultural significance and therefore worthy of preservation. For some owners of official landmarks, however, the designation can be a mixed blessing.

Officially, a landmark structure is forever. It cannot be demolished or even significantly altered, regardless of potential profits or maintenance costs. In a handful of cases, special exemptions have been obtained allowing owners to demolish landmark buildings, but such exceptions to the rules are rare, usually granted only when owners are able to demonstrate economic hardship.

A few years ago, the Unification Church was on the Landmarks Preservation Commission's list of buildings for designation. Located at 4 West Forty-third Street, the church was the UCA's principal place of worship in New York. The midtown location, with its easy access to the office towers of Madison and Park avenues to the east and the theatre district to the west, is also a prime piece of Manhattan real estate.

While the UCA had no immediate plans for demolishing or even modifying the property, like many a wise real estate investor it didn't want to have its options limited in perpetuity. The decision makers at the UCA were well aware that their lot would be worth millions if the structure were demolished and the land sold. Thus, the UCA opposed landmark designation for its church.

According to the Landmarks Preservation Commission, however, the building had originally been a club, one of several in the vicinity, including the Century Club (on the same block) and the Harvard, Yale, and Union League clubs (within a few blocks). The architect was thought to have been Bruce Price, a prominent New Yorker who worked at the turn of the century. The Unification Church was, in the estimation of the Commission, of sufficient historic, architectural, and cultural significance to merit landmark designation.

Gray was hired to look into the matter. He discovered that the Commission had missed the mark by a considerable margin. First, the building was not a club at all, but had been constructed as a hotel. Second, the architect wasn't the notable Mr. Price, but a less memorable practitioner. Gray's findings were crucial to the Commission's final decision. They did not choose to designate the Unification Church a landmark. As of this writing, the structure remains standing.

Gray has researched hundreds of other buildings over the years, but a second case provides a useful contrast to that of the Unification Church. In this instance, Gray's client was a group of residents on a street on New York's East Side. They had banded together to form a block association to advance their common interests and they hired Gray for a specific task. Once again, his job was to reinvestigate what the Landmarks Preservation Commission had already investigated.

The Commission had just designated twelve onetime stables on the block as landmarks. A thirteenth building, at 166 East Seventy-third Street, had been ignored as "not significant." The neighbors wanted to know what made that building an exception. It, too, had originally been a stable, but like its neighbors had become a residence.

The block association hired Gray.

He was fairly sure when he took on the task what the excepted building was, but he looked for formal corroboration. Once again, he fulfilled his charge.

Gray knew that the stables had originally been used to house the horses and carriages of residents of mansions to the west. Through his research, he was able to demonstrate not only that the undesignated stable was of merit but that it actually was the oldest on the block. In addition, he found that it had been designed by Richard Morris Hunt, an internationally known architect who had trained at the Ecole des Beaux-Arts in Paris. His client had been another notable, the art patron Henry Marquand, whose home had been two blocks over on Madison Avenue. In near-original condition, the building was, Gray concluded, "the most significant stable on the block."

Armed with Gray's findings, the block association was able to convince the Landmarks Preservation Commission to reconsider its decision. The Marquand Stable was subsequently designated a landmark.

Much of Gray's work today involves finding photos and drawings on a contingency basis. Sometimes the request is for an old photograph of a building or a streetscape at a certain time (he has perhaps 30,000 photos in his files). He finds evidence for legal cases, and often gets requests from architects and engineers who need the original drawings in planning a renovation or restoration. His customers, like the buildings he researches, are varied. Typical fees run about $750 plus reproduction costs for a photograph, while drawings are more, often around $2,000.

Gray is one of those people who need little prompting. He talks in paragraphs, with a minimum of dead air between his sentences. I asked him how he got into the business.

"I was a member of a fraternity at Columbia which had had an old chapter house downtown. I found the original drawings and learned that the building had been designed by James Renwick. I think in the long view he was probably a minor architect, but of course he did some nice buildings.

"Something clicked somehow. I was an utter novice in 1972 when I brought those minor Renwick drawings to Adolph Placzek at the Avery Library. He took my interest as seriously as that of an established scholar, and on that afternoon decided for me my life's work. His sensitive reception clued me in."

Placzek, who is now director emeritus at Columbia's Avery Library, gave Gray a lecture on Gothic Revival. Placzek has since recalled that meeting, remembering in Gray's eye a "glint of divine curiosity."

"By August 1975," Gray told me, "I had spent some time in Africa working as an architect even though I was not trained as one." (He managed to catch malaria, too.) "I had graduated from Columbia, but I was back at Avery Library doing some copy photography on Carrière and Hastings. I got talking to a researcher working for a woman doing her Ph.D. on Beaux-Arts architecture. The woman doing her dissertation was in Paris, and she desperately needed this information from the United States. I think this woman was also rich, and probably didn't feel like doing the grunt work.

"The researcher said to me, 'It's just research.' " Gray

repeated the phrase. " 'It's just research.' And she couldn't be bothered to do it." Gray was bemused by this attitude; it was clearly beyond his comprehension. I think he might also have been recalling his own sheer luck at stumbling into the situation.

"At that point I felt, 'Here is a market.' Somebody desperately needed this information, although as a practical matter I found out later the woman in Paris wasn't willing to pay very much to get it. But she *needed* it." From a chance conversation in a research library, a business was born.

Not all his research is done at the behest of clients. He's also a free-lance writer, contributing articles recounting the histories of certain buildings and neighborhoods. "It's really a way of marketing the research. I distribute research that way, but also create a demand for more of it."

He writes a weekly column for the Sunday *New York Times* Real Estate section, as well as a local-history column for an upscale Manhattan magazine called *Avenue*. He used to write one for *House & Garden* on private streets and enclaves. And somehow he consistently comes up with surprising finds about the buildings, the streets, and the people who lived there.

The Union Square Theatre dated from 1871. An interior remodeling in 1888 following a fire incorporated a horseshoe balcony, a gold-and-ivory-painted ceiling, and two large cupolas. In its heyday, the theatre featured burlesque, ballet, pantomime, and comedy; it was "the model temple of amusement," according to one theatre historian. Later, it became a vaudeville house and eventually a cinema.

During the Depression, the doors to the theatre were closed. The interior was walled off in 1936, when the landlord converted the street-level areas into retail space. Many tenants have come and gone in the intervening half century. Today, the familiar huge red-and-yellow logo of McDonald's obscures much of the building's façade.

Christopher Gray had read that the theatre balconies, boxes, and ceiling were intact, hidden above the dropped ceiling of

McDonald's. He had been told that no one in recent decades had actually seen those remnants of an earlier theatrical age. Exercising his architectural curiosity, Gray persuaded the owners of the building at 58 East Fourteenth Street to let him look around during the winter of 1989. He devoted a column in *The New York Times* to his findings.

He went in through a vacant storefront (McDonald's was long gone). He was alone, a condition insisted upon by the owner since portions of the structure are said to be unsafe and two people are heavier than one. Gray climbed a staircase at the back of the shop and found himself in the original stage area. It was, and probably always had been, a tall unadorned space. But a wall of firebrick separated him from the auditorium and the architectural details he sought. Still, he was undaunted.

As he reported in the *Times:* "A light inserted through a small hole in the brick disclosed that the 1936 alterations had not simply covered the original auditorium, but also had removed almost everything below the ceiling. On the walls there are only occasional fragments of composite capitals and painted decoration." The ceiling itself remained, but the cupolas had become receptacles for enormous ventilation ducts.

To read this and others of Gray's columns is to glimpse moments in New York's past. Virtually all his writings are building-specific. Gray's style is to recount the varied course of a building's history, citing architects, builders, dates, stylistic details, and the chronology of events surrounding the building's construction and subsequent history. For the New Yorker, to read Gray's writings is to encounter familiar structures. There's a pleasure in discovering (Gray prefers "uncovering") the stories behind the façades that one walks by in the city.

Individually or collectively, the columns concern broader issues, too. As an undergraduate, Gray took a course titled "Cities and Planning," taught by a professor named George Collins. "His course was probably the single greatest academic influence in my life. Collins discussed, in a primitive sense, real estate. He talked about the ring cities of Europe. They had ring fortifications, but as a city expanded outward, the ring was no

The Union Square Theatre: in 1875 (above) and 1990. It's hardly surprising that little is left of the old theatre's interior. *Luther Harris*

longer necessary. The ring was demolished, then there was a new localized building episode. That course of events explained why those cities looked the way they did.

"I found that very compelling. Having studied art history by that time, I knew the consensus among art historians about, oh, take Park Avenue apartment houses." Invariably, Gray brings the conversation back to New York. "The art historians said Park Avenue residential buildings developed the way they did because all the architects went to the Ecole des Beaux-Arts together and they thought it would be a nice idea if all their cornices matched.

"That is incredible cant and drivel. It's completely fictitious with no basis in history. Even as an undergraduate, I knew it didn't explain, in the way it pretended to, why Park Avenue looked the way it did.

"I saw that the cities-and-planning approach was really it. To study Alberti was not to learn anything about Park Avenue. Schwartz and Gross, who built a lot of the apartments on Park Avenue, may well have studied Alberti very closely at the Hebrew Technical Institute, but I doubt it. It was zoning, land values, why lots were plotted with certain orientations, and so on that explained why the city looked the way it did.

"The physical character of the city is a series of tableaux you can either understand or not. The removal of a stoop, the addition or removal of a cornice, the addition of fire escapes, the use of brick and stone—every physical element in the city is perfectly explicable, and often datable to a specific building event."

Gray cited further examples of this interplay of historical events and architecture. Referring again to the residential reaches of Park Avenue, he pointed out that the construction of private houses began there after the railroad tracks were sunk into the center of the avenue. Earlier construction in the neighborhood had been stimulated by the installation of the first railroad there in the 1830s, but steam-powered trains were too noisy and dirty to live near. Even after the trains were buried, Gray pointed out, the mall above was punctuated with vents for smoke and steam to escape the tunnel below. The façades of the early Park Avenue houses were oriented not to the avenue but to the perpendicular side streets. Who wants cinders and smoke staining the façade and floating through the front door?

Across town, Gray explained, the Upper West Side developed differently. The explanation isn't class differences, as many a novice historian today would guess from the remaining architectural evidence. To Gray, it's all explained by an understanding of real estate development.

Not much more than a century ago Manhattan's Upper West Side was virtually all farmland, while the East Side had already experienced fifty years of development. Among the differences were that the principal artery east of Central Park was the well-traveled Boston Post Road to New England. Another factor was geology, since the soil to the west was rocky and presented an obstacle to construction. The opening of the elevated railroad on Columbus Avenue in 1880 changed things, adding an important incentive to live and build on the West Side.

Gray decorates conversations with little revelations. He helped get the oldest operating stable in New York placed on the National Register of Historic Places. He also pointed out that its location, on West Eighty-ninth Street, was not accidental. At the time of the stable's construction in 1892, the street was a "stable street." It was common practice for builders and developers to designate, informally, certain streets as stable streets in order to confine the horses, carriages, and associated noise and odors to limited areas. To this day these streets have markedly fewer single-family houses and more garages, schools, and tenements.

In talking about wood-frame structures in New York, one learns that a fire code was adopted in 1866 that forbade the construction of wood buildings south of Eighty-sixth Street.

Gray pointed out that Manhattan's grid plan was laid out in 1811. He wondered out loud: "What is the effect of its endurance on the city?" One of his goals is to write a history of real estate and the market forces that determined the construction and development of Manhattan. A ring city it is not. Yet there are, no doubt, an array of other factors to be observed, interpreted, and translated.

I asked Gray if there is one particular house with which he feels a strong affinity. He answered immediately.

"No, I don't have a single building that I want to be connected with. I think of the marquee on Seventy-fifth and Lexington (over a coffee shop!) that was installed about 1905. I still want to know who did that. There's a building on Twenty-sixth Street that I wonder about. It was owned by the Astors. There are a couple of dozen buildings that I enjoy and love to see and walk by and think about.

"There are also facts that I savor having discovered, like the Marquand Stable. That worked out nicely," he added with a laugh. "But there's no one building that I hang my hat on."

Most often, Gray has found, it isn't style, chronology, or urban evolution that interests people. "They don't really care if their building was built in 1880 or 1900 or 1920. They want some sex and violence. They want to know that it was designed by Stanford White and it was a speakeasy and then a bordello and then there was a fire."

He continued: "Unfortunately, there weren't enough speak-easies, bordellos, and Stanford White buildings designed or built to go around."

Gray has spent years of his life looking at and researching New York streetscapes. Even before he became a professional architectural historian, he developed what he regards as his most important resource, a good basic knowledge of New York City. In part, he accumulated that knowledge while working as a part-time cabdriver and a post office driver. "And," he added, "just looking around."

Gray's consuming interest in preserving Manhattan's build-ings has served him well in another arena as well. In 1976, he read about an effort to save the New York Cancer Hospital, an eccentric Victorian brick structure, whose round "corner-less" rooms were thought (in 1885) to reduce the collection of germs. He contacted the preservationists to learn more. He was one of only two respondents to the newspaper article. The woman who answered was one Erin Drake, who today is also Mrs. Christopher Gray.

Not everyone can claim the good fortune of discovering a passion in college that, through a series of happy accidents, leads to a life's work and a family.

One of the "cornerless" turrets of the New York Cancer Hospital, a long-neglected yet still impressive structure. Perhaps one day . . .

Gray's attachment to old buildings is more than a matter of earning a living. As is true with most of the cultural conservators in these pages, Gray has managed as an adult to devise a means of transforming an inchoate childhood interest into a life's work.

"When I moved to New York in my early teenage years, I lived on Fifty-sixth Street and Sutton Place and went to school on Sixty-second and Park. Home and school formed, roughly speaking, a diagonal across a square section of the city's grid.

"Within that square there were many possible routes I could walk traveling back and forth to and from school. I remember in my obsessive-compulsive early teenagehood I would carefully and consciously follow different paths on a fairly even basis, trying not to favor one path over another. In the course of 'mapping' that, I noticed very quickly the buildings that were along those streets and that's how I differentiated one route from another."

At first, he merely "noticed" buildings; today, he knows those buildings and literally thousands of others. He's a researcher for hire, concerned with buildings, not so much for their own sake as for their role in history. His interest is less in preservation for preservation's sake than in the evolution of the larger canvas.

"I'm sometimes called a preservationist," he told me, "but I'm not. I'm a historian. That's what I'm interested in. Preservation, you know, is a political activity."

In some sense, Gray works both sides; yet he avoids advocacy work (in part because his relationship with *The New York Times* requires that he observe rather than participate in making news). Yet his is an open-eyed awareness of architectural history, one that more often than not pairs him with preservationists. Recognizing his aptitude for putting his infatuation with buildings to business use is important to appreciating Christopher Gray. But I suspect that, at bottom, to understand Gray is to accept that buildings matter to him more than motives do. They may even be more important than profits.

9
The Curator
of Class

*[L]ike any other "professional" man, the architect's talk will
be tinged with that class consciousness which is so frequently
mistaken for Conservatism.*
　　　　　　　　　　—*John Betjeman,* Ghastly Good Taste *(1933)*

Charles Lyle told me, "While I was getting my undergraduate
degree in history, I went to work part-time at the St. Louis
County Historical Society in Duluth, Minnesota. Until then, I
had planned to be a lawyer." He was answering my question
about how he got involved with old things.

To see him more than twenty years later, sitting at his highly
polished antique desk, dressed in a conservative suit and tie,
and protected by his secretary, it seemed for a moment as if he
had never veered from that course. But today he is a museum
director.

"I got the job at the local historical society my junior year
at the University of Minnesota and I stayed there for two years.
I just fell in love with it.

"It was a museum and library in a fine old house. They had
a whole mixture: a Victorian parlor, a wonderful little collection
of Eastman Johnson paintings of the Ojibwe Indians. It was
just one of those funny little places that had a mix of things
like all local historical societies do."

Lyle's speech is almost without accent. Over the last two decades, which he has spent in the mid-Atlantic states of New Jersey, Delaware, and Maryland, he's lost whatever of the flat, nasal quality of midwestern speech he may once have had. But he seems to have lost none of his enthusiasm for history museums.

"I decided during that period that I really wanted to be a director of a small historical society."

He has reached and even exceeded that goal. After getting his master's degree at the University of Delaware in museum administration, he got his first position in 1971 as director of the Monmouth County (N.J.) Historical Society. In addition to supervising a library and museum, his responsibilities included watching over four eighteenth-century Dutch farmhouses. "That's really how I got involved with architectural preservation," Lyle recalled.

"My career sort of spans the National Register of Historic Places. The Register was established in 1966, but it wasn't until the early seventies that much funding was available. Then museums and historic sites started to put their houses on the Register to try to qualify for matching grants-in-aid for restoration. We got a couple of those while I was working in New Jersey for the restoration of two of the Dutch houses."

In 1978, Lyle moved on to the National Trust for Historic Preservation. His job there was as director of historic properties, and he served on the board of advisers to the Trust from 1980 to 1989. Among other National Trust buildings of which he speaks with personal pride is Drayton Hall outside Charleston, South Carolina, surely one of the best American Palladian houses, dating from the early eighteenth century.

In 1980, he changed jobs again, this time to become executive director of the Historical Society of Delaware. "What really brought me to Delaware was the prospect of restoring the Read house, start to finish," he said.

Though he is in his mid-forties, you might think Lyle a decade or more younger. His hair is light-colored, with an age-defying quality about it—it's no longer quite blond, but it also hasn't gone to gray. He seemed younger still when he talked of the pet project of his Delaware years, the George Read II house.

Lyle left the Historical Society of Delaware and moved on to the directorship of the Maryland Historical Society (as of January 1990). But it is his decade in Delaware that will be the focus of this chapter.

Lyle's jobs have involved conserving and cherishing the past for the commonweal. Equally, he does so at the behest of key benefactors, many of whom are among the wealthy and powerful elite in the states in which he has worked. This makes him (quite appropriately, no doubt) a bit circumspect when he talks about the historical societies he has worked for and their collections. Dealing with the dual constituency of the hoi polloi and the well-to-do requires political savvy, and Lyle watches his footfalls carefully as he treads this territory.

"We have to come to terms here with the fact that we have been favored institutions among a lot of prominent old families," he told me.

"At the same time, we must somehow change people's attitudes toward such institutions. They aren't treasure houses of the rich, and they aren't unfriendly sorts of places. We need to convince people that they can be comfortable getting to appreciate the legacies, the quantity of quality things from the past."

It isn't that such prominent historical societies lack members, but it is a broader societal obligation with which Lyle is concerned. "There are a lot of people who are interested in our organizations; there are more people every year. At the same time, given the size of our population and what's happening in our cities, I think institutions like these are fixed resources that can never expand while populations are expanding geometrically. Given a very finite resource in a dynamic environment, I think it raises an issue of what American civilization is going to be.

"Will the past be respected? Will it be recognized? We've been involved in teaching history in the schools, and there's so much pressure put on school administrators to have computers and the like, to teach ethnic history and all the rest of it, that straight American history, even a basic appreciation of architecture, of something of the texture and the traditions of this society, those really don't find their way into standard curriculums anymore."

He concludes more bluntly: "We have to try to reach a whole ignorant generation of people out there who don't value and appreciate this kind of stuff."

Lyle and others try to reach, broaden, and serve their constituencies in a variety of ways. One architectural asset Lyle has used to good advantage is the George Read II house in New Castle, Delaware. The solutions he devised in restoring that house suggest something of Lyle, both as a preservationist and as a museum director confronted with certain political and educational realities. There's even an echo or two of the formative years he spent more than a thousand miles west in northern Minnesota.

The town of New Castle has a long and distinguished history. Peter Stuyvesant (who landed there in 1651) and his fellow Dutchmen called the place Sand-Hoek (Sand Hook). Stuyvesant decided it was the perfect site for a fortification with its vista south from the bend in the Delaware River, a fine vantage from which to view approaching ships, friendly and hostile alike. Fort Casimir was quickly raised. Stuyvesant laid out the orderly street plan that survives to this day, extending back from the waterfront to the village green.

The Swedes governed the town in 1654 and 1655, renaming it Fort Trinity, but the Dutch shortly took it back, and gave it the name New Amstel. The British and the Dutch took turns relinquishing the territory over the next few years. In 1682, William Penn landed there. He came armed with a lease from the Duke of York to New Castle and the surrounding land in a twelve-mile radius. The term was to be 10,000 years.

Despite such auspices, however, Penn ruled New Castle and what is now the state of Delaware only until 1704, when Pennsylvania's three lower counties (today's state of Delaware) separated. New Castle became the colony's capital and the site of the General Assembly and of the courts.

Though incorporated as a city in 1875, New Castle has never been much more than a village in size. At the time of the Revolution, the population was nearly 1,000; today it numbers roughly 5,000. Nevertheless, New Castle was an important trading center, especially in the eighteenth century. Penn had established it as a market town to which farmers came to sell their produce. Brickmaking and brewing were early industries.

International trade was transacted with ships passing on their way to the fast-growing metropolis of Philadelphia, forty miles to the north, and New Castle was the last port of call for ships bound for Canton in the China trade. The town was a stopping place for travelers moving by land or by ferry both north to Philadelphia and south to such influential eighteenth-century tidewater towns as Annapolis and Chestertown, Maryland, and Williamsburg, Virginia.

The town was essentially undamaged during the Revolution, though many a British warship sailed past. After the war, it remained on the well-traveled path from most southern cities to the nation's capital at Philadelphia. Despite its small size and the immense growth during the industrial revolution of Wilmington, six miles to the north, New Castle was the county seat until 1881. Turnpikes and stagecoach lines passed through, and an early railroad (1831) served the town. According to some sources, it was the first passenger rail service in the country—and the rails were initially made of wood. But by 1858, more direct routes bypassed New Castle, and rail services ceased. Like Essex, New York, and so many other well-preserved early towns, New Castle lost its once brilliant commercial future.

New Castle had no formal boundaries until 1797, when the Delaware Assembly enacted a statute mandating the creation of an official map. A commission of five men was appointed to survey the town, establish its formal limits, put in place such codes and regulations as were deemed necessary, and otherwise lay out the town with appropriate marking stones and posts,

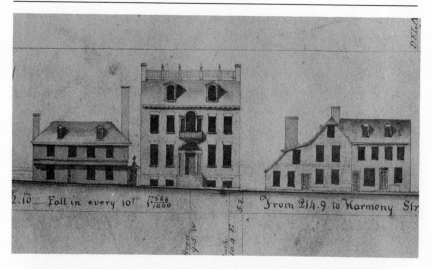

Benjamin Henry Latrobe painted this watercolor elevation of the Strand in 1804 for his street survey of New Castle, Delaware. At left is the George Read house (destroyed by fire in 1824), at center the George Read II house. *Delaware State Archives*

pavements, gutters, and fences. The process was completed in 1804 with the execution of a detailed set of plans that mapped streets and all of New Castle's buildings and included watercolor elevations of the streetscapes.

The paintings were done by Jefferson's friend Benjamin Henry Latrobe, a recent arrival from England, who, among other prestigious commissions, designed the Capitol in Washington and the Bank of Pennsylvania. In the survey, the elevation of the houses along the Strand revealed one house that stood tall above the others.

New Castle had a rival for "Mr. Jefferson." His name was George Read; his nickname, "the Signer." A New Castler since 1754, he was a lawyer, a framer of the Constitution, and a signatory to the Declaration of Independence. During the very years Latrobe was conducting his survey, one of the commission members, the scion of the signer, George Read II (1765–1836), was having a grand house built for himself. It is his tall New Castle home that draws the eye in Latrobe's watercolor.

What led me to visit New Castle was a recent reprint of a 1933 pamphlet published in the White Pine Series of Architectural Monographs. It described the George Read II house in detail and featured a number of photographs and measured drawings. I've learned since that the text has many minor errors, but the quality of the house was immediately apparent.

Most of the houses described in the White Pine Series (which was published from 1914 to 1940) are private homes. Many of them have long since disappeared, destroyed by fire or development. More than a few have fallen into the hands of the adversaries of preservation and been renovated beyond recognition. As a result, I was both pleased and surprised to find the Read house not only intact but open to the public. It had been lucky. But then grand houses often are.

Today, the place is no longer a residence. That is, no one lives there, although the house still has all the accoutrements of a home. On my first visit, one of the tour guides put it into perspective. We were standing in the mistress's bedroom with its towering bed and elegant furnishings. "If I ever got locked in this house, this is the room I'd stay in," she said. "But I have to remind myself that the mattress is actually Styrofoam peanuts."

It looks very much like a house, but don't be fooled. It's a museum.

The young George Read II had prospects. His father was perhaps the most important politician in Delaware, and George II showed all the signs of following in his father's significant footsteps. He passed the bar at twenty, and became United States Attorney for Delaware at twenty-four.

When Read commenced to build his grand house in 1797, he was only thirty-two. No doubt he anticipated its grandeur would be a reflection of his stature in the state and perhaps even of some future role in national affairs. While his larger ambitions remained unfulfilled (he was defeated in several congressional elections), he did get the privilege of living his life and running his law practice in his impressive home in New Castle.

How the plan for the house was developed is unclear, but correspondence exists between Read's father and his brother-in-law, Matthew Pearce, complete with four sketches of floor plans. The letters and plans were apparently exchanged in July and August 1797. None of the sketches is identical to the house that was eventually built, and no record exists of Read's own responses to them or of his own design notions. Yet, judging by the similarities between the plans and the house itself, no doubt those sketches played an important part in the design process.

Construction began in the fall of 1797. One entry in Read's account book for the time records that in September he made payments for "digging my cellar in New Castle." On October 14, he recorded: "Gave Richard Grubb [$1.00] to buy 1 Gallon of rum for hands on laying Corner Stone." However, for unknown reasons, work stopped shortly thereafter for nearly four years. Possible explanations abound, among them that

One more indicator of modernity is removed, as the power company takes down a telephone pole and attendant power lines that marred the elevation of the Read house. *Historical Society of Delaware*

Read may have had financial problems and that he was deeply saddened by the loss of his father, who died in 1798. The latter is Lyle's favorite answer, but no reason for the hiatus is certain.

Not until March 1801 were the basement walls completed. Over the next two years, work proceeded at a more precipitous rate. By mid-July 1801, the kitchen was finished, and the structure of the main house was done by year's end. The plasterer was hired in June 1802. Read reported in a letter: "I have this moment entered into articles of agreement with M. Thackera for plaistering my house—without reference to future measurement I have agreed to give him $700 for the work which is to be completed in the best manner . . ." In spring 1803, the Reads moved in.

The main building is of a five-bay configuration: As in John Curtis's "mansion house," the first-story entrance is at the center, flanked by pairs of large windows. Over the entrance on the second floor is a spectacular Palladian window. The attic story is lit by arched windows in a pair of dormers. The tall basement elevates the main story well above the street, providing an appropriately grand entry and enhanced view of the river.

Inside, the double-pile (two-room-deep) layout features a center hall that extends from front to back. On one side are two parlors, front and rear. On the other, an office for lawyer Read is at front, behind which a broad staircase leads to the second story. A large ell extends off the back of the house, containing the kitchen, wash room, and servants' quarters.

As with any high-style building, it is the details that distinguish the George Read II house. From without, decorative elements include stone lintels over the windows and the four arched openings (the doorway, topped by its semicircular fan sash; the Palladian window immediately above; and the pair of dormers with arched windows that light the third floor). On the roof, a balustrade decorated with Grecian urns safeguards anyone pacing the widow's walk.

The rooms inside loom large: the first-floor ceilings are thirteen feet high, the second-story ceilings fourteen. The grand staircase has extravagant finishing touches. Many of the window and door architraves, mantels, chair railings, and other woodwork feature punch-and-gouge decorations. The making of this sculptural molding was labor-intensive, involving alternating rows of hand-worked slots, made with the gouge, and rows of holes, which were punched. Today, the woodwork has been restored to perfection, after the laborious removal of as many as twenty-four layers of paint. The restoration process revealed that a thin layer of mahogany tops the chair rail and mantels, providing a contrasting texture and color to the painted surfaces beneath.

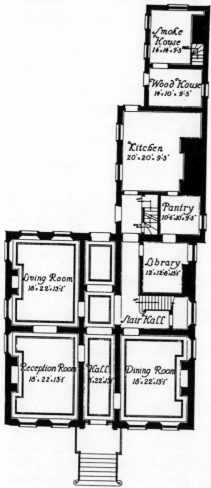

The plan of the first floor of the Read house as it was arranged during the Laird years. *Historical Society of Delaware*

The hand-worked punch-and-gouge decorations that adorn much of the woodwork on the first floor of the house. *Historical Society of Delaware*

Applied plaster reliefs of scenes from classical mythology adorn the mantelpieces. In the front parlor, the center panel of the mantelpiece, as described on the original bill of sale, depicts "the triumph of Mars returning from Battle."

This plaster ornamentation was the work of a Philadelphian, Robert Wellford. The bulk of the construction of the house was done by the crew of another Philadelphia craftsman, Peter Crowing, who probably functioned both as architect and as general contractor for Read. Thackera, the plasterer, was also from the nation's capital. In fact, it has been said of the house in its entirety that it "could not be a more Philadelphia house if it had been built there, loaded on a barge, and floated down the Delaware River." It nearly was. The materials arrived from Philadelphia on the Delaware River. The materials were off-loaded less than a hundred yards from the building site at a wharf that had been constructed specifically for this purpose.

George Read lived in the house until his death in 1836. For the restorers, the signal event of the years immediately following Read's passing was the preparation of a detailed inventory of the house and its contents. The document was to prove of inestimable value during the restoration process.

The house remained in the Read family for another decade, though for much of the time it was rented. Then, at a public auction in 1846, it was purchased by William Couper. While in the care of Couper and his heirs, the house remained largely unchanged. A merchant involved in the China trade, Couper decorated the house during the Victorian era with objects brought back from his travels. Following his death, a maiden niece of Couper's, Miss Hettie Smith, inherited the house and lived there until her death in 1919. The following year, the house was sold to a socially prominent Wilmington stockbroker and his wife for $9,000.

To many people, the Read house is better known as the Laird house, since Phillip and Lydia Laird lived there for much of this century (he died in 1945, but she remained until her death in 1975, when the Historical Society took over). Mrs. Laird's bequest of the house included all of the furnishings and a half-million-dollar endowment. The gift didn't arrive bound with endless strings, yet, Lyle decided, the Laird era in the house needed to be acknowledged, and not solely because of their generous gift.

"The Lairds bought the house in 1920, and a number of people in New Castle came here because they were either related to or friends of the Lairds," Lyle explained. "I think it would have been presumptuous to have erased the Lairds from the picture.

It also would have been difficult because there are a lot of people who fondly remember the house and being entertained in it."

The apparent conflict—namely, the opportunity to restore an exquisite 1804 house versus the need to respect its twentieth-century inhabitants and their effect on the place—could perhaps have posed an insurmountable contradiction. Lyle and his advisers actually turned the paradox to advantage. But that's getting ahead of the story.

The restoration of the house began with research, not workmen. Some preliminary study had already been done, as a great-great-great-great-granddaughter of Read's, Eliza Wolcott, had written her master's thesis on Read and his house in 1971. It summarized much of the existing original source material.

A further manuscript study was done by Historical Society staff members, resulting in over two hundred single-spaced typescript pages of precise transcripts of Read's letters, account books, and other source material. In his most understated manner, Charles Lyle observed, "There is quite a body of documentary evidence relating to the Read period."

Among other intriguing discoveries was the fact that, to judge from his letters to his brothers (who were charged with dispensing monies to numerous Philadelphia creditors), Read periodically had what we today would call cash-flow problems. He complained repeatedly of collecting from his debtors. "The difficulty of collecting money in this country is inconceivably great and as I am somewhat dependent on the ability of others to pay there is a degree of uncertainty of course attendant on collections." He also seemed to have had a certain fondness for haggling, as on many occasions he took issue with the sums for which he was billed.

A Historic Structure Report was done on the house in 1978. It included discussions of the house's condition, inside and out, and some educated guesswork about the physical changes made to the dwelling over the years. Drawings, an inventory of window types, X-ray analyses, and a paint analysis were conducted as part of the HSR.

The exterior restoration was begun in 1978. The shutters were removed. The toll taken by decades of inclement weather was erased from the entranceway, and it was repainted its original off-white color. The blackened masonry was cleaned and repointed, and the tones that emerged were warmer and lighter.

Just before the contract was let for the major exterior work, in March 1980, Charles Lyle arrived as newly appointed executive director of the Historical Society. Shortly thereafter, federal funding for architecture was radically cut and the major plans in place for the interior restoration had to be put on hold.

"We had to rethink the restoration at that point," said Lyle, "and we decided to do a thorough paint analysis. The earlier one was very disappointing. The results showed that all the trim color was cream and the plaster walls were to be painted white. Had all those federal monies flooded in and had we done the interior restoration then, that's what we would have had."

They had a major surprise coming to them. But in order to understand the findings, a bit of building history is necessary.

At about the turn of the eighteenth century, paint had been added to the list of decorating options in the colonies, though it didn't come into general use in America until perhaps 1750. Even then, paint in lesser houses was probably applied only to baseboards and wainscoting. In grander buildings, paint had been used earlier and in more places.

The colors were dictated by available pigments. Some pigments had existed for centuries, among them a green pigment called verdigris, made by applying acetic acid to copper. The use of red lead (litharge) produced a yellow-red color. A deep greenish blue known as Prussian blue (it was discovered in Berlin, capital of Prussia) first came into use in 1704 but remained relatively unknown until 1710. It was made from a salt compound of iron and potassium. When burned, a yellowish ocher soil turned red (thanks to its iron-ore content), producing "Venetian" red. There were also pigments made from reddish umber earth (it has manganese and iron oxides), and charcoal and lampblack. Little went to waste in Colonial America, as lampblack is the fine soot that was the residue on lamps or candles.

The pigments were mixed with a medium. One popular paint base for common people was milk, which produced casein paint. An old recipe for casein paint calls for a half gallon of skim milk, six ounces of lime, four ounces of neat's-foot oil, and a pound and one-half of color, all of which would have been at hand on the subsistence farm of the eighteenth century.

The wealthier householders had the option of purchasing paint materials, and making paint with a base of turpentine or linseed oil (a product of pressed flax seeds) or fish oils.

The successful marketing in recent years of "Williamsburg colors" has left many people with the mistaken impression that our ancestors lived in a world of "tasteful," subtle, muted shades. Recent research suggests that wasn't strictly true. Life was dark and dull enough, and bright colors were no doubt welcome.

One explanation for this misunderstanding is that until recently the tried-and-sort-of-true method of determining a paint chronology (that is, the sequence of colors applied to a surface) was simply to scrape, sand, or otherwise cut through the layers of paint. When done properly, the layers of paint are revealed in sequence and can be identified, sometimes by using a microscope. However, the colors as they emerge may only distantly resemble their original tones.

A case in point was the original paint color found in the center hall at the Read house. At the time of construction, the plaster wall had been sealed with a prime coat of linseed oil. Then the paint was applied. The original paint had never been overpainted, as the same coat had served throughout the Read residence, then had been covered with wallpaper by Couper and his heirs. The Lairds had applied a layer of canvas in their time of residence and painted that surface.

While the first paint analysis had concluded that the house was full of shades of white, the second paint analysis produced very different results. Matthew J. Mosca, a historic paint consultant noted for his work on Mount Vernon, arrived in July 1981 to collect samples from the house.

Mosca found that the deeply buried original paint in the hallway had become almost opaque, with just a tint of yellow. The aging had caused the paint to break down to a soaplike texture ("saponify" is the technical term), and the dim ocher tone that remained was essentially that of oxidized linseed oil. He then conducted chemical tests to determine the original color, applying sodium sulfide to reveal lead pigments and white lead, patent yellow, and zinc-white colors. A lime solution would reveal Prussian blue; distilled alcohol reveals shellac; and so on.

He discovered that a lime casein paint had been used. Indications of whiting, white lead, and patent yellow (lead oxychloride) pigments were present, leading Mosca to conclude that the hallway hadn't been white at all but rather a clear, light yellow.

Mosca proceeded throughout the house, taking woodwork and wall samples from every room and surface. He exposed the woodwork samples to ultraviolet light for one hundred twenty hours (to reduce the yellowing that oil paints undergo as they age). The chemical tests and microscopic examination were crucial to many of the findings.

The results were both copious and astonishing. To add to the mounting pages of research, Mosca delivered more than a hundred pages of detailed results, delineating every layer of paint on every surface in the house's interior. The colors were not limited to white, off-white, cream-white, and more white. Rather, downstairs the two parlors and the stair hall as well as the center hall had been brightly painted. The front parlor was an intense salmon pink, the rear parlor a strong blue-green of Prussian blue and verdigris pigments. The stairway was a light green made from a mix of Prussian blue, white, and patent yellow.

Still other findings were made. When the fire alarm system was being installed in 1983, a decorative border was found immediately below the cornice in the entry hall (during Mosca's initial study, a larger and later plaster cornice had covered the area). The discovery led to a reexamination of Read's account book, and the border, a hand-painted Greek key design, was found to have been applied in 1813. Payment had been made to Christian Jahns, who was listed in the Philadelphia directory of that year as an "Ornamental Wall Colourist."

In 1984, wallpaper removal in the front parlor revealed another border design, this one consisting of large oak leaves. Both borders have been painstakingly restored.

During restoration in the early 1980s, a workman laboriously removes some of the twenty-four layers of paint from the moldings in the entry hall of the Read house. Note the painted Greek key border beneath the cornice. *Historical Society of Delaware*

"The Read house has one of the best documentation collections in the country, with all the letters and contracts and information from the period of original construction," Lyle said. "And even with all of this stuff, all of this information, it was the physical investigation, the paint analysis, that completely changed everything. We had no idea that it was so stylish a house."

"Colonial" is a term common to real estate brokers and casual students of architecture. In its colloquial usage, it is taken to mean a house shaped like the main section of the Read, Hascall, and Curtis houses—that is, two full stories tall, with entrance and interior hall at center, with two bays on either side, a five-bay house. A so-called Colonial house may be one or two rooms deep (single- or double-pile).

The usage of the word has evolved a good deal over the years. Initially, the "Colonial" house was simply a Georgian house and much grander than the medieval buildings that inspired the likes of the Bixby house at Old Sturbridge Village. The Georgian house was the choice of well-off Americans for most of the eighteenth century, and it towered over simpler buildings, which tended to be one room deep, one story tall, and often lacked the details and finish of the Georgian.

Coincidental with the close of the Revolution, a new style emerged. The Federal style imposed thinner, lighter decorations on the same basic shape and arrangement, though some new wrinkles were introduced, such as elliptically shaped rooms and curved staircases. Today, however, both Georgian and Federal houses are commonly (though rather imprecisely) termed "Colonials." Some Greek Revival houses (a style common to the 1830–60 era), many twentieth-century Colonial Revival dwellings, and even some Victorian houses are also identified as Colonials. The deevolution of the Colonial has resulted in the term being applied to almost any house built five bays wide.

In common parlance, then, the Read house is a "Colonial." Making the more technical style designation of Georgian versus

Federal is a bit more complicated. While the usual era cited for the Federal style is 1780 to 1820, construction of houses in the older, Georgian style didn't cease all at once (as we saw with the Georgian-style Hascall house in Essex, New York, in 1810). For the most part, the Read house had been described in magazines as Georgian. In 1930, *Town & Country* went so far as to retrace its lineage to Palladio and to Inigo Jones, and concluded, "The style of [the Read] house is, of course, Georgian."

Not so fast, more recent students of the house have decided.

Adamesque, a label often used interchangeably with Federal, comes from a trio of English brothers. Their work, like Palladio's, has come down to us in printed as well as in built forms (*The Works in Architecture*, 1773). Also like Palladio, Robert Adam, the best known of the brothers, had spent time studying the classical monuments in Italy, having visited the recently discovered remains of the ancient civilizations at Pompeii and Herculaneum. As a result, he brought to English architecture a firsthand familiarity with classical antiquity. Previously the ancients had been seen only through the Renaissance eyes of Palladio and his English interpreter, Inigo Jones.

Though working with a reverence for the same models, the brothers Adam did not feel compelled to imitate strictly the classical structures that inspired them. While Palladio had measured and copied the proportions and detailing used in antiquity, Adamesque work is more interpretive. The ingredients were much the same, but their usage quite different.

The brothers Adam violated Palladio's rules. While Adamesque decorations are invariably refined and rich with plaster elements, they usually feature a range of elements beyond what Palladio would have prescribed. Swags and garlands were favored design elements, and are to be found on exterior cornices and architraves, as are urns and other geometric designs. The Adams not only employed a previously unheard-of mix-and-match approach; they also played fast and loose with Palladian proportion, thinning and narrowing and attenuating freely.

This decorative approach sets the Adamesque (or the Federal) apart from the Georgian. Rather than relying on curved moldings or architectural echoes of columns or other classical elements, the brothers Adam applied their urns and swags with abandon. The Georgian is certainly decorative architecture; the Adamesque is decorated architecture.

The Read house has many Adamesque details. One classic sign of an Adam-inspired decor is the carved fireplace surround; the Wellford-decorated mantels Read purchased are superb examples of such work. Rather than paneling the entire fireplace wall (as was characteristic in a Georgian parlor), Federal mantels in general, and the Read house's specifically, were accompanied by a chair rail and cornice, with plasterwork. The mantels resembled their classical sources, in the case of Read's complete with mythologic scenes, swags, festoons, and fruit baskets. However, the mantel itself retains its architectural

The plaster decorations on this mantel in the front parlor depict Mars returning from battle. Such classical scenes were characteristic of high-style Federal decoration. *Historical Society of Delaware*

inspiration, featuring pilasters, frieze, and other temple elements.

Until *The Works in Architecture,* pattern books made only passing mention of interior details, but Robert and James Adam specified not only precise trims for cornice, ceiling, and other moldings but colors as well. Among their favorites were Wedgwood blue, pale green, primrose, and lemon yellow, colors made possible by advances in paint manufacture.

In this country, it was left to their interpreters to carry the Adams' style to the people. The great Boston architect Charles Bulfinch, who designed numerous church and public buildings (including the Massachusetts State House) as well as residences, has been credited by many with introducing the style in America, but it was the writer and carpenter Asher Benjamin who made it widely available beyond the wealthy urban centers. His *The Country Builder's Assistant,* published in 1797, was the first building publication originated in America.

Benjamin was a working carpenter as well as author who had built widely in Connecticut, Vermont, and central Massachusetts when he moved to Boston in 1803. There, he found he had to keep up with the latest trends, and worked in the Federal manner of Bulfinch. With the publication of his next book, *The American Builder's Companion,* in 1806, he delineated a distinctly Federal style.

The American Builder's Companion reached a wide readership. Benjamin tailored his designs to the predominantly wooden American house. The style described was English, yet it was a thinner, more elongated version, one more in tune with the materials being used (namely, wooden boards rather than blocks of stone). Benjamin's slendering of proportion, though subtle, is one of the key characteristics of Federal buildings.

The interior details at the Read house in particular offer immediate visual evidence of its Federal qualities. As Matthew Mosca pointed out in his paint analysis: "The [plasterwork] decorations on the ceilings, such as the vines, branches and center medallion on the Center Hall (middle) ceiling, appear to relate to such sources as Asher Benjamin's *The American*

Builder's Companion (1806 and after) and would be a part of the architectural vocabulary of the time."

"The house has always been characterized as Georgian," Charles Lyle said. "It was considered to be sort of a holdover from earlier examples of the eighteenth-century house, mainly because of its conservative floor plan. But the paint analysis showed that it was indeed a high-style house, and of course there's also the punch-and-gouge work, a form of carving that came out of the Federal period. It's geometric and shallow versus the rich naturalistic carving seen in the earlier era. But somehow it had never quite clicked with people that this was a high-style house of the Federal period."

In the 1930s, the house was covered with ivy, and enjoyed the same unobstructed river view it did when Read lived there. Except that the seaplanes and yachts of their guests were moored on the bank of the Delaware in the time of the Lairds.

The house has always been a showplace. At the time of its construction, the Read house reached higher than the courthouse a few blocks away (its high ceilings made the Read house the equivalent of six stories tall). As Lyle put it, the house was "a pretty pretentious undertaking."

Phillip and Lydia Laird were proud of their house and treated it respectfully. They conducted no wholesale remodeling, and the basic configuration of the house remained much the same in their half century of domicile. They did perform a "restoration," at least insofar as the term was understood at the time. But the work consisted largely of refinishing interior surfaces to cover up the wallpaper and other signs of the Victorian era, giving the house the appearance of what was then understood to be Colonial style.

Bathrooms were also added, the largest one in the broad center hallway on the second story. The process of updating the kitchen continued (evidence was found suggesting that even within the Read years several major changes were made in cooking facilities, incorporating advances in cooking technology, with built-in masonry-and-metal ovens and steamers). But it is the dining room that best represents the Lairds' efforts.

"It's a wonderful, celebrated early-twentieth-century room with custom-designed wallpaper showing New Castle scenes," Lyle told me. "In fact, the dining room in the house is one of the most published twentieth-century Colonial Revival rooms in the country. *House Beautiful, The Ladies' Home Journal, House & Garden*—they all featured the house."

In the Read era, it had been an office for the man of the house. As such, it was a working space and, while handsomely finished, it had fewer decorative details than most of the rest of the house. The sculptural punch-and-gouge work and mahogany trim on the moldings are absent. The fireplace mantel is simpler and was never decorated with one of Wellford's plaster scenes from antiquity. Even the paint was plain, a cream-white all around, on moldings, walls, and ceiling.

A century later, the Lairds made the room their own. They commissioned the painting of a wallpaper mural that, in the spirit of the Colonial Revival era, celebrates the seventeenth- and eighteenth-century past of New Castle. There are local New Castle scenes, buildings, and even historical figures, including William Penn stepping ashore at New Castle in 1682. In the rather ponderous prose of *Town & Country:* "In all these pictorial comments it will be observed that the grandeur of the setting of the Read estate and of the town of New Castle on the very shore of the Delaware is concisely and entertainingly presented."

Just as the paint analysis presented a special challenge and opportunity to the restorers, so did the Lairds' dining room. The 1836 inventory of Read's furnishings offered no information about the original appearance of the room. As a result, Lyle said, "without documentary information on original furnishings, we would have had to speculate about the Read period as a law office. In contrast, we had this wonderful, celebrated early-twentieth-century room, all its furniture, and photographic documentation of every corner of the room." They decided to take advantage of what they had.

The Read house dining room, as it appeared circa 1930, complete with its hand-painted wallpaper depicting scenes from New Castle's history. *Historical Society of Delaware*

"By selecting the dining room to memorialize and, in a way, thank the Lairds for their generous gift, we solved a lot of problems when it came to doing the kind of restoration we were doing in the rest of the house. I also think it is a very important document of Colonial Revival taste that will become more important as time goes on."

The wallpaper makes it work. Installed in 1927 by a Philadelphia decorator, the paper extends from chair rail to cornice, on all four sides of the room. Though the portrayal of different times and characters features numerous anachronisms, the total effect of the painting is surprisingly powerful.

Oddly, the room has a more museumlike feel than any other in the house. For the most part, the mix of early-nineteenth- and early-twentieth-century furniture isn't museum quality. Yet being surrounded by the painted walls gives one the feeling of being inside the painting. It reminded me of the odd sensation I get all too rarely upon being taken in by a painting. Suddenly you are having a picnic with Manet's rather demure naked lady in the forest. Or you're there in Gilbert Stuart's studio watching him paint George Washington: he isn't done yet, of course, but the likeness of the Great Man is surely there.

The Lairds' wallpaper isn't great painting. The identities of the workers who painted it are unknown (the records only extend as far as the decorating firm, the Chapman Decorative Company). During the complex restoration process, not only was the wallpaper stabilized but much inpainting was done by students from the Art Conservation Program of the University of Delaware and Winterthur Museum.

The total effect of the room is considerable. The time warp is made all the more palpable by restoration steps that weren't taken. While radiators and electrical switches were removed in the Read era rooms, they remain in the dining room. The floors, stripped back to their original bare wood elsewhere, are stained and carefully waxed and buffed in the dining room. The rug, the glassware and china—they're all from the Lairds. Since the Lairds never used the dining-room fireplace, even the logs in the firebox are the very same ones pictured in a 1938 photograph.

Two other spaces in the house have also been restored to their early-twentieth-century appearance. In the basement is a taproom, one of three original such areas installed during Prohibition. The room is finished and decorated in the manner of a German basement bar-restaurant, a rathskeller, and features a trestle table and benches, false beams, a brick floor, and stained glass. Designed by a well-known local architect, the space, now restored to its 1940 appearance from photographic evidence, recalls a more casual side of life in the Laird household.

On the second story is the Lairds' master bedroom. Its mantelpiece had disappeared, so restoration of the chimney breast would have had to have been, at best, speculative. Lyle also noted that there was a certain symmetry in doing one Colonial

Revival era room on each level. "It makes for continuity and variety."

Treating the Colonial Revival era with seriousness is a rather new approach in restoration circles. Just as it took nearly three-quarters of a century to develop a taste for Victoriana, an appreciation for the Colonial Revival has come slowly.

It's hardly accidental that Charles Lyle has been a pioneer in this area. In talking about how he came to develop a taste for architecture, he said, "My brother's an architect, for one thing. And my mother was artistically inclined, so there was always emphasis on looking around you and *seeing*.

"But there was another thing that fixed my interest in houses very early in my life. In Duluth there were a number of wonderful, grand estates that were built in the Colonial Revival period, the teens and twenties. I didn't grow up in one, but as a kid I always had a special attraction to those houses."

One that, decades later, he got to exercise to very good advantage.

The restoration of the house took roughly ten years and cost just over $900,000. It involved a great deal more than research and decision making. At times, as many as twenty-five workmen were busy in the house. Unwanted remodeling was demolished. All signs of the modern kitchen on the main floor and the bathrooms were erased. Wallpaper, floor stain, and other surface finishes had to be eliminated. The removal of as many as twenty-four layers of paint from the punch-and-gouge woodwork required thousands of painstaking man-hours. New shutters, new and carefully obscured mechanical systems, and a thousand other installations and changes were required.

Highly trained craftspeople were hired to replicate the grain painting on the exterior doors and the painted borders. Another expert was hired to restore the plaster ornamentation on the mantels. Replacement materials had to be found. New moldings for the few missing pieces were fabricated and matching floorboards bought at salvage.

Restoring the house turned into something of an exercise in historiography. As it stands today, the house is in itself a sort of history of history. The task required more than the usual close examination of what was originally there. It was more than "a matter of subtraction," to borrow John Mesick's words regarding the Hascall house. Today, the era of George Read II exists alongside a composite of reverential and historical thinking dating from the second quarter of the twentieth century and the so-called Colonial Revival. Under one roof, the near and distant American pasts are compared and contrasted.

Transforming the grand brick house at 42, The Strand, New Castle, from a home to a museum involved more than preservation decisions. Practical considerations figured in, too, like the need for offices for the site administrator (on the third, attic floor). Basic amenities for the public were also required, so a reception area was built in the basement, incorporating bathrooms and a museum shop to service the needs of an anticipated 30,000 annual visitors. Updated working systems are today unobtrusively functioning, since central heating and air conditioning were not to be found at the turn of the nineteenth century, but are essential for maintaining a museum house full of valuable furniture and other artifacts.

A new entrance was needed, one that would avoid unnecessary wear and tear on the original front entrance. Architect Martin J. Rosenblum came up with a solution that was convenient but would not interfere with the front elevation of the house. A stairway to the basement was installed on the side, with access from the garden. Discreetly obscured behind a fence, it was the only element added to the exterior of the house during the restoration process.

The above recounting of a few of the findings and decisions involved in the Read house restoration only suggests the challenge of the task taken on by Lyle and his advisers. Telling the full story might well require several volumes and profiles of a disparate array of experts: Philadelphia-based architect Martin J. Rosenblum; Anne F. Clapp, the conservator who oversaw the restoration of the mural; paint consultant Matthew J. Mosca;

furnishings consultant Page Talbott; and an army of researchers, painters, masons, and specialized conservators.

Even now, no one can say with any assurance that all the mysteries have been solved. There are, for example, many signs that the house had an early (circa 1850) hot-air heating system of quite revolutionary design. And the bedroom that is at present in the Colonial Revival style may not remain that way forever. "Should evidence in the future come to light," admitted Lyle, "it may be necessary to rethink that room."

"The challenge of the Read house," said Lyle, "was not only to take good advantage of the privilege and opportunity to restore one of the great buildings in the country. It was the whole issue of the way people perceive historic houses as museums.

"I have thought a great deal about taking what has always been considered to be a rather static, boring experience of visiting the historic house and turning it into something else. I think we accomplished that by using a couple of different strategies.

"One strategy we employed involved making use of two periods. It was something we more or less fell into because the documentation wasn't there for us to redo Read's law office. Plus, that wallpaper was important and it was a very published room.

"It was a departure doing those three rooms as Colonial Revival spaces, but I think it has been a success in some measure. Most of the public may not be knowledgeable enough that they can really understand what we're attempting, but the sophisticated visitors appreciate that juxtaposition of the two very well-documented periods."

I suspect he understates their success. Even an uninitiated visitor can't help but perceive the changes in floor color and the presence (or absence) of such signs of modernity as light switches and radiators. Not every visitor can explain what he or she has seen, but there has to be at least an intuitive understanding that something is different, that something has changed over time and from room to room.

Another notable difference from many house museums is the flexibility and continuing changes the house is undergoing. At the time of his departure from the Historical Society of Delaware, the Read house was being put to use, as Lyle put it, "for a series of changing exhibitions and changes within the house itself.

"It was more than going from winter dress to summer dress (we did that, too). For example, we did something in the fall of 1989 which took a lot of people by surprise.

"We sent out an invitation to the membership for the funeral of Louisa Dorsey Read. The whole house was draped in mourning and there was a casket in the back parlor, and the bedroom upstairs was interpreted as a sickbed with a doctor's kit next to it. We talked about early medical practices, circa 1820. We were able to build a special exhibit within the existing house with a whole different layer of interpretation.

"We have also done special holiday and seasonal exhibits using both the 1820 and the 1920 periods. We introduced into the house some manikins, not pink-skinned manikins but modern abstract ones in period clothing. That way we were able to get into servants, clothing, social customs.

"Those are ways we've been trying to address the classic 'velvet rope' problem where you create a pretty picture in setting up a place and then announce: 'It's done, it's documented, and I as a curator will now leave it, and this is the best we can do with what we have in the collections.'

"Instead, we tried to create within a strictly accurate historical and cultural framework a dynamic and attractive place for people to go again and again and again."

For now, however, the restoration is completed. In the spring of 1989, the last piece of the architectural restoration was put in place: the balustrade on the roof, rather like the candles on a cake.

Why is the house important? I asked Lyle how it relates to his mission as a director of a historical society.

"As somebody who is an administrator, a bit of a curator, and a bit of this and a bit of that, I'm a pretty matter-of-fact kind of person. But quite honestly, I think that history museums are critical right now.

"We are looking at a society that is changing dramatically and quickly. We are looking at the built environment, which is constantly being threatened and changed. We're looking at the erosion of the family and a country where there is little sense of place anymore . . ." His voice trailed off.

"In Europe you find a deep-seated sense of tradition and a great respect for the past. I'm not sure that's the case in this country. Americans don't understand history, and I'm not sure that they understand what its impact is on their daily lives.

"There's a group of people who love going to museums, expanding their knowledge, and reading the books. We try to serve them. And there are, of course, people you'll never reach. It's just a fact of life that some people are not oriented toward these things. But there are others we need to talk to, to help protect the culture.

"So I feel like I am, hopefully, a custodian of what's left of America's past and culture and civilization.

"I don't mean to sound pretentious," Lyle added. "But I think history museums are seriously threatened today by a lack of interest, money, and professional standards."

Lyle may work as a curator of class, benefiting from the generosity and bequests of the upper crust. Yet I believe his understanding of the past concerns preservation for all classes. He seeks to conserve and to understand the past, for what he hopes will be a widening constituency.

10
The Academic Provocateur

To be is to have been, and to project our messy, malleable past into our unknown future.
—*J. H. Plumb,* The Death of the Past *(1969)*

The building—red, rectangular, and about three inches high—was immersed in water inside a plain, wide-necked bottle. It was a variation on the old ship-in-the-bottle theme.

When I asked him about it, University of Vermont professor Chester H. Liebs swiveled in his chair and brought the bottle from the windowsill behind him to the desktop between us.

"A sculptor friend made me this building just about the time I began the Historic Preservation Graduate Program here in the summer of 1975. I asked her if it was waterproof. She said she wasn't sure, so I stuck it in this jar with plain tap water," Liebs told me.

"It was a 'preserved building,' obviously. That was the pun. But I was curious to see what would happen to it over time."

I looked at it closely. It appeared to be a chunk of brick. The imprecise black markings painted on it to represent windows and doors suggested that it was supposed to be a generic building rather than a copy of a particular structure. The water had a few floaters in it, specks of dust or mold that clouded the medium

211

slightly. As far as I could tell, the building was just as it was when it was immersed fifteen-odd years before.

"What has happened several times," Liebs continued, "is that cleaning people at the university have come in and not understood that what I was doing was a little experiment. So they've changed the water once in a while. I've even had a couple of industrious people who I think have *cleaned off* the building."

The original "experiment" involved sealing the building in the bottle, untouched, with the expectation that it would stay there indefinitely. Like the scientist intent on one finding who stumbles onto another quite accidentally, Liebs found his experiment transformed. The university housekeeping crew had unknowingly redefined the parameters of his investigation.

In its way, the experiment proved to be quite successful. As Liebs remarked to me: "I'm always curious to see what people notice." They most certainly did notice the building in the bottle and, of their own volition, chose to intervene in the "preservation" process. That little captive building, like just about every full-sized building in creation, proved to be subject to the impulses of the people charged with its care.

Without regard to intentions, good or bad, buildings seem forever to be at the mercy of those who take care of them. Quite accidentally, I think, we stumbled onto a tangible symbol of what fascinates Chester Liebs most as he surveys the world of preservation today.

Like Don Carpentier and John Mesick and thousands of others, Liebs is concerned with preserving and protecting old buildings. However, he has a slightly different idea of what the shoulds and should-nots are. The issue isn't whether to save, as he's in favor of saving many structures that more traditional preservationists couldn't care less about, including gas stations, drive-in theatres, and eccentric buildings of all sorts. The question for him is: Whom do you trust?

It's always dangerous to put words into people's mouths—especially when they are as quotable as Liebs—but it seems to me that his answer to that question might be characterized as "trust time." He argues against second-guessing the passage of time, is adamant that it is often a mistake to try to turn the clock back, and insists we should not try to rewrite history. In general, he believes you should trust what you see *today* in yesterday's buildings. Save them—but don't try to make them into something they never were.

But don't take my simplifications in place of Liebs's own arguments.

Chester Liebs and I had talked on the phone a couple of times about the Hascall house in Essex when I was writing a story about that house and its porches. Liebs had felt it was something of a crime against history to "erase" whole eras of time in restoring the house to its earliest appearance.

My conversations with him had left me with the clear impression that he was a voluble talker. It was also apparent, to judge from his opinions on the Hascall house, that he saw things very differently than many of the people with whom I had been talking. So I went to see him.

Liebs's base hasn't always been Burlington, where the University of Vermont is located. He's lived there for most of the last two decades, yet he still describes himself as a New Yorker. He grew up in the New York City metropolitan area, where his father, the president of a printing concern, introduced him to the changes occurring in the landscape around him. When he was a boy, Liebs and his father looked on when Roosevelt Field on Long Island, whence Lindbergh and *The Spirit of St. Louis* had embarked, was turned into a shopping center. They followed the changing fortunes of some of the grand estates on Long Island that were demolished or subdivided.

While attending the City College of New York, he witnessed the razing of Pennsylvania Station in Manhattan in 1964. That event helped awaken his preservation consciousness. "It seemed like an absolutely incredible absurdity, tearing down that building. Now I understand how that happens. But then . . ." He shook his head silently.

Liebs took courses in biology and geology, but he majored

in history. "I was very much drawn, ultimately, to the history of architecture," he recalled. He enrolled in the fall of 1969 in the Historic Preservation Program at Columbia University. "I was in the first wave of graduates."

Next, he took a job as curator of history for the New York State Historic Trust (now called the Division for Historic Preservation). There he worked on preserving, and getting entered on the National Register of Historic Places, Albany Union Station, the New York State Capitol, and a number of other buildings in Albany. Then he went on to a position as field historian for the Historic American Engineering Record. Liebs served, in his late twenties, as president of an organization he helped found called the Society for Industrial Archaeology, whose purpose was to call attention to the nation's technological past.

Liebs moved to Vermont to sell his skills in preservation, initially working for the state as supervisor of historic sites. He found himself gravitating to the University of Vermont, and launched his first preservation course off-campus in Montpelier.

"Those courses were like Russian roulette," he recalled of the first courses he gave in Vermont. "You didn't know whether they would go off or not. It was always a gamble.

"But my first one drew people from as far away as Albany and Massachusetts as well as from New Hampshire and Vermont. I had this wonderful group with all sorts of skills and backgrounds, and not only in architecture; we had schoolteachers, a photographer, a whole mix of people.

"It was a time when urban renewal had trickled down to the smaller cities. It was the last gasp of the American urban clearance programs. It was trickling even to places like Vermont.

"Vermont had—and still does to some degree—a very strong sense of itself that isn't based on what it is but on the myth of what outsiders want. It had a self-image of small towns, with little white buildings grouped around a church, yet Vermont was a place of small cities. While efforts were being taken to preserve the former, for the latter it was 'anything goes.'

"So what was happening was that all sorts of plans were beginning to be floated about destroying Vermont's little city centers and moving commerce over to the interstate. That was the period of time when this course took place.

"I marched these students into the village of Randolph. I had just read an article in the paper reporting that an architect had told the city fathers that if they wanted to save their downtown with its Victorian commercial blocks clustered around a railroad station, probably the only course was to paint all the buildings sky blue, put up a canopy, and hope for the best. It sounds incredible now.

"So we did a project—we *looked* at Randolph and how it had changed through time. We tried to get people enthusiastic about it. Today, it sounds obvious enough, but then it was a pioneering awareness project.

"We started with this enthusiastic group of students, but gradually more and more townspeople came to see our presentation. Within a year, the town started advertising itself as a historic downtown.

"This was just a holding action. There was also a plan to tear down an old firehouse and hose tower that officials had said was totally unsafe. It was to be demolished to make way for several parking spots. But within two years, because of the holding action and the conceptual interest we were able to stir up, the times had changed. Urban renewal was on the wane, it was the middle of the energy crisis, interest in the Bicentennial was building, and Randolph managed to get some funds it could use on the building.

"So the old firehouse wasn't demolished. It is now proudly the town offices. There was a whole change: Randolph has never become a cutesified, yuppie town; it's still a working town. It still has its basic stores.

"I had long been interested in the nuts and bolts of buildings. But what we did at Randolph was the sort of thing that showed me the potential of people to recognize that buildings *signify* something. There's a human aspect to buildings and landscapes that I think interests people.

"Anyway, I went on to do a series of these classes. A lot of people thought this was a good site for a graduate program. It was easier said than done, but we began the Historic Preservation Program here."

Chester Liebs is the sort of man who might have inspired the cliché of the professor in a tweed jacket with leather elbow patches. Seated behind his desk or at the front of a classroom, he takes his listeners for a nonstop ride, moving from one subject to the next. You get the feeling he knows the topography very well, as he points out an issue or tells an anecdote. Yet he is conscious of his audience, often seeming to peek out from behind his professorial mask, without interrupting the flow, to make sure you're following him, that you're looking in the direction he wants you to look.

His manner suits his subject, which is, broadly speaking, the built environment. He describes himself as an environmentalist, though of a different sort than usually comes to mind when we hear that term. He's less concerned with nature's landscape than with the landscape that has evolved, the built environment that has been shaped and changed by humankind. He is concerned with preserving a forest of buildings and structures, complete with its undergrowth of roads and walkways and plantings and the rest. He is at his most provocative when he applies his nonstop talk to the built environment, the man-made landscape.

In his book *Main Street to Miracle Mile*, Liebs describes going for a drive as "a trip along a vast linear time line in three dimensions, each passing scene a clue for unraveling the larger puzzle of how and why twentieth-century society has chosen to reorganize its civilization around the highway." In his book he wrote at length about how the roadside landscape has changed, about how downtowns in eighteenth-century port towns featured a "form of primordial Main Street that served as a corridor for trade." He described how, in the early nineteenth century, turnpikes and inland waterways produced hundreds of new communities and how the coming of the railroad once again centralized commerce, this time in the vicinity not of the docks but of the downtown railroad depot.

Liebs's book, subtitled *American Roadside Architecture,* traces in detail the complex evolution in the twentieth century of commercial and residential development, thanks to the automobile, along strips of highway. These are the "miracle miles" (one of the first such booming commercial strips was Wilshire Boulevard in Los Angeles). Equally important are the 40,000 miles of interstates, the early shopping centers and then the malls, the massive interchanges, and, finally, in the 1970s, the ironic return to Main Street with, as Liebs wrote, its "dash of historic preservation."

"When I came to Vermont," he told me, "it wasn't yet popular to talk about 'reading' places. Most architectural historians were still concerned with the great modernist architects and defending them. 'Cultural landscape' and all those other terms had not evolved.

"In the years since, I've benefited from an excitement in history. We've begun to synthesize history again. The sea change was beginning to affect the historian, the architectural historian, the geographer, the archaeologist. All these people began talking to each other. We began to see a town not just as good, bad, ugly, or just as design. We saw that the beauty in towns was in history, in their evolution."

Not everybody sees what is before them when they regard a town or street or a house. "When people teach history as social studies," Liebs complained, "it rarely is taught with any reference to physical surroundings. Many people have come to think about architecture (the same thing is true with their reaction to paintings) that they need to be connoisseurs. They think that one needs to have an opinion of what or how good something is. That's very intimidating, that you can't just rely on your ability to understand what something means.

"I do an exercise in the course I've taught for the last twenty years now called 'The Architectural Landscape in History.' Everyone comes in at the beginning and I show them certain images of buildings and places. Quite predictably, almost everyone will say, 'Oh, I like this' or 'I don't like that.' When asked why they like something, people will say, 'Oh, that's old, so I think that's better,' or 'That's Colonial, so that's good.' Which makes no sense, necessarily."

Liebs has given this phenomenon a calculatedly ironic name. "I call this the 'tyranny of the present.' You're showing pictures to people who have never regarded a preservation problem, and they come out with a prejudice that's been beaten into them: 'Old is better.' They don't see the building as a text full of knowledge but rather something to have off-hand opinions about. Instead of seeing it as an individual structure that has its own personality, it's just a stereotype."

One role Liebs plays today is helping to foster a less inhibited way of seeing buildings and landscapes. In a sense, he is still influencing public thinking, just as he did back in Randolph. But today circumstances have changed so that he is not just concerned about saving buildings from the blade of the bulldozer. Today's added worry is to save structures from their saviors.

"As soon as you start to see a house, you must let your mind wander over it to understand what it really means. Not just what your house means for yourself, but what it means on the street and in the city. Then your interest starts to become different and your opinions start to reach out.

"If you say, 'I like that house' or 'I don't like that house' or 'I think Colonial is best' or 'I like Victorian best,' the options are narrowed. You become very closed down, focused on that one little thing.

"On the other hand, if you begin to look at a town and buildings and how they relate to one another, your mind begins to open up.

"I think that fixing up an old building should not be a self-centered exercise of 'I own my beauty, and I'm going to show I spent a lot of money on it.' It also can be a way of learning about yourself and the past and the whole world around you. I think both things can happen.

"But sometimes this other side of architecture is not as well known. So people limit themselves to their initial reactions about buildings, whether they're pretty or ugly. Often that sort of opinion is irrelevant. I know personally the things I think are pretty or ugly, but I also know what they mean. I believe there's far more freedom in beginning to understand what the context is. There's a much larger point of view that spins out of it."

Liebs pointed out that there are other pressures on the novice preservationist. "There's always the tug: to scrape or not to scrape, whether to restore, to preserve, to conserve. There are many people who work on houses—you should always bear this in mind—and the more changes that are made, the more money changes hands. The more work that can be done, the more changes that can be made, the larger the project. Even with responsible people who work with old buildings there's always some pressure or profit motive to change things.

"The homeowner often feels it, too. One buys a house and says, 'Oh, this is a lovely old house,' but doesn't understand the qualities that make that loveliness special. And if people are beginning to spend money or are being advised to invest a lot in the property, there is also some desire to make it look like money has been spent.

"It's just like a buying a new car. You don't want a dull old car, you want a shiny car. I think there's a lot of pressure both to spend money and to make it look like money is spent.

"That's how you can get a new old house."

For many people concerned with old houses, the manual work and tool skills of preservation and restoration are of paramount importance. I asked Liebs how crucial he thought the "hands-on" was to the study of historic preservation.

"It's hands-on and brains-on," he replied. "You have to do both. Hands-on is easy, because ultimately it's knowing what to do with your hands that's hardest. I'm not saying that—whoa—back up on that, don't get that wrong."

He paused. His concern was clearly that he might be offending the craftsmen of the restoration world. "I am a great supporter of restoration crafts and craftspeople. We give courses in it, too." That said, he started again. "Look at it another way. The hands-on is easier in the sense that it's linear and can be learned. There are a lot of things from the past that we revere now because they haven't become commonplace. There are skills today, like, say, those of a computer programmer, that might seem to some future generation terribly esoteric, so at that time they can relearn how to make computers."

He searched for another example.

"I see this circumstance often in beginners at an auction. I'll hear someone say"—Liebs changed to an exaggerated and excited high-pitched voice—' "Oh my God, the carving! You'll never get that again!' And I'll see that this person is admiring a piece of mass-produced turn-of-the-century oak furniture. What this person doesn't realize is *how* that chair was made. He or she has simply never done carving and doesn't realize the 'carving' is merely pressed on a machine.

"But when you hand someone a molding plane and you teach them to make a molded edge by hand, then it starts to fit together.

"I think that hands-on is very important. It leads to some brains-on, as questions emerge: 'What does this mean?' and 'Why are we doing it?' When we get to 'Is it appropriate to re-create the past?' and 'Are we doing this for our own egos or are we doing it for something larger?'—then we've begun to ask and consider the good questions."

In his book *The Brown Decades*, Lewis Mumford wrote: "The commonest axiom of history is that every generation revolts against its fathers and makes friends with its grand-fathers." Liebs cited this quote in his book, so I asked him, as a man who has written and lectured often about the work of his father's generation, if he wasn't an exception to Mumford's proposed rule.

"I don't think so."

He was thoughtful.

"I dispute that," he added agreeably. "I'd say as a historian, I don't love the father any more than the grandfather. I think I have an even-handed interest in beginning to look at any period of time—age alone is not a good rule of thumb.

"The best time to begin to conserve a place is when it is old enough to be out of vogue but young enough for its original design to be completely intact. Visual evidence, certain types of visual evidence, disappears very rapidly.

"Like now. Now's the time to look at the later American suburb. Historians are beginning to look at the 1920s and 1930s suburbs, but I think it's time to look at the 1950s suburbs. As historians, we should at least begin to collect materials or photograph them. We might not be able to understand them fully right now, but there are lots of things that are simply not going to be around when in the normal course historians get to them.

"I'm a relativist with all of this. I don't have absolutes. I think it's very important not to treat the environment in a monolithic way. If you do, you end up with whole gaps of time. There is a fairly standard and accepted restoration approach that asserts that if you are to restore, then the evidence should be there. If you don't have the evidence, then you're not restoring.

"But when you do restore—and the decision to restore is a separate issue—I think you run the risk of lobotomizing the past. Because to restore is not to deal with history. Restoration is often done out of people's prejudices for a certain type of design at a different period of time. Often to restore is a denial within a community of itself."

An example?

"It's an old one, but still the best. Newburyport, Massachusetts, was a town where they built great clipper ships. It has an incredible Colonial-period-to-pre-Civil War downtown. A whole part of it was lopped off by urban renewal in the late 1960s, but then it became a place where the early phase of adaptive use caught on. It went from urban renewal to preservation, as a lot of it was preserved. I think the town won an award for its pioneering reuse of early buildings.

"But it got to the point where every building was being cleaned, where the visual references in the town were limited to either pre-Civil War or the cute sign. The town was trying to be the past but really being the present.

"There's a luncheonette downtown in the middle of this, Fowles' News Store and Soda Shop. It has a Carrara-marble storefront that was put in right at the end of World War II. It was really well done, with a projecting marbleized sign.

"They cooked up a plan to Colonialize that. But there was an outcry of local residents saying that they felt that this place represented the imprint of their parents and grandparents. They recognized that a whole period of time had been denied in this town, that this familiar lunch place represented an important part of their lives. It was about the roar of the twentieth century, evoking the hope things modern represented in the Depression and during World War II. It was something they remembered.

"Ultimately it was restored and saved. They were even able to find the craftsmen—not somebody playing at craftsman years later—but the actual craftsmen who knew how to crumple up newspaper and use it to roll paint on the sign to make it look like marble. So there's an example of where a conscious attempt was made not to lobotomize the visual evidence.

"But there isn't any 'they.' This isn't some awful conspiracy. It's just what happens when you're working in the built environment. You're dealing with real estate, you're working with people's values.

"Again, you can't have one right way of doing things. There are many philosophical arguments, there are many philosophical approaches. Even if you think you have the 'right' way, it's sure to eliminate a lot of things. There needs to be a lot of ways to approach this.

"You also have to remember that, in a broad sense, different parts of the nation's heritage have been favored over others at different times in our history. You get a skewing of what people perceive as historic, and it changes over the years. The turn-of-the-century Colonial Revival is the classic example.

"Today's Victorian Revival in our suburbs is another skewing of history. Right now, ironically, you have twentieth-century American suburbs that are beginning to be Victorianized. The trickle-down of the restoration movement has affected a lot of new construction. And I can show you neighborhoods here where the integrity of the suburb and its original design is being Victorianized, both with new 'Victorian' houses and things like, you know, the iron porch railings are being taken out and replaced with spindly wooden Victorian posts and little sunburst decorations where they never were. I would maintain that what is going on will be fascinating in the future as cultural evidence."

A recurring concern of Liebs's is that we are creating a fictitious time that never was. But he's also worried about today's world, about how we will see it tomorrow.

"Right now we have the *Leave It to Beaver* neighborhoods, the Levittowns, the planned suburbs that are intact as cultural evidence. If we believe in subtraction, then we must believe, I suppose, in cordoning off whole areas and making them time-capsule zones. Then you won't have to subtract in the future. You can save the stuff and make sure it's around."

He laughed at that, perhaps a bit mischievously.

"But that won't happen," he added.

Liebs's talk of saving today's suburbs may seem a bit extreme coming from a preservationist. In fact, a prominent restoration professional once said to me, "Every movement needs a lunatic fringe, and for those of us in preservation, it's Chester." It was said jokingly, with a mix of affection and respect.

In contrast, after I shared this remark with another preservationist, she commented, "Well, there are those of us who think of him as the cutting edge." A third professional in the preservation field said to me, "Liebs has a philosophical position which everybody sees some truth in, but which he sees as gospel." Clearly, Liebs inspires strong feelings among the denizens of the restoration world.

But each of these characterizations is to the point. Liebs isn't afraid of being provocative. At times, he seems to take positions for the sake of argument or effect. On the other hand, I found him at times very persuasive. Yet it was his historical-cum-psychological argument that affected me most.

In Liebs's words: "We need to develop a sense of ourselves to preserve from the past enough to give us the context. Without those roots you can easily run away from yourself."

11
Four Private Possibilities

_____

Time the destroyer is time the preserver.
                    —*T. S. Eliot, "The Dry Salvages" (1943)*

For the preservationist, the ultimate challenge is the abandoned dwelling.

Molds and dust mites may be its only denizens, but a deserted house often appears, as if by some natural process, to have regressed in time. There seems almost to have been a ripening, in which an unidentified mechanism has enhanced the possibilities of the place.

Here follow four stories, true tales of houses found bereft of human habitation that have presented their owners with great opportunities.

Restored to its simple eighteenth-century elegance and framed by an open field and a copse of trees, the little mustard-colored Cape Cod house looks like a million dollars. Robert Herron bought it for one dollar in 1981.

Today, the house, located in Austerlitz, New York, looks like it was quite a bargain, but the building Bob Herron bought was little more than a shell scheduled for demolition. He had to arrange for it to be moved, then utterly reconstructed from foundation to roof.

Herron was born and brought up in Austerlitz. He returned there after working in a military hospital outside Washington, D.C., during World War II and going to college in Colorado. His life's work has been buying, selling, and collecting early American antiques.

While looking at his house one day, I asked him if he remembered it from his childhood. "I knew the son of the owners of the house," he said, "but when I bought it I hadn't been in the house since I was a kid." So the house Herron bought decades later was largely a mystery. "The parlor I'd only seen once when the boy's father died and he was laid out."

When he first visited the house as an adult, it had decorative Victorian shingling on the exterior. The original twelve-over-

A Polaroid Robert Herron took as his house was being moved. Note the Victorian shingling, subsequently removed to reveal early attributes of the house. *Robert Herron*

eight windows had been replaced with two-over-twos. There was an ell off the back with no foundation.

Still, he thought, the place did hold promise. The parlor had raised paneling around the fireplace (later, a matching chair rail and wainscoting were found around the rest of the room, buried beneath layers of wallboard). In the old kitchen, the hearth remained and, beneath a later wall covering, he found the bake oven. "Then I got interested," recalled Herron.

So he bought the place and began the process of moving the neglected house to his property about one mile away from its original site. "I thought I'd be able to restore it for $40,000 or $50,000," he said. "When I got to $50,000, I had a well, a septic system, and the house moved, but almost nothing done on the house itself."

He had his carpenters restore the original floor plan. At the front, there's the formal parlor (on the right) and a bed chamber (to the left). The rear in the main structure is the old kitchen (used today as a dining room) and a pantry. The shed addition off the dining room gives the house the shape of a Saltbox-style dwelling and houses a modern kitchen and bathroom. (Technically, the house isn't a Saltbox, however, as it has but one full story.) The upstairs of the main structure within the steeply pitched roof is the master bedroom and study.

Herron found one original window hidden in the coal bin and had it copied. Most of the original doors were still there but had been moved around, so more than a little detective work was necessary to reconstruct which went where.

Herron estimates that the house dates from between 1760 and 1790. The town graveyard has headstones with dates in the 1760s, and a very similar house nearby was built in 1790. Those facts established the range.

When he bought the house, it had no plumbing, electricity, or central heating. "We lowered the pantry ceiling four inches to hide the plumbing for the upstairs bathroom," Herron said. He also pointed out that the house is clear of obvious intrusions into its original fabric. At the same time, in place of the dirt floor and porous fieldstone walls of the original crawl space, the relocated house sits atop an insulated (poured-concrete) foundation containing plumbing, electrical service, and a central air-conditioning and heating system.

As is usually the case with such top-to-bottom restorations, numerous discoveries were made in Herron's house. Stenciling emerged on the parlor floor. Some unexplained wooden stubs were found in the wall over the front door. Only by accident, when browsing through *Early Domestic Architecture of Connecticut,* a classic 1924 book on New England-style houses, did Herron learn what the stubs had been for. The arc sawn into them was the continuation of what had been a sprung roof over the front door, probably a borrowing from Dutch-style dwellings. Ironically, though Austerlitz is in the Hudson River valley, where Dutch houses are common, the inspiration for the roof is thought to have traveled from Long Island to Connecticut and, finally, to Austerlitz, brought by settlers of English extraction.

One reason there was so much left to discover, Herron observed, is that the house was in the hands of people without

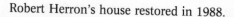
Robert Herron's house restored in 1988.

great financial means. "The thing about an old house," he said, "is that if people have had money, it's been modernized. With no money it's a mess, but it remains original."

Robert Herron's house sits squarer on its new foundation than it did before its move. The aged oak beams of its original frame now rest astride steel I beams. Little else about the house suggests that it is other than aged. When I visited one day to ask Bob Herron about its restoration, I was comfortable in a period wing chair. The rest of the furniture, too, dates from the eighteenth century. The fabrics, the colors, the accretion of details in the house made the past seem almost real. My host, glancing out a window, pointed out a red fox. It ran across an adjacent hayfield, oblivious to the passage of time.

Most houses that date from the first half of the nineteenth century have already been visited more than a few times by remodelers. Occasionally, usually in out-of-the-way rural areas, there are houses that have been empty for decades and that have remained basically unchanged.

The Trapp house in Oak Hill, New York, is one. It has been given something resembling foster care in recent years, but has yet to receive a full measure of preservation attention.

Located in the Catskill Mountains, the house was built by a successful local merchant family. It's a small but elegant brick structure that, when I saw it, was owned by an antiques dealer from a nearby town. He didn't live there. No one has for more than fifty years. But he gave me a tour.

We walked around the exterior of the building first, and noted that some of the brickwork needed repointing (that is, the joints between the bricks needed new mortar where the old, lime-base mortar had crumbled to dust). For the same reason, one chimney had collapsed into the roof. The front doorway was covered with a layer of black plastic to protect it from the elements until proper restoration could be undertaken. My tour guide pulled the covering aside and a picture-perfect Federal entrance emerged, with an elliptical fan sash in a sunrise configuration.

The front entry of the Trapp house in Oak Hill, New York. Though unrestored, the delicate fan sash, thin pilasters and sidelights, and eight-panel door are the chief display on the house's façade.

Since the front door was sealed, we went around to the rear entrance. A door in the pantry led into a kitchen with a large fireplace and a bake oven. The wall surfaces were all grain-painted. Although well over a century old, the graining work was in perfect condition.

As we walked through the house, I felt like a blind person in an unfamiliar room. We had no light other than a few streaks of the sun's rays that shot through narrow gaps in the shuttered windows. As my eyes adjusted, outlines and shapes appeared.

I realized then that it's not a bad way to get a first look at a house. Since the memory tends to dim details anyway, perhaps it is an advantage to see relatively few of them and be less distracted from the whole.

I noticed the floors. They had never been varnished or finished with any sealer. Some were still covered with the tattered narrow strips of early Victorian carpeting. We walked up the center staircase and something seemed strange about it. Only upon reaching the top did I realize that the staircase—and the whole house—seemed reduced in scale. The banister on the landing that looked back down the stairs was only about two feet high.

The house is truly a little gem. The owner at the time believed the architect was Philip Hooker, a Federal architect of note from Albany, less than fifty miles away. Whether or not Hooker was responsible, the house was surely the work of an informed designer. More significant to me, however, was that there were very few mysteries to uncover: the original was virtually all there. Uncompromised by time, it hadn't been removed or obscured by remodelings.

No one had substantially renovated the house since its construction. Each downstairs room had one electric light at its center but no outlets. There was no bathroom. The kitchen had a hand pump, but no modern appliances. Stovepipe sleeves led directly into the old chimneys, and floor vents allowed the heat to rise to the bedrooms upstairs. Those signs of wood or coal stove installations were the only hints of change in the heating system. The original fireplaces were all in place. The mantels had been repainted. Close examination revealed the original marbleized finish beneath the peeling paint.

The Oak Hill house is a document in itself, a rare experience that richly deserves preservation. It was sold once again in 1989; its future is still unclear.

Some of us imagine we can read into the clothes people wear something of their personalities; in occasional instances, houses can be interpreted in the same way. Enoch Robinson's house in the suburban town of Somerville, Massachusetts, is so unusual that I came away from a tour of it with a sense of his personality. He's been dead for about a hundred years, but once you see his house, you immediately get a strong sense of the man.

A Boston hardware manufacturer, he was an individualist. He resigned from the Masons and the Odd Fellows when, in his judgment, those organizations became too popular. He had something of the same reaction when the Greek Revival house he had built for himself, complete with an octagonal cupola on top, was copied by a neighbor. Far from being flattered, Robinson immediately sold that house and proceeded to build himself another, one that has never been duplicated by anyone.

At the time of the Robinson house's construction, the octagonal-house style had had a brief vogue. Those houses had multiple flat sides (usually eight, as the name suggests, though some six-sided variants were built). The popularity of the octagon style resulted from the success of a book titled *A Home for All* by Orson Fowler, another Victorian eccentric.

Though there is a distant resemblance to Fowler's octagon designs, Robinson's house had no flat sides; it was and is literally round. Round buildings were not unheard of at the time. A brief vogue in round barns produced, among other buildings, the cleverly laid-out barn at the Shaker community in Hancock, Massachusetts. In England, the same trend had been seen a century earlier. But most round buildings are made of stone or brick, whereas the Round House, as Robinson's house has come to be called, is wooden.

The frame of the house consists of wooden planks. Rather than being applied side to side to a framework of vertical wooden members, the boards are stacked like bricks on top of one another. While no record has been discovered that proves Robinson knew of Fowler's writing, the method of piled-board construction was almost certainly a borrowing from Fowler, since in the first edition of *A Home for All*, published in 1848, he recommended the technique. However, Fowler was advo-

A turn-of-the-century photograph of the Round House in Somerville, Massachusetts. Its shape and elaborate Victorian window architraves lend it the appearance of an elegant wedding cake. *Robert Adam*

cating the use of straight-cut boards, whereas in the Round House an arc was cut onto the outside edge of every board. The result was a solid, curved wall of wood.

If the Round House sounds a bit like a log cabin, think again. The only thing this house has in common with a rough-hewn cabin is the impressive quantity of trees that gave their lives to build it. Decorated with carved window architraves, this is an elegant, high-style dwelling. The pine clapboards that make up the siding are curved, with their ends wedged beneath vertical moldings.

There is evidence in the house of an early indoor bathtub, probably a part of a gravity water system. An investigation of the frame of the building reveals a complete set of rafters between the second and third stories. This suggests that the third story was not original; it was added perhaps ten years after the first and second stories were constructed.

Robinson's house once sat isolated in rural Somerville with a view of the city and harbor of Boston. An oddity in its time, the Round House is certainly one now. While it was lived in as recently as the early 1980s, today it sits uninhabited, cold and damp, awaiting what would be an expensive restoration.

Its location is a liability, its original site now little more than a shrunken piece of a complicated suburban puzzle. The house is surrounded by two-family dwellings. Many of them are Queen Anne houses that arose as the last century drew to a close. Most of them are sided with homogenizing aluminum or vinyl.

They date from different decades and their sites couldn't be more different, yet the Enoch Robinson house and the Trapp house in Oak Hill share, at least for the moment, the same fate. While both have been owned in recent years by people sympathetic to the historic nature and value of those buildings, neither has yet benefited from more than custodial care.

"When we took possession of the house, the fireplace was bricked up and for many years we simply used a stove in cold weather. But it had always been my intense desire to have an open fire with blazing logs."

So wrote Mary Medbury MacKaye in 1923, in an unpublished manuscript. Titled "Chronicles of the Cottage," the little memoir was, the title page asserts, "written for her dear children."

When she spoke of her desire for an open fire to a family friend, Frank Lawton, he told her, "I know that there used to be a fireplace. . . . I am quite sure I remember my father speaking of the fact that he had sold the fire frame, which had originally stood there, for old iron many years ago." A fire frame is a metal firebox, common in the second quarter of the nineteenth century, which was built into a masonry fireplace to extend it out into the room, enhancing efficiency.

"Well," Mrs. MacKaye responded, "we must find another fire frame because I am determined to have my crackling logs."

The "Chronicles" continue: "Then began a search which lasted nearly two years. He not only looked everywhere in the region all about, but he also wrote to several places in regard to a frame, because this fire frame was smaller than the usual one. But all to no avail. One day while I was in New York . . . I received a letter from Frank beginning 'Eureka,' emphasized by a dozen exclamation points. Then followed the story of the successful ending of our search.

"He had been taking one of [his] long tramps over the fields. The snow was still on the ground. Presently [he] found himself beside an old dump heap. Frank, in accordance with his usual custom whenever he encountered anything so fraught with treasure possibilities, began to poke about with his cane among the debris. In a few minutes he had unearthed an old piece of rusty iron. The shape of the iron aroused his interest and further 'pokings' soon disclosed that it was a part of a fire frame. Its size interested him still more as it was unusually small, and the thought occurred 'Can this be a part of Betsy Kelsey's fire frame?' Lo and behold! when he unearthed the whole thing it proved to be a complete fire frame! Well, to make a long story short, it was found to fit the parlor fireplace exactly."

When Mary Medbury MacKaye wrote her "Chronicles of the

Cottage," she was an old woman, recording the history of the little house in Shirley Center, Massachusetts, in which she and her family had spent many happy summers. The children for whom she wrote the book included her sons Percy, a playwright and poet, and Benton, a naturalist and outdoorsman best remembered for his role in helping establish the Appalachian Trail. But the history of the cottage starts earlier.

The house was built for a maiden lady named Betsy Kelsey in 1835. The date is established by the original deed, handwritten on a tattered and yellowed sheet of paper, framed in the entryway today. The house had two small rooms downstairs, a parlor and a kitchen. Upstairs there was a bedroom and a workroom, where Miss Kelsey made her living braiding hat straw, as had Emerson Bixby's daughters. Given the overall shape, proportion, moldings, mantels, and other details, it is obviously a vernacular Greek Revival house.

After Miss Kelsey's death, the house was owned for more than eighty years by the MacKaye family. An aunt owned it first; then it became the property of Steele MacKaye, the patriarch of the MacKaye family (and Mary's husband, who, among other distinctions, held a patent for the theatre folding chair). The house was too small for the MacKayes, so during the 1890s additions were attached to the building, nearly doubling its original size.

Benton MacKaye lived in the house off and on until his death in 1975 at age ninety-six. The house stood empty until 1977, when a surviving niece of MacKaye's called a local man of her acquaintance named Robert Adam. She asked if he would like to be the caretaker, and told him she was planning to establish a MacKaye museum there. Adam decided to have a look.

In his early twenties, Robert Adam went to work teaching in a trade school for secondary school students. After a dozen years of spending more time dealing with hormones than hardwood, he left. He tried selling his skills directly to the consumer, but the insulation contractor for whom he went to work sold the company to a competitor, who proceeded to lay off all the employees. Then he found the perfect job.

Adam went back to teaching, this time amid the Victorian brick buildings in Boston's North End. Adam teaches preservation carpentry at the North Bennet Street School to students well beyond secondary school. When I visited during the 1987–88 academic year (it's a thirty-six-week program) his students included an engineer, an architect, and an urban planner. Each pays a tuition of $7,000 to learn about pre-twentieth-century architectural styles and the tools and equipment needed for working on old structures.

The school catalogue promises that students will get to work on a pre-twentieth-century building, and it was Robert Adam who showed me the Robinson house; he and his class were stabilizing it. However, it is the MacKaye house that has benefited the most from his restoration energies.

When he first looked at the place, it was badly deteriorated. It was so damp that the wallpaper was peeling off the walls. The roof had a large hole in it, and the house was chockablock with books and Victorian furniture. Although Benton Mac-Kaye had worked for the TVA and its electrification program in the 1930s, he hadn't wanted modern utilities at the cottage. When a town water system had been installed in the 1940s, a line was brought into the tiny stone basement, but was sealed off. The house Adam inspected had no electricity or central heating, and its primitive plumbing relied upon a backyard cistern.

"It was a house I didn't want," Robert Adam recalled. "It was late, and back then I thought I wanted an eighteenth-century house." The offer to live there was appealing, but he couldn't quite imagine doing a vast amount of work on a house he didn't own. Somehow he found himself making a $7,500 offer that he was sure would be refused. It wasn't and the house was his.

"Before I moved in, I wanted a record of what was here," Adam went on. He took roll after roll of film. "My next concern was to get it cleared out so I could work on the place." Benton's books and papers went to the library at Dartmouth College. Other papers and goods went to the Shirley Historical Society. Members of the family took some, too, and much of the rest was auctioned. Adam held a brief ceremony to spread Benton MacKaye's ashes. They had been left unclaimed, at the time of his death two years before, in their urn at the funeral home. Then the reconstruction of the house began.

"For the most part," says Adam, "I felt a responsibility to keep the character of the house à la MacKaye." Though the original building had been built more than a century and a half earlier for Betsy Kelsey, the cottage was clearly of a later time. The house was a document to the energy and activity of the MacKayes. So in painting the kitchen Adam chose a color scheme from the MacKaye era. He installed an enormous gas-and-coal cookstove and a soapstone sink consistent with the 1890 MacKaye habitation.

Few of us have the materials he had at his disposal, from MacKaye family photographs to the other sources his research uncovered, including surviving relatives and neighbors. Houses that have had the benefit of a storyteller like Mary Medbury MacKaye are rare indeed. In fact, the parlor in the cottage is still filled with furniture from the MacKayes' years in the house, including a handsome Empire secretary of mahogany and a Chippendale mirror. Most appropriate of all is a large primitive painting of Mary herself and her siblings as small children.

Robert Herron and Robert Adam have spent years studying and restoring their houses. Unlike the professionals we met earlier in this book, they have been concerned with following their instincts to be true to the actual past of their houses at the same time as they adapt the dwellings for their own personal uses.

They are different from the likes of most of the cultural conservators in this book. Most likely, if the Enoch Robinson and Trapp houses are to be restored, it won't be by an organization or a group of restoration professionals; rather the task will be taken on by people like Herron and Adam, men and women who wish to live a contemporary home life in a historic structure. We can only hope that such theoretical restorers approach those two structures with the good sense and intelligence of Robert Herron and Robert Adam. But another thread binds these four houses.

The four houses offer remarkable visual and physical evidence of the kind of patience preservation requires. Restoration work doesn't always have to be done today. Not that there isn't an immediacy about certain projects; there often is a need to act now. But preservationists must exercise a clarity of vision that allows for blending yesterday's qualities with today's resources and skills—and, in turn, with an understanding of how to serve our obligations to tomorrow, too.

Preservation isn't merely today's answer to renovation problems. Rather preservation, unlike some easy answers that are abandoned almost as quickly as they are offered, must focus on the future to nearly the same degree it emphasizes the past.

To me, the theme that links the four houses in this chapter is conveyed by T. S. Eliot's line: "Time the destroyer is time the preserver." His context was entirely apart from preservation, of course, but it is the allusory way of poetry to suit other, unanticipated schemes.

Eliot's words capture the ultimate irony of each of the four houses described in this chapter. They are indeed fine houses, all of a certain age yet not subjected to the willful destruction of recent unthinking renovations. By virtue of neglect they have survived. Had they been "cared for" in a time when restoration and renovation were essentially interchangeable terms, the opportunities for preservation later would have been less or even negligible.

All four houses, examined from a future time remote from our own, may well be seen to have shared the same fortuitous fate. The phenomenon might be termed the irony of neglect. It allowed these houses to be preserved into the late twentieth century, not because people cared for them, but because people did not.

12
The Future
Requires a Past

—————

Every art that finds a penetrating pathway to the mind, and whose foundations are profoundly set, must needs have precedent and parallel, ancestors and heirs.
—Geoffrey Scott, The Architecture of Humanism *(1914)*

Very few things touched by the human hand outlast the hand that touches them.

Think about that a moment. It's true, isn't it? What of the childhood furniture you knew, your toys, your first radio or television, your bicycle?

There's an essential cruelty, it would seem, to the human hand, and not only to the hand of the child. Cars, furniture, clothing, and a great variety of everyday objects are regarded as disposable. Americans in particular are guilty of such callousness in most phases of their lives. Look at it from a reverse angle: How many objects, small or large, do you own today that were the possessions of your parents or other, earlier ancestors?

This book portrays individuals who have chosen to obey principles that run counter to this observed reality. They believe that it is possible to treat objects, especially old ones, with some respect and care. These people assign a significance to old things, buildings in particular.

Carpentier, Curtis, Labine, Lyle, and the rest have much in

common with one another, yet there is no single profile that
fits them. They're not all from small towns or a single geographical region. Their places of birth include a hamlet in Minnesota, Kansas City, urban and rural Massachusetts, New York
City, and even Oregon. They range in age from their mid-thirties
to their sixties. No two of them would be likely to perform the
same function at a given restoration. Some push paper, others
are more comfortable pushing hand planes.

Aside from a fascination with antique architecture, there
seems to be only one common denominator. Each of these men
made friends with old things as a young person, whether the
objects befriended were photos in a book, drawings of Monticello, or a Model T. As with my boots, it was not later than
the teenage years that, in almost every case, a father, mother,
or grandfather introduced the old objects.

Unfortunately, that doesn't really tell us much. It's almost a
cliché that most of one's interests in life are discovered before
the age of consent, often at the behest of one's elders.

Yet the very diversity of these cultural conservators, as well
as other factors, leads me to think that they are representative
of a population far greater than just the relatively small coterie
that works at preservation tasks. I have also come to believe
that there is today a climate congenial to architectural preservation.

I date the present preservationist era as having begun in the
winter of 1963. It was then that Philip Johnson and other prominent members of New York's architectural community picketed
to draw attention to the imminent destruction of Pennsylvania
Station.

Sadly, seven lonely picketers trudging through the snow were
not enough, as the building was destroyed. It was an event that,
in architecture critic Paul Goldberger's words, constituted "the
single greatest act of architectural vandalism the city [of New
York] has ever seen."

More happily, the late 1960s and early 1970s proved to be

watershed years for preservation. In the aftermath of the demolition of Penn Station, New York became the first major city
to pass a strong landmark ordinance, creating the Landmarks
Preservation Commission in 1965. One of its early acts was to
designate another railroad terminus, Grand Central Station, as
a protected landmark. The Commission did so none too soon,
since, in 1968, the building's owner, the Penn Central Railroad,
sought permission to alter the building radically in order to
construct a 5,000-foot-high tower on top.

Having been designated as an official landmark, the station
was the beneficiary of a body of law that guided the ensuing
confrontation. It still required ten years, a widely publicized
fight led by Jacqueline Kennedy Onassis, and a trip to the
Supreme Court. This time the public and the courts acted, and
Grand Central Station was preserved. In the process, the Court
established that "states and cities may enact land-use restrictions or controls to enhance the quality of life by preserving
the character and desirable aesthetic features of a city . . ." That
is, individual buildings and neighborhoods can be protected
lawfully.

Not only New Yorkers but a geographically diverse spectrum
of Americans experienced a change of mind during those years.
We have come to regard older buildings differently, and not
solely because our judicial system validated such feelings. And
it isn't only magnificent mansions, monuments, and public edifices that draw our concern and attention. This historical consciousness—and, just as important, *conscience*—now
influences virtually everyone who owns, visits, or is concerned
with older buildings.

In the 1950s, we obliterated whole city blocks under the
guise of "urban renewal"; in the case of individual structures
during that earlier era, the notion of gutting and replacing the
old was synonymous with "new and improved." Those
approaches have been superseded in many instances by a desire
to preserve as we go about making our spaces suit our needs.
The nature of the debate has changed. In general, it isn't so
much the all-powerful and moneyed developers versus the pres-

ervationists, nor is the opposition between "scrap it" and "save it" for the homeowner. As often as not, almost everyone is on the side of saving the older structure, in whole or in part, and the question is not whether to do it but how.

Chester Liebs put it another way when he said, "There isn't any 'they.' This isn't some awful conspiracy. It's just what happens when you're working in the built environment."

Remember, too, Clem Labine's words: "The concept of preservation has a lot of political capital inherent in it." He also added, "We've gotten to a point where a politician has to think twice about opposing a preservation project. That's an incredible step."

Increasingly, preservationists are finding themselves working from within the system rather than without. As well as finding employment in the traditional niches at universities and museums, professional historic preservationists (distinguished by degrees earned in academic programs established in the last twenty-five years) are beginning to forge a new infrastructure in which preservationists are assuming regulatory roles in government. Others are going to work as independent consultants to commercial and real estate concerns. Preservation is a young business, but for many it has become exactly that, a business.

This has come to mean that more often than not, at least in the case of public buildings, voices for preservation will be raised when a building project is being contemplated. Consideration is routinely given in most cases to what is already there in the face of the ubiquitous and seemingly involuntary urge to destroy and begin anew. As Labine said, it is an incredible step.

Preservation may have become a potent public force, but countless skirmishes have been and continue to be fought. Some of them occur on surprising fronts.

While visiting a dairy farm a few years ago, I was given a tour of a new barn. It was a pole barn—that is, its foundation consisted of concrete footings at roughly eight-foot intervals. Resting on the footings were a series of vertical members (the "poles") to which the walls and roof were attached.

The owner of the efficient new barn told me its builder had boasted upon finishing the building, "You know, Ken, this will last you a generation."

Something is terribly wrong with that sentiment. Until the post-World War II building boom, barns and houses were built with a sense of permanence in mind. Since then, we have adopted more and more temporary building materials. Asphalt shingles, vinyl and aluminum sidings, and a variety of plastic products all require replacement in a generation or less. Compare that with, say, an 1850 house which has its original slate roof and pine siding.

We are about to enter another age, one in which we will be forced to consider matters of permanence and the ecological impact of the let's-rebuild-it-in-twenty-years tactic. We are beginning to recognize that a spendthrift approach to our resources won't work. It creates more waste than we know what to do with (witness our waste-disposal problems nationwide), and we are starting to accept that our resources are finite. Unlike that barn builder, some people are thinking about houses new and old within a longer time frame.

It has been estimated that it takes sixteen times more energy to construct a building than to operate it for a year. So, in a sense, if you use an existing building rather than constructing a new one, you get sixteen years of energy conservation by taking advantage of its "embodied energy." There is good ecological sense in preserving structures already standing.

These are the forces in opposition: The spendthrift, the disposable—the pole-barners, if you will—are meeting up with an emerging coalition of loosely allied conservationists. Some of these people call themselves preservationists, others are environmentalists or even entrepreneurs. But there is an ever more apparent commonality of interest when it comes to concerns about conserving energy, ecological balance, and the built environment.

In the opening pages of this book, I offered a glib pairing of categorizations, the "savers" and the "throwers." We see the same opposing factions doing battle daily in the wilderness and in the cities, in the United States and the Third World, at sea and in the sky. We know one side as the cultural conservators, the preservationists, or, for want of a better umbrella term, the "savers." They are confronting the throwers, the pole-barners, the advocates of change, those who think that progress will solve our problems.

Understanding the nature of the confrontation is important, both in appreciating the advances of preservation and in helping us think about how we are to live in our world in the future. One way to consider the matter is to examine the word "progress." It cropped up in talking with several of the preservationists in this book and seems to be at the heart of the opposition between the savers and the throwers.

When asked about his notions of progress, John Mesick remarked, "I don't believe in progress—each generation has to enter the lists anew."

Clem Labine told me, "I think we're getting much more humble, much more careful about how we get behind progress."

Most people I spoke to in writing this book share those sentiments. In fact, there's a certain unanimity among these men. They categorize progress as a false icon.

"Progress" is another one of those words, like "cute" and "conservative," that have undergone changes in their meaning. It was first used to describe physical movement, usually a journey. From the beginning it had echoes of moving forward, of advancing. Only gradually did progress come to be synonymous with improvement.

Later still it took on other, more political connotations. People who described themselves as progressives advocated change, improvement, or reform; this was in opposition to those who wanted to maintain things as they were—that is, to conserve.

I believe progress is a largely political notion and cannot be trusted. As historian C. Vann Woodward pointed out in his book *The Future of the Past,* "progressive historians [have] demanded that history be written in accordance with some vision of the future . . ." Hand in hand with progress, then, there too often comes a distortion of the past in service to a political vision of the future.

To believe that progress offers a solution to the social, environmental, or other ills of our time is wrongheaded. Visits to the countless ghost towns in the West, once booming and brimming with confidence and optimism at what the future would bring, offer a certain perspective on how unreliable progress can be.

Growth and development, we now realize, are not always beneficial. Unbridled economic growth may produce wealth, but too often that wealth is of a temporal kind, of which the bubble of the junk-bond market is the most obvious recent example. The price of profits can be great, including damage to the ecosystem, growth in the gap between the haves and the have-nots, and other long-term costs.

We simply aren't always moving forward. For every problem we solve we come up against a new one, either of our own making or one previously unnoticed. It isn't that I lack confidence in the future. On the contrary, I am by nature optimistic, choosing to think that tomorrow can indeed provide us with opportunities to improve our lives and our world. But in order for that to be so, I believe absolutely in the need to regard the past and its lessons for what they are: a body of experience that can guide us. Rejecting the past or the present for the future is reckless and unnecessary. Distorting the past or our expectations of the future is needless and perhaps even dangerous.

So we are back, once again, to the opposing forces. The savers and the throwers, the preservationists and the pole-barners, the conservatives and the progressives. I cannot plant myself squarely in either camp, though emotionally I seem to have some kind of autonomic rooting interest in the savers.

But my intellect tells me the commonweal will best be served by seeking some kind of balance. In general, the lessons of the past are not incompatible with our learning of the future; we aren't asked to take an all-or-nothing position. A clarity of vision, both forward and backward, is a necessity.

Robert Frost observed that writing free verse was like playing tennis without a net. In the same way, I would argue, abandoning thousands of years of architectural lessons is more than audacious, it is presumptuous in the extreme. Yet it is among the claims of modern architecture to have left behind the pallid and pedestrian past.

The experience of the last few decades has, however, left many of us feeling that a great deal has been lost. Modern architecture has consistently failed to satisfy the human desire for a sense of place, of comfort, of that hard-to-define notion of home.

I don't believe for a moment that when Louis Sullivan wrote about form following function he ever dreamt of banishing all echoes of man's architectural past from his or anybody else's work. His greatest buildings are all rich with allusions to classical, Gothic, and Romanesque works. Yet his words have been used to justify the most mechanical and unappealing of modernist structures.

Our century has witnessed the full swing of the pendulum. The opening decades of this century saw the construction of a range of buildings in neo-classical styles. They were built within a crafts tradition that produced fine workmanship and with materials that could be expected to endure. But at some point, the historicalness became unimportant, as the progressive pendulum swung. Short-term profit came to outweigh long-term practicalities. The passing fancy of contemporary tastes suddenly dwarfed the developments of millennia. The great traditions of Western architecture were abandoned almost overnight. In their stead, buildings of temporary materials were constructed with characterless moldings, in shapes and configurations that often proved less than functional. They were and are artless structures.

Compare them with the structures with which the preservationists in this book are concerned. In Thomas Jefferson's time, a man regarded himself as wealthy if he had a large house filled with fine furnishings and containing a substantial library. The house was intended to attract the eye of the passerby, and to provide pleasure to its owner each and every day. And it did. We've seen numerous examples of that in the preceding chapters.

In contrast, a look at most new construction is to understand that we really don't care much about how our houses look. No self-respecting builder of an earlier century would have dreamt of presenting the carriage house or barn as the principal façade. Yet today even houses of impressive design are often displayed garage-first to the visitor. To my way of thinking, being confronted by yawning garage doors instead of the front of a house is rather like being greeted by someone with his mouth open, offering you a view of his dental work.

All too many modern houses lack detail. They are usually asymmetrical, patternless, and textureless. Too often there is little or no evidence of craftsmanship, with prefabricated materials applied with a minimum of imagination or skill.

Yet we cannot assign the blame to the machinery or mass-production methods, as so much that we admire about Victorian architecture arrived from the factory prefabricated. The mass-produced house today leaves one with the ever present feeling that the finish work was executed with more of a consciousness of the next job than of doing this one well enough so that it would make sense to hang around for a few pats on the back.

The sorry truth is that the experience of the last fifty years has led intelligent people to realize that if an existing building of a certain age is to be replaced with a new one, then, given the quality of materials and workmanship today, the new one will almost certainly be less worthy. That's a nearly universal judgment, even if you banish aesthetics from the argument.

The Preservationist's Progress—that is, the journey, the pilgrimage, if you will, that these cultural conservators have been on for some years—is not solely about recapturing the old. Old in and of itself is not necessarily desirable; it is the qualities of style and craftsmanship that distinguish it.

One reason for the search is to understand—to comprehend

how and why certain things were done and the complex inter-relationships of technology, culture, taste, and basic human needs and desires. Another reason has to do with the continuing appeal of the sort of beauty that some buildings offer.

There's an economic factor, too; there always is in our world. In the case of private homes, a general understanding has been reached among homeowners and real estate agents alike that using a house's history effectively—rather than striving to deny or to erase it—is to enhance one's investment.

There are small indications that we may be able to position ourselves more wisely with respect to our architectural past. Thousands of restoration professionals are out there, respond-ing to a demand from individual and corporate clients who want to respect the original qualities of their buildings. Design-ers are exploring historical styles in new construction. Our streetscapes are enhanced by the proper treatment being given to historic structures and, to some degree, by a renewed interest in architectural style, in form for its own sake.

For me, though, the wandering into history that our pres-ervationists have embarked upon—and that millions of us have at least a passing interest in sharing—has another virtue, too. Looking backward enables us to appreciate time as more than a point and even more than as a time line.

Time is precious, and we must not try to think of this moment or any other as a frozen single instant but as part of an endless string of images. Like the good chess player who always must think a half dozen moves ahead at all times, we must consider the changes that will result from this move or that. We would do well to contemplate as well the first game we played and what our last one might be like.

One day in the summer of 1988, I took a hike in Adirondack Park. The terrain was rugged, with a dense undergrowth that provided cover to countless wild animals. Deer and bear are hunted there every fall.

I left the footpath and made my way through the forest for

several miles. I surprised an owl on the limb of a tall hemlock, and saw the big-bodied bird fly away almost soundlessly. I could imagine my surroundings were a primeval wilderness like that Daniel Boone and the other frontiersmen faced. Modern times seemed incomprehensibly far away.

I picked up a trail, and at one point it broke into a clearing and a long valley spread before me. Suddenly, for a moment, I thought the sky was falling. With a roar peculiar to the jet age, a B-52 lumbered into view at an altitude of some five hundred feet. Its giant shadow seemed to fly through me, shading me for an instant from the summer sun. Later I learned that the Strategic Air Command was practicing bombing runs, as it has done off and on for more than twenty years in the Adirondacks.

That trail was a few miles from Essex, the little town where this book began with the Ralph Hascall house. The juxtaposition of the B-52 and the town made me think, and it wasn't because the immense jet was scary or even irritating. I'm awed and thrilled by aircraft, especially the behemoths that seem too big ever to take flight.

Unwelcome as it might have seemed in the middle of my mountainside reverie, that B-52 represented to me the pure and undeniable power of the present. At times, we try to immerse ourselves in the past—I know I do, and if you've gotten this far in this book, you probably share the same yearning, at least occasionally. Yet we all know that it is ultimately unattainable.

Even at Sturbridge we can't really pretend the clock has stopped. Paying visitors push baby carriages made of space-age materials, and the Villagers, despite their period attire, go home at sundown to their microwaves and satellite dishes.

The changes are undeniable and unending. New generations of students have been arriving at the Academical Village for nearly two centuries. But don't think for a minute that the place is truly the same from one generation to the next.

The simple truth is that we have no more chance of capturing and bottling any given time—today or yesterday—than I did of plucking that B-52 from the sky with a butterfly net. On the other hand, the presence of the jet only made the hidden valley amid those rugged peaks all the more wonderful. The initial shock gave way to a recognition that times can collide and yet be one.

I have come to believe that it is the role of the preservationists profiled in this book to enable us to glimpse other times within the context of our own modern world. It is their insistence on the importance of the physical presence of the past, of its artifacts and architecture, that preserves something of that past.

The preservationists provide us with a range of snapshots of the past, which bring us to some understanding and appreciation of earlier eras. I believe the value of that must not be underestimated. After all, our ability to appreciate history as the passage of time helps makes us human.

Notes on Sources

———

In researching and writing this book, I have relied upon numerous interviews and a wide range of written materials. The interviewing demonstrated that people are likely to be generous with their time and opinions when they are discussing matters about which they care. Almost everyone I asked for help offered it unreservedly and in most cases with a certain passion for the subject at hand.

I confirmed another pet notion of mine, too. There's nothing under the sun that hasn't had something written about it. Thus, I must acknowledge my debt not only to the interviewees but to printed sources as well. Both are cited in the chapter-by-chapter notes that follow.

1. Cultural Conservatism
The only source for the coffin story is family lore, but for material about Shays's Rebellion, I've drawn upon several sources, in particular *History of the Town of Hubbardston* (Hubbardston, Mass., 1881). Santayana's famous words are from his *The Life of Reason* (1905); Henry James's words, here taken slightly out of context, appeared in his *Hawthorne* (1879).

2. An Architectural Assay

Among those who have talked to me about Essex are Robert Hammerslag, Lauren Murphy, John Mesick, Chester H. Liebs, and Philip C. Marshall. For the whos and whats and whens of the Hascall house history, I drew upon the Historic Structure Report (unpublished) prepared by Dale Clark, Colin Fink, and Janice Peden. My source for the material on Essex's history was *Essex: An Architectural Guide* (Essex, N.Y.: ECHO, 1986). Other ECHO materials, including the *Echo Diary* and the minutes of its monthly directors meetings, were also invaluable in understanding Essex today.

3. The Admirable Craftsman

Donald G. Carpentier, the so-called Squire of Eastfield Village, was not only the subject but also the most valuable source for this chapter. The stories here are drawn largely from those he has told me and what I have learned in frequent visits to the Village.

William McMillen, too, taught me much both in East Nassau and on his home turf at the Richmondtown Restoration on Staten Island, New York. Perhaps a dozen or more of the Eastfield Irregulars have also shared with me their recollections. The quote from Morgan Phillips appeared in *The New York Times* on July 10, 1980.

The play *The Admirable Crichton* (1902) was written by James Matthew Barrie, later the author of *Peter Pan*.

4. The Village Historian

John Curtis on numerous occasions answered my questions and guided my tours of both his own home and the Bixby house. His guidance and considered words were crucial to this chapter, though in writing about the Bixby house, I must acknowledge a key documentary source, an unpublished study prepared by John Worrel for Old Sturbridge Village called "Life in the Countryside: The Bixby Family Moves from Barre Four Corners into Our Mill Neighborhood." The main source for facts about the evolution of Old Sturbridge Village was *The Wells Family* by

Ruth Dyer Wells, a privately printed family biography (Southbridge, Mass., 1979).

For many of the facts and details regarding the restoration of his home, I also have drawn upon Curtis's extraordinary documentation, the three, thick ring binders packed with photos, hundreds of pages of carefully typed and articulately rendered notes, drawings, and other materials.

The Shingle Style and the Stick Style: Architectural Theory and Design from Downing to the Origins of Wright, by Vincent J. Scully, Jr. (New Haven: Yale University Press, 1955; rev. ed., 1971), provided much of the factual information in the discussion of the birth of the Colonial Revival and Messrs. McKim, Mead, White, and Bigelow. I also found stimulating reading in the pages of Oswald Spengler's *The Decline of the West* (1926) and a number of Lewis Mumford's writings, including *Sticks and Stones* (1924), *The Brown Decades* (1931), and *Technics and Civilization* (1934). In the same vein, I found myself absorbed by several of John Ruskin's books, in particular *The Stones of Venice* (and its chapter "The Nature of Gothic") and *The Seven Lamps of Architecture* (1853 and 1848, respectively).

For the discussion of "paper hangings," I relied upon *Wallpaper in New England* by Richard C. Nylander, Elizabeth Redmond, and Penny J. Sander, with essays by Abbot Lowell Cummings and Karen A. Guffey (Boston: Society for the Preservation of New England Antiquities, 1986).

For this chapter and those that follow, the material about the evolution of the American house was drawn from many sources. Among them were *Early American Architecture: From the First Colonial Settlements to the National Period,* by Hugh Morrison (New York: Dover, 1987; original edition, 1952); *The Framed Houses of Massachusetts Bay: 1625–1725,* by Abbot Lowell Cummings (Cambridge, Mass.: Harvard University Press, 1979); Talbot Hamlin's *Greek Revival Architecture in America* (New York: Dover, 1944); James Marston Fitch, *American Building 1: The Historical Forces That Shaped It* (2nd ed.; Boston: Houghton Mifflin, 1966); and *American*

Building 2: The Environmental Forces That Shaped It (2nd ed.; Boston: Houghton Mifflin, 1972); *American Building: Materials and Techniques from the First Colonial Settlements to the Present,* by Carl W. Condit (Chicago: University of Chicago Press, 1968, 1982); *History of Building,* by Jack Bowyer (2nd ed.; London: Granada, 1973). Though necessarily abbreviated, this reading list could well constitute something of a basic syllabus for an introduction to the history of American architecture.

5. The Epochal Carrier

John Mesick made possible the research and writing of this chapter by granting an ongoing series of interviews and less formal conversations in person and by phone. James Murray Howard spent a morning with me touring the Academical Village and introducing me to the nuances of the restoration process there. He and Mary Helen Detmer showed me through Pavilion I.

My printed sources for this chapter included the Historic Structure Report on Pavilion I, as well as *The Lawn: A Guide to Jefferson's University,* by Pendleton Hogan (Charlottesville, Va.: University Press of Virginia, 1987). For details of the roof restoration, I drew upon both Mesick's account and an article titled "Reroofing a Landmark" in *The Architectural Record* (February 1989). I found additional material about Mesick, Cohen & Waite in the March–April 1989 issue of *Clem Labine's Traditional Building.*

The bibliography on Palladio is extensive, but it begins with his own *The Four Books of Architecture* (New York: Dover, 1965; original edition, 1570; original Isaac Ware edition, 1738). I drew upon *Andrea Palladio: The Complete Works,* by Lionello Puppi (New York: Rizzoli, 1973, 1986), as well as several other volumes.

In seeking to understand the pattern-book phenomenon, I learned much from Helen Park's classic "A List of Architectural Books Available in America Before the Revolution," (published in 1961 in the *Journal of the Society of Architectural His-*

torians) and Janice G. Schimmelman's *Architectural Treatises and Building Handbooks Available in American Libraries and Bookstores Through 1800* (Worcester, Mass.: American Antiquarian Society, 1986). Some of the reprints of the original pattern books were also invaluable, including Asher Benjamin's *The American Builder's Companion* (New York: Dover, 1969; original edition, 1827) and *The Architect, or Practical House Carpenter* (New York: Dover, 1988; original edition, 1830) and Minard Lafever's *The Beauties of Modern Architecture* (New York: Da Capo Press, 1968; original edition 1835).

6. The Victorian Merchant
Clem Labine has talked into my little black tape machine on several occasions. In addition to him, however, I have drawn upon other sources, including articles in *The New York Times* that appeared on August 18, 1977, and February 5, 1987.

In writing about Labine, I could not help but have in my mind hundreds of images and lessons from his publications, the *Old House Journal* and *Clem Labine's Traditional Building*. The article by Charles Howell appeared in *Traditional Building* in the March–April 1990 issue.

7. The Artist's Collector
I was helped here by Bruno Freschi, Thomas Monaghan, John O'Hern, Sara-Ann Briggs, and Julia Stokes. I'm indebted to the written literature as well. On Wright, the extensive bibliography includes dozens of volumes, but the books on which I drew included *Years with Frank Lloyd Wright: Apprentice to Genius,* by Edgar Tafel (New York: Dover, 1979), a volume rich with anecdote about Mr. Wright; *In the Nature of Materials: The Buildings of Frank Lloyd Wright 1887–1941,* by Henry-Russell Hitchcock (New York: Da Capo Press, 1942), a book on which Wright himself collaborated; *The Architecture of Frank Lloyd Wright: A Complete Catalog,* by William Allin Storrer (2nd ed., Cambridge, Mass.: MIT Press, 1974, 1978), a valuable survey of Wright's built designs; and the best biography to date, *Many Masks: A Life of Frank Lloyd Wight,* by Brendan

Gill (New York: Putnam, 1987). A thoughtful paper given by UCLA professor Thomas S. Hines ("The Search for Wright") at the July 1989 symposium titled "Wright: The Reality and Myth of Frank Lloyd Wright" also helped me better understand Wright the mythmaker.

In writing about Thomas Monaghan, I have drawn upon not only the facts and anecdotes he himself told me but a number of articles about him in the popular press, including those in *Gentlemen's Quarterly* (July 1989), *Time* (April 4, 1988), and *Parade* (June 11, 1989). In considering the marketing of Wright's objects, articles in *Progressive Architecture* (November 1987), *Newsweek* (February 1, 1988), *Business Week* (December 5, 1988), and *The New York Times* (March 24, 1988) proved useful.

8. The Man Who Sells History

Christopher Gray talked to me but also provided me with a sheaf of articles, some by him and some about him. Especially useful were his "Streetscapes" columns from the Sunday *New York Times* Real Estate section, in particular the one devoted to the Union Square Theatre (January 29, 1989). Week by week, he is composing an invaluable if idiosyncratic history of the city of New York, featuring a blend of the past and the present, and correcting no small number of errors along the way.

9. The Curator of Class

For the history of New Castle, I have drawn upon *New Castle on the Delaware,* a volume assembled by Jeannette Eckman and Anthony Higgins for the Delaware Federal Writers' Project in the American Guide Series (New Castle: New Castle Historical Society, 1936, 1950, 1973).

As for the White Pine Series, it was funded by the White Pine Bureau, a trade association based in St. Paul, Minnesota, but which represented lumber companies nationwide. It is a unique collection of photographs and architectural drawings of early

American buildings from 1630 to about 1840, with accompanying text of varying accuracy by a variety of writers. Because of the quality of its drawings and its breadth—hundreds of buildings from up and down the east coast are covered—it has become a basic reference for preservationists of early American architecture. Its importance has been enhanced by the fact that it is the only surviving record of many lost or altered dwellings.

The series was originally published between 1914 and 1940, but has been republished in recent years in multiple-volume sets. At present, the series is in print as *Survey of Early American Design* (Hicksville, N.Y: The National Historical Society).

Charles T. Lyle generously granted me interview time and has answered numerous follow-up queries by post and phone and in person. His monograph *The George Read II House: Notes on Its History and Restoration* (Wilmington: The Historical Society of Delaware, 1986) was an invaluable source for many names, dates, and other facts concerning the restoration process.

Unpublished sources on the Read house included Matthew J. Mosca's paint analysis of the Read house; Eliza Wolcott's thesis, "George Read (II) and His House"; the Historic Structure Report prepared by Alvin H. Holm, Jr., AIA, and Robert M. Levy; and the manuscript study conducted by Richard R. Stryker, Jr., and Carol Jane Flahart. All were made available to me at the Historical Society of Delaware library and archives in Wilmington. Also of value, particularly in giving me a sense of the atmosphere of the time, were articles about the house that appeared in *Country Life* (October 1920), *House & Garden* (November 1923), *Town & Country* (February 1930), and *House Beautiful* (August 1935 and May 1940).

10. The Academic Provocateur

My debt here is to the effusive Chester H. Liebs. His words constitute the bulk of this chapter, largely from time spent interviewing him. However, his book *Main Street to Miracle Mile: American Roadside Architecture* (Boston: New York

Graphic Society, 1985) is an invaluable resource for looking at and thinking about the American landscape. A handful of biographical facts have also been drawn from a profile of Liebs by Richard Wolkomir that appeared in *Smithsonian Magazine*.

11. Four Private Possibilities

The principal sources for this chapter were the men themselves, Robert Adam (for both the Kelsey/MacKaye house and the Robinson house) and Robert Herron. Norman Young showed me the Trapp house and told me what he knew of its history.

The source Herron cited for his sprung-roof porch was *Early Domestic Architecture of Connecticut* by J. Frederick Kelly (New York: Dover, 1924). Orson S. Fowler's *A Home for All* is available in a reprint of its 1853 edition (New York: Dover, 1973). A copy of the unpublished 1923 manuscript by Mary Medbury MacKaye, "Chronicles of the Cottage," was loaned to me by Robert Adam.

12. The Future Requires a Past

More than Clem Labine, Chester Liebs, John Mesick, and the other preservationists quoted and named in this chapter influenced my thinking; to some degree, everyone who talked to me as I was researching and writing this book helped me formulate the opinions contained in this chapter.

Numerous printed sources made me think, too, notably C. Vann Woodward in his collection of essays *The Future of the Past* (New York: Oxford University Press, 1989); Geoffrey Scott in *The Architecture of Humanism: A Study in the History of Taste* (New York: Norton, originally published in 1914); and Henry Hope Reed in *The Golden City* (New York: Norton, 1970, 1959).

Among the factual sources I drew upon were *Grand Central Terminal: City Within the City,* Deborah Nevins, ed. (New York: Municipal Art Society of New York, 1982); *The History of the National Trust for Historic Preservation 1963–1973,* by Elizabeth D. Mulloy (Washington, D.C.: Preservation Press,

1976); and David Lowenthal's *The Past Is a Foreign Country* (Cambridge, England: Cambridge University Press, 1985).

I also owe a debt to the late Richard Stein for the calculation that constructing a building requires the energy equivalent of sixteen years of running it; I borrowed the term "embodied energy" from Charles Howell (see above, Chapter 6).

INDEX

Page references in boldface indicate the page number of an illustration or its caption.

265

About the Author

Born and bred in the central Massachusetts town of Westminster, Hugh Howard has written books on a variety of subjects, ranging from medicine to baseball to home renovation. Among his previous writings are the book *How Old Is This House?* and many magazine and newspaper articles about preservation for such publications as *The New York Times, Preservation News,* and *House Beautiful.*

He lives in New York City and the upstate New York hamlet of Red Rock with his wife, writer Elizabeth Lawrence, and their infant daughter.